Test Yourself

Elementary Algebra

Lawrence A. Trivieri, M.A.
DeKalb Community College
Clarkston, GA

Contributing Editors

Mark Weinfeld, M.A.
President
MathWorks Corporation
New York, NY

Charles M. Jones, M.S.
Department of Mathematics
East Texas State University
Commerce, TX

Douglas G. Smith
Arthur P. Schalick High School
, NJ

NTC LearningWorks
a division of NTC Publishing Group
Lincolnwood, Illinois

Library of Congress Cataloging-in-Publication Data

Trivieri, Lawrence A.
    Elementary algebra / Lawrence A. Trivieri ; contributing editors,
Mark Weinfeld, Douglas G. Smith.
        p.   cm. — (Test yourself)
    ISBN 0-8442-2356-5   (alk. paper)
    1. Algebra—Examinations, questions, etc. I. Weinfeld, Mark.
II. Smith, Douglas G. (Douglas George)   III. Title.   IV. Series:
Test yourself (Lincolnwood, Ill.)
    QA 157.T73   1996
512.9'076—dc20   96-6080
                                                    CIP

A *Test Yourself Books, Inc.* Project

Published by NTC Publishing Group
© 1996 NTC Publishing Group, 4255 West Touhy Avenue
Lincolnwood (Chicago), Illinois 60646-1975 U.S.A.

6 7 8 9 ML 0 9 8 7 6 5 4 3 2 1

Contents

Preface

This book has been written so that you can test your knowledge of elementary algebra. It is not a textbook but is based upon the leading texts for such a course. You can use this book in conjunction with your own textbook if you are currently enrolled in an elementary algebra course. It can also be used as a review book to refresh your knowledge of the subject material if you have been out of school for a while.

In the first section of each chapter of this book you will find a brief discussion of the material introduced or reviewed in the chapter. Included are definitions, terminology, basic properties, and exercises. In the second section of each chapter you will find completed solutions for each of the exercises given in the first section. Each solution is indexed to the appropriate section where the material is found in the chapter. In the final section of each chapter you will find a summary of all the exercises by section number. Check the questions you missed and go back and review the appropriate sections of your text.

Study the chapters of this book as you cover the corresponding material in your class. If used as intended, this book will help you meet with great success.

I wish to thank Fred N. Grayson for encouraging me to write this book and for his careful and thorough guidance leading to the completion of the project.

You have my very best wishes for a successful experience.

Lawrence A. Trivieri

How to Use this Book

This "Test Yourself" book is part of a unique series designed to help you improve your test scores on almost any type of examination you will face. Too often, you will study for a test—quiz, midterm, or final—and come away with a score that is lower than anticipated. Why? Because there is no way for you to really know how much you understand a topic until you've taken a test. The *purpose* of the test, after all, is to test your complete understanding of the material.

The "Test Yourself" series offers you a way to improve your scores and to actually test your knowledge at the time you use this book. Consider each chapter a diagnostic pretest in a specific topic. Answer the questions, check your answers, and then give yourself a grade. Then, and only then, will you know where your strengths and, more importantly, weaknesses are. Once these areas are identified, you can strategically focus your study on those topics that need additional work.

Each book in this series presents a specific subject in an organized manner, and although each "Test Yourself" chapter may not correspond exactly to the same chapter in your textbook, you should have little difficulty in locating the specific topic you are studying. Written by educators in the field, each book is designed to correspond, as much as possible, to the leading textbooks. This means that you can feel confident in using this book, and that regardless of your textbook, professor, or school, you will be much better prepared for anything you will encounter on your test.

Each chapter has four parts:

 Brief Yourself. All chapters contain a brief overview of the topic that is intended to give you a more thorough understanding of the material with which you need to be familiar. Sometimes this information is presented at the beginning of the chapter, and sometimes it flows throughout the chapter, to review your understanding of various *units* within the chapter.

 Test Yourself. Each chapter covers a specific topic corresponding to one that you will find in your textbook. Answer the questions, either on a separate page or directly in the book, if there is room.

 Check Yourself. Check your answers. Every question is fully answered and explained. These answers will be the key to your increased understanding. If you answered the question incorrectly, read the explanations to *learn* and *understand* the material. You will note that at the end of every answer you will be referred to a specific subtopic within that chapter, so you can focus your studying and prepare more efficiently.

 Grade Yourself. At the end of each chapter is a self-diagnostic key. By indicating on this form the numbers of those questions you answered incorrectly, you will have a clear picture of your weak areas.

There are no secrets to test success. Only good preparation can guarantee higher grades. By utilizing this "Test Yourself" book, you will have a better chance of improving your scores and understanding the subject more fully.

The Real Numbers and Their Properties

Test Yourself

1.1 Sets of Numbers

In this section, we review the various subsets of the real numbers.

The counting numbers are also called the **natural numbers**. There are infinitely many natural numbers. The smallest natural number is 1; there is no largest natural number. Denoting the set of natural numbers by the symbol N, we have

$$N = \{ 1, 2, 3, 4, 5, 6, 7, 8, ... \}$$

where the dots indicate that the numbers continue in the pattern.

The set of **whole numbers**, denoted by the symbol W, consists of the natural numbers together with 0. There are infinitely many whole numbers. The smallest whole number is 0; there is no largest whole number. We have

$$W = \{ 0, 1, 2, 3, 4, 5, 6, 7, 8, ... \}.$$

Each natural number has an opposite. The opposite of 4 is −4; the opposite of 9 is −9. The set of **integers**, denoted by Z, consists of all of the natural numbers, their opposites, and the whole number 0. There are infinitely many integers. There is no smallest integer or largest integer. We have

$$Z = \{ ..., −6, −5, −4, −3, −2, −1, 0, 1, 2, 3, 4, 5, 6, ... \}.$$

The set of integers can be subdivided into three disjoint sets as follows:

The **positive integers**, or $\{1, 2, 3, 4, 5, 6, ... \}$

The **negative integers**, or $\{ ..., −6, −5, −4, −3, −2, -1\}$

The **integer zero**, or $\{ 0 \}$

Notice that the set of positive integers and the set of natural numbers are the same.

The set of **rational numbers**, denoted by Q, is the set of all numbers that can be expressed as the quotient of two integers, provided that the denominator is not equal to 0. We have

$$Q = \left\{ \left\{ \frac{a}{b} \right\} \mid a \text{ and } b \text{ are integers}, b \neq 0 \right\}.$$

Examples of rational numbers are $\frac{-3}{7}, \frac{17}{-4}, \frac{-39}{-41}$, and $\frac{0}{17}$. Note, also, that every integer is a rational number. For instance, the integers 5 and −11 can be written as $\frac{5}{1}$ and $\frac{-11}{1}$, respectively.

Further, terminating decimals (*e.g.*, 3.56, 0.0067, 126.19) and repeating decimals (*e.g.*, $2.\overline{78}$, $0.\overline{33}$, $14.\overline{14}$) are also rational numbers. The bar over the digits indicates that the digits

1

repeat indefinitely. For example, $3.56 = \dfrac{356}{100}$ and $0.\overline{33} = \dfrac{1}{3}$. There are infinitely many rational numbers. There is no smallest rational number or largest rational number.

The set of **irrational** numbers, denoted by J, is the set of all numbers that have decimal representations that neither terminate nor repeat. Examples of irrational numbers are $\sqrt{2}$, $-\sqrt{19}$, $3 + 2\sqrt{13}$, and π. The irrational number $\sqrt{2}$ can be approximated by the rational number 1.414 to three decimal places. Similarly, the irrational number π can be approximated by the rational number 3.1416, to four decimal places.

The set of **real numbers**, denoted by R, is the set of all numbers that are either rational or irrational.

Note: Not all numbers are real numbers. In chapter 9, we will see solutions of quadratic equations, such as $\sqrt{-5}$ and $\sqrt{-23}$, that are not real numbers.

In Exercises 1-15, determine to which of the sets N, W, Z, Q, J, or R the given number belongs. If none of these, so state.

1. 6

2. −13

3. 4.16

4. $\dfrac{1}{9}$

5. $\sqrt{23}$

6. $\dfrac{19}{-2}$

7. $\sqrt{16}$

8. $\sqrt{0.012}$

9. 3π

10. $\sqrt{-8}$

11. $\dfrac{-17}{-3}$

12. $2.8\overline{3}$

13. $(-3)^2$

14. $4 - 11$

15. 0×13

1.2 Ordering of the Real Numbers

On the real number line, the positive numbers are to the right of 0 and the negative numbers are to the left of 0. (See Fig. 1.1)

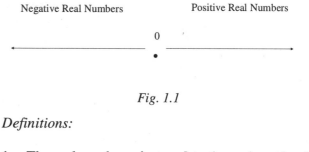

Fig. 1.1

Definitions:

1. The real number a **is equal to** the real number b, denoted by a = b, if and only if the two numbers are graphed at the same point on the real number line.

2. The real number c **is less than** the real number d, denoted by c < d, if and only if c is to the left of d on the number line.

3. The real number r **is greater than** the real number s, denoted by r > s, if and only if r is to the right of s on the number line.

In Exercises 16-30, order each of the given pairs of real numbers.

16. −7, −2

17. 5, 3

18. −5, 0

19. 0.23, 0.39

20. $\sqrt{2.5}$, 4

21. 7, 0

22. $\dfrac{1}{5}, \dfrac{3}{8}$

23. $\dfrac{-1}{2}, \dfrac{-1}{4}$

24. $3.01, 3.001$

25. $-4.9, -4.91$

26. $\pi, 2.7$

27. $-\pi, -4.1$

28. $5.6, \sqrt{25}$

29. $0.89, 0.097$

30. $-\sqrt{26}, -\sqrt{30}$

1.3   Addition of Real Numbers

Definition: The **absolute value** of the real number x, denoted by | x |, is the distance that the number x is from 0 on the number line.

Note: The absolute value of a real number is never negative; it is always positive or zero.

In Exercises 31-40, write each expression without absolute value symbols, and simplify if possible.

31. $| 7 |$

32. $| -13 |$

33. $| -3.5 |$

34. $| 8 | - | 5 |$

35. $| 8 - 5 |$

36. $| -13 | + | 17 |$

37. $| -11 | - | -8 |$

38. $| -3 | \times | -6 |$

39. $| 7 - 2 | - | 9 - 7 |$

40. $| 12 - 2 | \div | 6 - 1 |$

Rules for Adding Two Real Numbers

1. If the two real numbers have the **same** sign, add their absolute values and use the common sign as the sign of the sum.

2. If the two real numbers have **different** signs, take their absolute values and subtract the smaller absolute value from the larger absolute value. The sum will have the sign of the number with the larger absolute value.

Note: If a is any real number, then a + 0 = 0 + a = a. That is, the sum of any real number and 0 is that real number.

In Exercises 41-50, add as indicated.

41. $7 + (-9)$

42. $9 + (-7)$

43. $(1.6) + (-2.3)$

44. $\left(\dfrac{-1}{2}\right) + \left(\dfrac{-1}{3}\right)$

45. $(-4.9) + 0$

46. $(+12) + (+21)$

47. $\left(\dfrac{+4}{5}\right) + \left(-2\dfrac{1}{4}\right)$

48. $(-6) + (+8) + (-10)$

49. $(+1.2) + (+1.3) + (-2.5)$

50. $(-12) + (-9) + (-17)$

1.4   Subtraction of Real Numbers

Definition: Numbers that are the same distance from 0 on the number line, but in opposite directions, are called **opposites** of each other.

Rule for Subtracting Real Numbers

To subtract one real number from another real number, replace the number to be subtracted by its opposite and add.

In Exercises 51-60, subtract as indicated.

51. $(-18) - (-7)$

52. $(+23) - (+27)$

53. $(-7.9) - (+5.6)$

54. $\left(1\frac{1}{3}\right) - \left(+3\frac{2}{5}\right)$

55. $(-39) - (+17)$

56. $(-3.09) - (+4.78)$

57. $(-3.6) - (-0.72)$

58. $(+5.16) - (+8.09)$

59. $\left(-3\frac{1}{4}\right) - \left(+4\frac{1}{5}\right)$

60. $\left(-2\frac{1}{2}\right) - \left(-4\frac{1}{3}\right)$

In Exercises 61-65, perform the indicated operations.

61. $(-6.02) - (-8.7) - (+3.17)$

62. $(3.81) + (+8.1) - (5.9)$

63. $\left(+5\frac{1}{2}\right) - \left(-3\frac{2}{3}\right) + \left(-2\frac{1}{4}\right)$

64. $(-17) + (+19) - (-14) + (-11) - (+16)$

65. $(-9.4) - (+5.16) + (-0.69) + (-7.18) - (-0.29)$

1.5 Multiplication of Real Numbers

Rules for Multiplying Two Real Numbers

1. Disregard the signs and multiply the two real numbers as though they were positive numbers.

2. The product will be:

   a. 0, if either of the real numbers is 0.

   b. positive, if the two real numbers have the same sign (that is, both positive or both negative).

c. negative, if the two real numbers have **different** signs (that is, one positive and the other negative).

In Exercises 66-75, multiply as indicated.

66. $(-3)(+5)$

67. $(+11)(+7)$

68. $(-12)(-8)$

69. $(+9)(-13)$

70. $(-1.2)(-4)$

71. $(+3.1)(-4.2)$

72. $(+21.2)(+0.12)$

73. $(-3.1)(-5.3)$

74. $\left(\frac{-2}{3}\right)\left(\frac{+4}{5}\right)$

75. $\left(-3\frac{1}{2}\right)\left(-4\frac{4}{5}\right)$

1.6 Division of Real Numbers

Rules for Dividing Real Numbers

1. Disregard the signs and divide the two real numbers as though they were positive numbers.

2. The quotient will be:

   a. 0, if the numerator is 0 and the denominator is different from 0.

   b. positive, if the numerator and the denominator have the **same** sign.

   c. negative, if the numerator and the denominator have **different** signs.

3. The quotient does not exist if the denominator is 0.

In Exercises 76-85, divide as indicated.

76. $(+36) \div (-9)$

77. $(-49) \div (-7)$

78. $(-56) \div (-14)$

79. $0 \div (-113)$

80. $(+7.2) \div (-0.08)$

81. $(-0.25) \div (+0.05)$

82. $(-0.06) \div (-1.2)$

83. $(+0.05) \div (-0.005)$

84. $\left(+\frac{3}{8}\right) \div \left(\frac{-2}{5}\right)$

85. $\left(\frac{0}{-7}\right) \div \left(\frac{-13}{29}\right)$

In Exercises 86-90, perform the indicated operations.

86. $[(-11) + (+17)] \times [(-23) - (-31)]$

87. $[(+23.1) \times (-0.01)] - [(-24) \div (-1.2)]$

88. $[(-48) \div (-16)] \times [(-56) \div (-14)]$

89. $\left(-3\frac{1}{4}\right) \times \left(-5\frac{1}{2} - 4\frac{2}{3}\right)$

90. $\left(\frac{-4}{7} - \frac{-2}{5}\right) \times \left(\frac{-3}{8} + \frac{-1}{9}\right)$

1.7   Order of Operations on Real Numbers

Rules for Performing Operations on Real Numbers

1. First, do all operations within parentheses, if any.

2. Next, evaluate all expressions with exponents.

3. Then, do all multiplications and divisions, **in order from left to right.**

4. Finally, do all additions and subtractions, **in order from left to right**.

In Exercises 91–95, perform the indicated operations.

91. $2^4 - 3^2 \times 4 \div (2 \times 3) - 3 \times (4 + 5)$

92. $(2 + 7)^2 \div (5 + 4) + 9 - 4 \times 5 + 3^2$

93. $(9 - 4) \times (36 \div 9) \div 2^2 - (2 \times 3)^2$

94. $3^3 - (4^3 \div 4^2) + 4 \times 5 - 2^3$

95. $(5^4 \div 5^2) \div (5^3 \div 5^2) - 3 \times 2^2 - 8$

1.8 Properties of Real Numbers

Commutative Properties

For addition: The order in which we add two real numbers is not important. That is, if x and y are any real numbers, then x + y = y + x.

For multiplication: The order in which we multiply two real numbers is not important. That is, if u and v are any real numbers, then uv = vu.

Associative Properties

For addition: The order in which we group real numbers for addition is not important. That is, if p, q, and r are any real numbers, then (p + q) + r = p + (q + r).

For multiplication: The order in which we group real numbers for multiplication is not important. That is, if u, v, and w are any real numbers, then (uv)w = u(vw).

Distributive Properties

Left Distributive: If a, b, and c are any real numbers, then a(b + c) = ab + ac.

Right Distributive: If u, v, and w are any real numbers, then (u + v)w = uw + vw.

Identity Properties

For addition: The real number 0 is the **additive identity** such that a + 0 = 0 + a = a where a is any real number. The additive identity is unique. (That is, there is only one such real number with this property.)

For multiplication: The real number 1 is the **multiplicative identity** such that (b)(1) = (1)(b) = b where b is any real number. The multiplicative identity is unique.

Inverse Properties

For addition: For each real number x, there exists a unique real number −x, called the **additive inverse** of x, such that x + (−x) = (−x) + x = 0. (The additive inverse of a real number is also called its **opposite**.)

For multiplication: For each *nonzero* real number y, there exists a unique real number $\frac{1}{y}$, called the **multiplicative inverse** of y, such that $y(\frac{1}{y}) = (\frac{1}{y})y = 1$. (The multiplicative inverse of a real number is also called its **reciprocal**. Note that the real number 0 does not have a multiplicative inverse.)

In Exercises 96-100, state the additive identity for the given set, if it exists, or indicate that none exists.

96. N

97. W

98. J

99. The set of all nonnegative integers.

100. The set of all rational numbers greater than −3.

In Exercises 101-105, state the multiplicative identity for the given set, if it exists, or indicate that none exists.

101. W

102. Z

103. Q

104. The set of all irrational numbers less than 3.

105. The set { −3, −2, −1, 0, 1, 2, 3 }.

In Exercises 106-110, state the additive inverse for each of the indicated real numbers, if it exists, or indicate that none exists.

106. −9

107. $\sqrt{71}$

108. 0

109. $\frac{-13}{21}$

110. | 3 − 7 |

In Exercises 111-115, state the multiplicative inverse for each of the indicated real numbers, if it exists, or indicate that none exists.

111. −5

112. −| −3 |

113. $\sqrt{19}$

114. −$\sqrt{121}$

115. $\frac{87}{-8}$

In Exercises 116-125, indicate which property of real numbers is being used.

116. 0 + (−142) = −142

117. (2)(−5) = (−5)(2)

118. (−17) + (17) = 0

119. (−7)[6 + (−9)] = (−7)(6) + (−7)(−9)

120. $\left(\frac{-4}{9}\right)\left(\frac{-9}{4}\right) = 1$

121. (3 x 4) x 5 = 5 x (3 x 4)

122. (−5 + 7)(1) = −5 + 7

123. (−3 + 8)(−11) = (−3)(−11) + (8)(−11)

124. [(21)(−39)](42) = 21[(−39)(42)]

125. (11 − 3) + (11 + 3) = (11 + 3) + (11 − 3)

✓ Check Yourself

1. 6 belongs to N, W, Z, Q, and R. **(Sets of numbers)**

2. −13 belong to Z, Q, and R. **(Sets of numbers)**

3. 4.16 belongs to Q and R. **(Sets of numbers)**

4. $\frac{1}{9}$ belongs to Q and R. **(Sets of numbers)**

5. $\sqrt{23}$ belongs to J and R. **(Sets of numbers)**

6. $\frac{19}{-2}$ belongs to Q and R. **(Sets of numbers)**

7. $\sqrt{16} = 4$ belongs to N, W, Z, Q, and R. **(Sets of numbers)**

8. $\sqrt{0.012}$ belongs to J and R. **(Sets of numbers)**

9. 3π belongs to J and R. **(Sets of numbers)**

10. $\sqrt{-8}$ belongs to none of the indicated sets. It is not a real number. **(Sets of numbers)**

11. $\frac{-17}{-3}$ belongs to Q and R. **(Sets of numbers)**

12. $2.8\overline{3}$ is a repeating decimal. It belongs to Q and R. **(Sets of numbers)**

13. $(-3)^2 = 9$ belongs to N, W, Z, Q, and R. **(Sets of numbers)**

14. $4 - 11 = -7$ belongs to Z, Q, and R. **(Sets of numbers)**

15. $0 \times 13 = 0$ belongs to W, Z, Q, and R. **(Sets of numbers)**

16. $-7 < -2$ **(Ordering of real numbers)**

17. $5 > 3$ **(Ordering of real numbers)**

18. $-5 < 0$ **(Ordering of real numbers)**

19. $0.23 < 0.39$ **(Ordering of real numbers)**

20. $\sqrt{2.5} < 4$ **(Ordering of real numbers)**

21. $7 > 0$ **(Ordering of real numbers)**

22. $\frac{1}{5} < \frac{3}{8}$ **(Ordering of real numbers)**

23. $\dfrac{-1}{2} < \dfrac{-1}{4}$ **(Ordering of real numbers)**

24. $3.01 > 3.001$ **(Ordering of real numbers)**

25. $-4.9 > -4.91$ **(Ordering of real numbers)**

26. $\pi < 2.7$ **(Ordering of real numbers)**

27. $-\pi > -4.1$ **(Ordering of real numbers)**

28. $5.6 > \sqrt{25}$ **(Ordering of real numbers)**

29. $0.89 > 0.097$ **(Ordering of real numbers)**

30. $-\sqrt{26} > -\sqrt{30}$ **(Ordering of real numbers)**

31. $|\,7\,| = 7$ **(Absolute value)**

32. $|-13\,| = 13$ **(Absolute value)**

33. $|-3.5\,| = 3.5$ **(Absolute value)**

34. $|\,8\,| - |\,5\,| = 8 - 5 = 3$ **(Absolute value)**

35. $|\,8 - 5\,| = |\,3\,| = 3$ **(Absolute value)**

36. $|-13\,| + |\,17\,| = 13 + 17 = 30$ **(Absolute value)**

37. $|-11\,| - |-8\,| = 11 - 8 = 3$ **(Absolute value)**

38. $|-3\,| \times |-6\,| = 3 \times 6 = 18$ **(Absolute value)**

39. $|\,7 - 2\,| - |\,9 - 7\,| = |\,5\,| - |\,2\,| = 5 - 2 = 3$ **(Absolute value)**

40. $|\,12 - 2\,| \div |\,6 - 1\,| = |\,10\,| \div |\,5\,| = 10 \div 5 = 2$ **(Absolute value)**

41. $7 + (-9) = -(9 - 7)$ (Different Signs)

        $= -2$ **(Addition of real numbers)**

42. $9 + (-7) = +(9 - 7)$ (Different Signs)

        $= +2$ **(Addition of real numbers)**

43. $(1.6) + (-2.3) = -(2.3 - 1.6)$ (Different Signs)

        $= -0.7$ **(Addition of real numbers)**

44. $\left(\dfrac{-1}{2}\right) + \left(\dfrac{-1}{3}\right) = -\left(\dfrac{1}{2} + \dfrac{1}{3}\right)$ (Same Signs)

        $= \dfrac{-5}{6}$ **(Addition of real numbers)**

45. $(+4.9) + 0 = +4.9$ (Addition Involving 0) **(Addition of real numbers)**

46. $(+12) + (+21) = +(12 + 21)$ (Same Signs)

         $= +33$ **(Addition of real numbers)**

47. $\left(+\dfrac{4}{5}\right) + \left(-2\dfrac{1}{4}\right) = -\left(2\dfrac{1}{4} - \dfrac{4}{5}\right)$ (Different Signs)

         $= -1\dfrac{9}{20}$ **(Addition of real numbers)**

48. $(-6) + (+8) + (-10) = +(8 - 6) + (-10)$ (Different Signs)

         $= (+2) + (-10)$ (Simplifying)

         $= -(10 - 2)$ (Different Signs)

         $= -8$ **(Addition of real numbers)**

49. $(+1.2) + (+1.3) + (-2.5) = +(1.2 + 1.3) + (-2.5)$ (Same Signs)

         $= (2.5) + (-2.5)$ (Simplifying)

         $= 0$ (Addition of Opposites)

         (Addition of real numbers)

50. $(-12) + (-9) + (-17) = -(12 + 9 + 17)$ (Same Signs)

         $= -38$ **(Addition of real numbers)**

51. $(-18) - (-7) = (-18) + (+7)$ (Adding the opposite of -7)

         $= -(18 - 7)$ (Different Signs)

         $= -11$ **(Subtraction of real numbers)**

52. $(+23) - (+27) = (+23) + (-27)$ (Adding the opposite of $+27$)

         $= -(27 - 23)$ (Different Signs)

         $= -4$ **(Subtraction of real numbers)**

53. $(-7.9) - (+5.6) = (-7.9) + (-5.6)$ (Adding the opposite of $+5.6$)

         $= -(7.9 + 5.6)$ (Same Signs)

         $= -13.5$ **(Subtraction of real numbers)**

54. $\left(-1\dfrac{1}{3}\right) - \left(+3\dfrac{2}{5}\right) = \left(-1\dfrac{1}{3}\right) + \left(-3\dfrac{2}{5}\right)$ (Adding the opposite of $+3\dfrac{2}{5}$)

         $= -\left(1\dfrac{1}{3} + 3\dfrac{2}{5}\right)$ (Same Signs)

         $= -4\dfrac{11}{15}$ **(Subtraction of real numbers)**

55. $(-39) - (+17) = (-39) + (-17)$ (Adding the opposite of $+17$)

         $= -(39 + 17)$ (Same Signs)

         $= -56$ **(Subtraction of real numbers)**

56. $(-3.09) - (+4.78) = (-3.09) + (-4.78)$ (Adding the opposite of +4.78)

                     $= -(3.09 + 4.78)$ (Same Signs)

                     $= -7.87$ **(Subtraction of real numbers)**

57. $(-3.6) - (-0.72) = (-3.6) + (+0.72)$ (Adding the opposite of –0.72)

                    $= -(3.6 - 0.72)$ (Different Signs)

                    $= -2.88$ **(Subtraction of real numbers)**

58. $(+5.16) - (+8.09) = (+5.16) + (-8.09)$ (Adding the opposite of +8.09)

                     $= -(8.09 - 5.16)$ (Different Signs)

                     $= -2.93$ **(Subtraction of real numbers)**

59. $\left(-3\frac{1}{4}\right) - \left(+4\frac{1}{5}\right) = \left(-3\frac{1}{4}\right) + \left(-4\frac{1}{5}\right)$ (Adding the opposite of $+4\frac{1}{5}$)

                  $= -\left(3\frac{1}{4} + 4\frac{1}{5}\right)$ (Same Signs)

                  $= -7\frac{9}{20}$ **(Subtraction of real numbers)**

60. $\left(-2\frac{1}{2}\right) - \left(-4\frac{1}{3}\right) = \left(-2\frac{1}{2}\right) + \left(+4\frac{1}{3}\right)$ (Adding the opposite of $-4\frac{1}{3}$)

                  $= +\left(4\frac{1}{3} - 2\frac{1}{2}\right)$ (Different Signs)

                  $= 1\frac{5}{6}$ **(Subtraction of real numbers)**

61. $(-6.02) - (-8.7) - (+3.17) = (-6.02) \underline{+ (+8.7)} - (+3.17)$

                        $= +(8.7 - 6.02) - (+3.17)$

                        $= (+2.68) - (+3.17)$

                        $= (+2.68) \underline{+ (- 3.17)}$

                        $= -(3.17 - 2.68)$

                        $= -0.49$ **(Addition and subtraction of real numbers)**

62. $(3.81) + (+8.1) - (5.9) = +(3.81 + 8.1) - (5.9)$

                        $= (+11.91) - (5.9)$

                        $= (+11.91) \underline{+ (-5.9)}$

                        $= +(11.91 - 5.9)$

                        $= 6.01$ **(Addition and subtraction of real numbers)**

63. $\left(+5\frac{1}{2}\right) - \left(-3\frac{2}{3}\right) + \left(-2\frac{1}{4}\right) = \left(+5\frac{1}{2}\right) + \left(\underline{+3\frac{2}{3}}\right) + \left(-2\frac{1}{4}\right)$

      $= +\left(5\frac{1}{2} + 3\frac{2}{3}\right) + \left(-2\frac{1}{4}\right)$

$$= \left(+9\frac{1}{6}\right) + \left(-2\frac{1}{4}\right)$$

$$= +\left(9\frac{1}{6} - 2\frac{1}{4}\right)$$

$$= 6\frac{11}{12} \quad \textbf{(Addition and subtraction of real numbers)}$$

64. $(-17) + (+19) - (-14) + (-11) - (+16)$

$$= (-17) + (+19) \underline{+ (+14)} + (-11) \underline{+ (-16)}$$

$$= [(-17) + (-11) + (-16)] + [(+19) + (+14)]$$

$$= -(17 + 11 + 16) + [+(19 + 14)]$$

$$= (-44) + (+33)$$

$$= -(44 - 33)$$

$$= -11 \textbf{ (Addition and subtraction of real numbers)}$$

65. $(-9.4) - (+5.16) + (-0.69) + (-7.18) - (-0.29)$

$$= (-9.4) + (-5.16) + (-0.69) + (-7.18) \underline{+ (+0.29)}$$

$$= [(-9.4) + (-5.16) + (-0.69) + (-7.18)] + (+0.29)$$

$$= (-22.43) + (+0.29)$$

$$= -(22.43 - 0.29)$$

$$= -22.14 \textbf{ (Addition and subtraction of real numbers)}$$

66. $(-3)(+5) = -(3 \times 5) \qquad$ (Different Signs)

$$= -15 \textbf{ (Multiplication of real numbers)}$$

67. $(+11)(+7) = +(11 \times 7) \qquad$ (Same Signs)

$$= 77 \textbf{ (Multiplication of real numbers)}$$

68. $(-12)(-8) = +(12 \times 8) \qquad$ (Same Signs)

$$= 96 \textbf{ (Multiplication of real numbers)}$$

69. $(+9)(-13) = -(9 \times 13) \qquad$ (Different Signs)

$$= -117 \textbf{ (Multiplication of real numbers)}$$

70. $(-1.2)(-4) = +(1.2 \times 4) \qquad$ (Same Signs)

$$= 4.8 \textbf{ (Multiplication of real numbers)}$$

71. $(+3.1)(-4.2) = -(3.1 \times 4.2) \qquad$ (Different Signs)

$$= -13.02 \textbf{ (Multiplication of real numbers)}$$

72. $(+21.2)(+0.12) = +(21.2 \times 0.12) \quad$ (Same Signs)

$$= 2.544 \textbf{ (Multiplication of real numbers)}$$

73. $(-3.1)(-5.3) = +(3.1 \times 5.3) \qquad$ (Same Signs)

$$= 16.43 \textbf{ (Multiplication of real numbers)}$$

74. $\left(\dfrac{-2}{3}\right)\left(\dfrac{+4}{5}\right) = -\left(\dfrac{2}{3} \times \dfrac{4}{5}\right)$ (Different Signs)

    $= \dfrac{-8}{15}$ **(Multiplication of real numbers)**

75. $\left(-3\dfrac{1}{2}\right)\left(-4\dfrac{4}{5}\right) = +\left(3\dfrac{1}{2} \times 4\dfrac{4}{5}\right)$ (Same Signs)

    $= 16\dfrac{4}{5}$ **(Multiplication of real numbers)**

76. $(+36) \div (-9) = -(36 \div 9)$ (Different Signs)

    $= -4$ **(Division of real numbers)**

77. $(-49) \div (-7) = +(49 \div 7)$ (Same Signs)

    $= 7$ **(Division of real numbers)**

78. $(-56) \div (-14) = +(56 \div 14)$ (Same Signs)

    $= 4$ **(Division of real numbers)**

79. $0 \div (-113) = 0$ (0 Divided by a Nonzero Number)

    (Division of real numbers)

80. $(+7.2) \div (-0.08) = -(7.2 \div 0.08)$ (Different Signs)

    $= -90$ **(Division of real numbers)**

81. $(-0.25) \div (+0.05) = -(0.25 \div 0.05)$ (Different Signs)

    $= -5$ **(Division of real numbers)**

82. $(-0.06) \div (-1.2) = +(0.06 \div 1.2)$ (Same Signs)

    $= 0.05$ **(Division of real numbers)**

83. $(+0.05) \div (-0.005) = -(0.05 \div 0.005)$ (Different Signs)

    $= -10$ **(Division of real numbers)**

84. $\left(\dfrac{+3}{8}\right) \div \left(\dfrac{-2}{5}\right) = -\left(\dfrac{3}{8} \div \dfrac{2}{5}\right)$ (Different Signs)

    $= -\left(\dfrac{3}{8} \times \dfrac{5}{2}\right)$

    $= \dfrac{-15}{16}$ **(Division of real numbers)**

85. $\left(\dfrac{0}{-7}\right) \div \left(\dfrac{-13}{29}\right) = -\left(\dfrac{0}{7} \div \dfrac{13}{29}\right)$ (0 Divided by a Nonzero Number)

    $= 0$ **(Division of real numbers)**

86. $[(-11) + (+17)] \times [(-23) - (-31)]$

    $= (+6) \times (+8)$

    $= 48$ **(Mixed operations on real numbers)**

87. $[(+23.1) \times (-0.01)] - [(-24) \div (-1.2)]$

$$= (-0.231) - (+20)$$

$$= -20.231 \textbf{ (Mixed operations on real numbers)}$$

88. $[(-48) \div (-16)] \times [(-56) \div (-14)]$

$$= (+3) \times (+4)$$

$$= 12 \textbf{ (Mixed operations on real numbers)}$$

89. $\left(-3\frac{1}{4}\right) \times \left(-5\frac{1}{2} - 4\frac{2}{3}\right)$

$$= \left(-3\frac{1}{4}\right) \times \left(-10\frac{1}{6}\right)$$

$$= 33\frac{1}{24} \textbf{ (Mixed operations on real numbers)}$$

90. $\left(\frac{-4}{7} - \frac{-2}{5}\right) \times \left(\frac{-3}{8} + \frac{-1}{9}\right)$

$$= \left(\frac{-6}{35}\right) \times \left(\frac{-35}{72}\right)$$

$$= \frac{1}{12} \textbf{ (Mixed operations on real numbers)}$$

91. $2^4 - 3^2 \times 4 \div \underline{(2 \times 3)} - 3 \times \underline{(4 + 5)}$

$$= \underline{2^4} - \underline{3^2} \times 4 \ 6 - 3 \times 9$$

$$= 16 - \underline{9 \times 4} \div 6 - 3 \times 9$$

$$= 16 - \underline{36 \div 6} - 3 \times 9$$

$$= 16 - 6 - \underline{3 \times 9}$$

$$= \underline{16 - 6} - 27$$

$$= 10 - 27$$

$$= -17 \textbf{ (Order of operations)}$$

92. $\underline{(2 + 7)}^2 \div \underline{(5 + 4)} + 9 - 4 \times 5 + 3^2$

$$= \underline{9^2} \div 9 + 9 - 4 \times 5 + \underline{3^2}$$

$$= \underline{81 \div 9} + 9 - 4 \times 5 + 9$$

$$= 9 + 9 - \underline{4 \times 5} + 9$$

$$= \underline{9 + 9} - 20 + 9$$

$$= \underline{18 - 20} + 9$$

$$= -2 + 9$$

$$= 7 \textbf{ (Order of operations)}$$

93. $\underline{(9-4)} \times \underline{(36 \div 9)} \div 2^2 - \underline{(2 \times 3)}^2$

$= 5 \times 4 \div \underline{2^2} - \underline{6^2}$

$= \underline{5 \times 4} \div 4 - 36$

$= \underline{20 \div 4} - 36$

$= 5 - 36$

$= -31$ **(Order of operations)**

94. $3^3 - (\underline{4^3} \div \underline{4^2}) + 4 \times 5 - 2^3$

$= 3^3 - (\underline{64} \div \underline{16}) + 4 \times 5 - 2^3$

$= 3^3 - 4 + 4 \times 5 - \underline{2^2}$

$= 27 - 4 + \underline{4 \times 5} - 8$

$= \underline{27 - 4} + 20 - 8$

$= \underline{23 + 20} - 8$

$= 43 - 8$

$= 35$ **(Order of operations)**

95. $(\underline{5^4} \div \underline{5^2}) \div (\underline{5^3} \div \underline{5^2}) - 3 \times 2^2 - 8$

$= \underline{(625 \div 25)} \div \underline{(125 \div 25)} - 3 \times 2^2 - 8$

$= 25 \div 5 - 3 \times \underline{2^2} - 8$

$= \underline{25 \div 5} - 3 \times 4 - 8$

$= 5 - \underline{3 \times 4} - 8$

$= \underline{5 - 12} - 8$

$= -7 - 8$

$= -15$ **(Order of operations)**

96. None. 0 is not a natural number. **(Properties of real numbers)**

97. The additive identity for the set W is 0. **(Properties of real numbers)**

98. None. 0 is not an irrational number. **(Properties of real numbers)**

99. The nonnegative integers are all of the positive integers and the integer zero. Hence, 0 is the additive identity for the set of all nonnegative integers. **(Properties of real numbers)**

100. 0 is the additive identity for the set of all rational numbers greater than -3, since 0 is a rational number and $0 > -3$. **(Properties of real numbers)**

101. The multiplicative identity for the set W is 1. **(Properties of real numbers)**

102. The multiplicative identity for the set Z is 1. **(Properties of real numbers)**

103. The multiplicative identity for the set Q is 1. **(Properties of real numbers)**

104. None. $1 < 3$, but 1 is not an irrational number. **(Properties of real numbers)**

105. The multiplicative identity for the set { −3, −2, −1, 0, 1, 2, 3 } is 1. **(Properties of real numbers)**

106. The additive inverse for −9 is 9. **(Properties of real numbers)**

107. The additive inverse for $\sqrt{71}$ is $-\sqrt{71}$. **(Properties of real numbers)**

108. The additive inverse for 0 is 0. **(Properties of real numbers)**

109. The additive inverse for $\dfrac{-13}{21}$ is $\dfrac{13}{21}$. **(Properties of real numbers)**

110. $|\,3 − 7\,| = |\,{-4}\,| = 4$. Hence, the additive inverse for $|\,3 − 7\,|$ is −4. **(Properties of real numbers)**

111. The multiplicative inverse for −5 is $\dfrac{-1}{5}$. **(Properties of real numbers)**

112. $-|\,{-3}\,| = -3$. Hence, the multiplicative inverse for $-|\,{-3}\,|$ is $\dfrac{-1}{3}$. **(Properties of real numbers)**

113. The multiplicative inverse for $\sqrt{19}$ is $\dfrac{1}{\sqrt{19}}$. **(Properties of real numbers)**

114. $-\sqrt{121} = -11$. Hence, the multiplicative inverse for $-\sqrt{121}$ is $\dfrac{-1}{11}$. **(Properties of real numbers)**

115. The multiplicative inverse for $\dfrac{87}{-8}$ is $\dfrac{-8}{87}$. **(Properties of real numbers)**

116. $0 + (−142) = −142$ illustrates the additive identity property. **(Properties of real numbers)**

117. $(2)(−5) = (−5)(2)$ illustrates the commutative property for multiplication. **(Properties of real numbers)**

118. $(−17) + (17) = 0$ illustrates the additive inverse property. **(Properties of real numbers)**

119. $(−7)[6 + (−9)] = (−7)(6) + (−7)(−9)$ illustrates the left distributive property. **(Properties of real numbers)**

120. $\left(\dfrac{-4}{9}\right)\left(\dfrac{-9}{4}\right) = 1$ illustrates the multiplicative inverse property. **(Properties of real numbers)**

121. $(3 \times 4) \times 5 = 5 \times (3 \times 4)$ illustrates the commutative property for multiplication. **(Properties of real numbers)**

122. $(−5 + 7)(1) = −5 + 7$ illustrates the multiplicative identity property. **(Properties of real numbers)**

123. $(−3 + 8)(−11) = (−3)(−11) + (8)(−11)$ illustrates the right distributive property. **(Properties of real numbers)**

124. $[(21)(−39)](42) = 21[(−39)(42)]$ illustrates the associative property for multiplication. **(Properties of real numbers)**

125. $(11 − 3) + (11 + 3) = (11 + 3) + (11 − 3)$ illustrates the commutative property for addition. **(Properties of real numbers)**

Grade Yourself

Circle the numbers of the questions you missed, then fill in the total incorrect for each topic. If you answered more than three questions incorrectly, you need to focus on that topic. (If a topic has less than three questions and you had at least one wrong, we suggest you study that topic also. Read your textbook, a review book, or ask your teacher for help.)

Subject: The Real Numbers and Their Properties

Topic	Question Numbers	Number Incorrect
Sets of numbers	1, 2, 3, 4, 5, 6, 7, 8, 9, 10, 11, 12, 13, 14, 15	
Ordering of real numbers	16, 17, 18, 19, 20, 21, 22, 23, 24, 25, 26, 27, 28, 29, 30	
Absolute Value	31, 32, 33, 34, 35, 36, 37, 38, 39, 40	
Addition of real numbers	41, 42, 43, 44, 45, 46, 47, 48, 49, 50	
Subtraction of real numbers	51, 52, 53, 54, 55, 56, 57, 58, 59, 60	
Addition and subtraction of real numbers	61, 62, 63, 64, 65	
Multiplication of real numbers	66, 67, 68, 69, 70, 71, 72, 73, 74, 75	
Division of real numbers	76, 77, 78, 79, 80, 81, 82, 83, 84, 85	
Mixed operations on real numbers	86, 87, 88, 89, 90	
Order of operations	91, 92, 93, 94, 95	
Properties of real numbers	96, 97, 98, 99, 100, 101, 102, 103, 104, 105, 106, 107, 108, 109, 110, 111, 112, 113, 114, 115, 116, 117, 118, 119, 120, 121, 122, 123, 124, 125	

Linear Equations and Inequalities

2

Test Yourself

2.1 Simplifying Expressions

Definition: A **linear equation in the variable x** is an equation of the form ax + b = 0, such that $a \neq 0$.

The following are examples of linear equations in a single variable.

$2x - 3 = 0$ (linear in the variable x)

$2(y - 1) = -3y$ (linear in the variable y)

$t - 3(4 - 5t) = 6t - 2(t + 3)$ (linear in the variable t)

To solve a linear equation, we try to simplify both sides as much as possible. We now consider ways of simplying expressions.

Definitions:

1. A **term** is an expression that is part of a sum. (5, −9, 2x, −7y, and 14z are all terms.)

2. **Like terms** are terms that contain the same variable with the same exponents. (2x, −3x, and 15x are like terms.)

3. **Unlike terms** are terms that are not like terms. (3x and 2y are unlike terms. −5u and $7u^2$ are unlike terms.)

In Exercises 1-5, determine if the indicated expressions are like or unlike terms.

1. $1.2x, -3x, 17x, 0.5x$

2. $-4r, 5s, 11r$

3. $\frac{1}{7}y^2, \frac{-2}{9}y^2, -6y^2, y^2$

4. $2x^4, 3x^2, -5x$

5. $-3, 14, \sqrt{7}, \pi, 8.1$

Rules for Combining Like Terms

To combine like terms:

1. Add the numerical coefficients.

2. Multiply the sum by the common variable part.

In Exercises 6-10, combine the indicated like terms.

6. $11x + 8x$

7. $-2y - 5y + 10y$

8. $-5u^3 + 7u^3 - 21u^3$

9. $3a + 2b - 4a - 6b + 9a$

10. $10uv - 3uw + uv + 6uv - 7uw$

Definition: To solve an equation containing a variable means to determine all values of the variable that will make the equation a true statement. Each such value of the variable is called a **solution** to the equation.

To determine if a number is a solution for an equation, replace the variable by the number and determine whether the statement is true or false.

In Exercises 11-15, determine if the given number is a solution for the indicated equation.

11. $4; x - 3 = 2$

12. $2; 2y + 6 = 10$

13. $6; 3(2 - r) = -12$

14. $-3; \dfrac{3u - 5}{-2} = 5$

15. $0; -3(t - 4) = 3(2t - 1) + 15$

2.2 Addition/Subtraction Rules for Solving Linear Equations

Definition: **Equivalent equations** are equations in the same variable that have the same solutions.

Addition Rule for Solving Linear Equations

We can *add* the *same* quantity to *both* sides of a linear equation to obtain an equivalent equation. That is, if

$$x - a = b,$$

then $(x - a) + a = b + a,$
or $x = b + a.$

In Exercises 16–20, solve each of the given equations for the indicated variable.

16. $p - 7 = 3$

17. $x - 5 = -2$

18. $q - 1.2 = 0.1$

19. $m - \dfrac{1}{2} = \dfrac{2}{3}$

20. $t - 5 = 3.9$

Subtraction Rule for Solving Linear Equations

We can *subtract* the *same* quantity from *both* sides of a linear equation to obtain an equivalent equation. That is, if

$$y + a = b,$$

then $(y + a) - a = b - a,$
or $y = b - a.$

In Exercises 21-25, solve each of the given equations for the indicated variable.

21. $q + 11 = -4$

22. $x + 1.7 = -3.9$

23. $y + \sqrt{3} = -4\sqrt{3}$

24. $t + 5.6 = -9$

25. $w + \dfrac{2}{9} = \dfrac{-1}{4}$

2.3 Multiplication/Division Rules for Solving Linear Equations

Multiplication Rule for Solving Linear Equations

We can *multiply both* sides of a linear equation by the *same nonzero* quantity to obtain an equivalent equation. That is, if

$$\frac{x}{a} = b \ (a \neq 0),$$

then $a\left(\dfrac{x}{a}\right) = (a)(b),$
or $x = ab.$

In Exercises 26-30, solve each of the given equations for the indicated variable.

26. $\dfrac{x}{5} = -2$

27. $\dfrac{y}{0.3} = 1.2$

28. $\dfrac{q}{5} = \dfrac{-1}{4}$

29. $\dfrac{u}{-5} = -2.6$

30. $\dfrac{t}{-3.1} = \dfrac{2}{5}$

Division Rule for Solving Linear Equations

We can *divide both* sides of a linear equation by the *same nonzero* quantity to obtain an equivalent equation. That is, if

$$ax = b \ (a \neq 0),$$

then $\qquad \dfrac{ax}{a} = \dfrac{b}{a},$

or $\qquad x = \dfrac{b}{a}.$

In Exercises 31-35, solve each of the given equations for the indicated variable.

31. $3p = -4$

32. $-2t = 8$

33. $1.2x = 0.36$

34. $-2.1q = 0.7$

35. $\dfrac{-3}{5}y = \dfrac{-4}{7}$

2.4 Solving Linear Equations Using More Than One Operation

It is sometimes necessary to use more than one operation to solve an equation. In doing so, we try to obtain an equivalent equation in which all terms containing the variable are on one side of the equation and all other terms are on the other side of the equation.

For example, to solve the equation $3x - 5 = 2$, we observe that on the left side

1. x is multiplied by 3, yielding 3x, and

2. 5 is subtracted from 3x, yielding $3x - 5$.

To solve the equation, perform the inverse or opposite operation in each of the steps above but in reverse order. (That is, start with step 2, then go to step 1.) Solving the equation, we do the following:

1. Add 5 to $3x - 5$ (and also to 2). Hence,

$$3x - 5 = 2$$

becomes $\quad (3x - 5) + 5 = 2 + 5,$

or $\qquad\qquad 3x = 7.$

2. Divide 3x by 3 (and also divide 7 by 3). Hence,

$$3x = 7$$

becomes $\qquad \dfrac{3x}{3} = \dfrac{7}{3},$

or $\qquad\qquad x = \dfrac{7}{3}.$

Therefore, $\dfrac{7}{3}$ is the required solution.

In Exercises 36-43, solve each of the given equations for the indicated variable.

36. $4x - 1 = 5$

37. $\dfrac{2}{3}y + 3 = 1$

38. $\dfrac{q-5}{4} = -3$

39. $4 - 3t = 5$

40. $5(p - 6) = 1$

41. $\dfrac{2x-1}{2} = -9$

42. $\dfrac{3-4u}{-5} = \dfrac{2}{3}$

43. $\dfrac{2}{5}m - 4\dfrac{1}{3} = -3\dfrac{1}{2}$

2.5 Simplifying First Before Solving Linear Equations

Sometimes a linear equation in a single variable will contain more than one variable term. To solve the equation, we first combine all like terms on each side of the equation and then proceed as in the previous section. To combine like terms on each side of the equation, it may be necessary to remove parentheses.

For example, to solve the equation $3(x - 2) - 3 = 5x - 1$, we proceed as follows:

$3(x-2) - 3 = 5x - 1$

$3x - 6 - 3 = 5x - 1$ (removing parentheses)

$3x - 9 = 5x - 1$ (combining like terms)

$-9 = 2x - 1$ (subtracting 3x from *both* sides)

$-8 = 2x$ (adding 1 to *both* sides)

$-4 = x$ (dividing *both* sides by 2)

Substituting −4 for x in the original equation does lead to a true statement. Therefore, −4 is the required solution.

In Exercises 44-51, solve each of the given equations for the indicated variable.

44. $2y - 3 = -3(2 + y)$

45. $-5(u + 1) = 4(1 - u)$

46. $6(z - 4) + 5 = -2z$

47. $\frac{1}{2}(t - 3) = \frac{2}{3}(4 - t)$

48. $\frac{w + 1}{3} = 2(5 - w)$

49. $1 - 3(q - 5) = 4(2 - 3q)$

50. $-2(x - 3) + 5 = 3(1 - 4x) - 7$

51. $4(r - 5) - 2(3 - r) = 3 - 5(r + 4)$

2.6 Applications Involving Linear Equations

We now use linear equations to solve some application (word) problems. The following procedure is used.

Procedure for Solving Word Problems

1. Read (and, if necessary, reread) the word problem very carefully.

2. Determine what it is that you are asked to find.

3. Identify all unknown quantities and assign a variable to each.

4. Draw a diagram or set up a chart to help you organize all of the given information.

5. Rewrite the word statement(s) as an equation.

6. Determine if there is enough information to solve the problem.

7. Solve the equation.

8. Check your results.

For each of the Exercises 52-58, solve the problem.

52. The sum of 21 and twice a certain number is 45. What is the number?

53. A rectangular region has a length of 21 yards. If the perimeter of the region is 67 yards, what is the width of the region?

54. Determine the selling price for an electric can opener that costs $14.60, if the profit is 0.4 of the selling price.

55. Consecutive whole numbers are whole numbers that differ by 1. (6 and 7 are consecutive whole numbers.) Determine three consecutive whole numbers whose sum is 144.

56. The sum of the three angles of a triangle is 180°. If the largest angle of a triangle is three times as large as the smallest angle and the third angle is 15° more than the smallest angle, how many degrees are in each of the angles of the triangle?

57. Maria has some nickels, dimes, and quarters. She has three more nickels than twice the number of dimes, and twice as many quarters as dimes. If the total value of her money is $14.85, how many of each kind of coin does Maria have?

58. There are freshmen, sophomores, and juniors enrolled in a general biology course. There are three times as many freshmen as there are juniors. The number of sophomores is twenty-one more than twice the number of juniors. If the total enrollment in the course is 357, how many juniors are enrolled?

2.7 Formulas

Definition: A mathematical formula is an equation that relates two or more variables. It states a rule or method for doing something.

For example, the equation d = rt expresses the relationship between the distance (d) traveled by an object in uniform motion, and the rate (r) and time (t). If all but one of the variables in a formula is known, the resulting variable can be determined by using the following rule.

Rule for Evaluating a Variable in a Formula

1. Replace all of the other variables in the formula with the given or known value(s).

2. Solve for the unknown variable.

In Exercises 59-60, use the formula d = rt.

59. Evaluate d, if r = 55 mph and t = $2\frac{1}{4}$ hr.

60. Evaluate r (in km/hr), if d = 300 km and t = 150 min.

In Exercises 61-62, use the formula P = 2L + 2W, where P represents perimeter, L represents length, and W represents width. P, L, and W are all in the same units of measurement.

61. Evaluate P (in feet), if L = 33 ft and W = 9 yd.

62. Evaluate W (in yards), if P = 24 yd and L = 27 ft.

In Exercises 63-64, use the formula $A = \frac{a+b+c}{3}$, which represents the average (A) of three numbers a, b, and c.

63. Evaluate A, if a = 63, b = 72, and c = 59.

64. Evaluate c, if A = 242, a = 91, and b = 62.

2.8 Ratio and Proportion

When we order two real numbers, we are comparing them to determine which number is larger. Using subtraction, we can also compare the two numbers to determine how much larger one number is than the other. We can also compare two numbers by division.

Definition: Given two numbers a and b, the ratio a to b is the quotient of the two numbers and is written as $\frac{a}{b}$ or a:b.

The ratio 5 to 3 is written as $\frac{5}{3}$ or as 5:3. Similarly, the ratio −11 to 17 is written as $\frac{-11}{17}$, or as −11:17.

65. On a community affairs committee, there are 13 female members and 11 male members. Write a ratio for each of the following:

    a. the number of females to the number of males.

    b. the number of females to the total number of members.

66. A baseball player gets 8 hits out of 21 times at bat. Write a ratio for each of the following:

    a. the number of hits to the number of misses.

    b. the number of times at bat to the number of hits.

67. A bookcase is 46 inches wide and 64 inches tall. Write a ratio for each of the following:

    a. the height of the bookcase to its width.

    b. the width of the bookcase to the sum of its width and length.

68. On the faculty of Merit College, 72 faculty members are tenured and 101 faculty members are nontenured. Write a ratio for each of the following:

    a. the number of tenured faculty to the number of nontenured faculty.

    b. the number of tenured faculty to the total number of faculty.

We sometimes have ratios that are equal. For instance, the ratio 4:6 is equal to the ratio 2:3, since the fractions $\frac{4}{6}$ and $\frac{2}{3}$ are equivalent fractions.

Definition: If a:b and c:d are two *equal* ratios, then

the equation $\dfrac{a}{b} = \dfrac{c}{d}$ is called a **proportion**, and is read "a is to b as c is to d." The proportion can also be written as a:b::c:d.

Basic Property for a Proportion

In the proportion $\dfrac{a}{b} = \dfrac{c}{d}$, the quantities a and d are called the extremes. The quantities b and c are called the **means**. In a proportion, the product of the **extremes** is equal to the product of the means. That is, **ad = bc**.

In Exercises 69-72, identify the extremes and the means for the indicated proportions.

69. $\dfrac{3}{7} = \dfrac{9}{21}$

70. 6:3::49: 4.5

71. 5:u::25:3

72. $\dfrac{t+4}{-3} = \dfrac{3-t}{4}$

In Exercises 73-76, determine if the given ratios form a proportion.

73. $\dfrac{4}{8} ? \dfrac{15}{30}$

74. $\dfrac{12}{9} ? \dfrac{8}{5}$

75. $\dfrac{19}{7} ? \dfrac{51}{11}$

76. $\dfrac{101}{303} ? \dfrac{6}{18}$

In Exercises 77-80, solve each of the given proportions for the indicated variable.

77. $\dfrac{x}{5} = \dfrac{15}{10}$

78. $\dfrac{-4}{t} = \dfrac{13}{21}$

79. $\dfrac{5}{12} = \dfrac{t}{1.2}$

80. $\dfrac{-7}{9} = \dfrac{11}{w}$

2.9 Linear Inequalities

If a and b are real numbers, then either a < b, a = b, or a > b. Each of the statements "a < b" and "a > b" is called an **inequality**. The symbols "<" and ">" are called the **inequality signs**. We also can use either of these inequality symbols together with the symbol for equality. The symbol "a ≤ b" means that a < b (a is less than b) or a = b (a is equal to b). Similarly, the symbol "a ≥ b" means that a > b or a = b. The inequality symbol always points toward the smaller of the two real numbers.

Definition: Two inequalities are said to be of the **same sense** if their inequality signs point in the same direction. Two inequalities are said to be of the **opposite sense** if the inequality signs point in different directions.

In Exercises 81-84, determine whether the indicated pairs of inequalities are of the same or opposite sense.

81. x < 3 and x < −7

82. y < −9 and y > 2

83. u ≤ −5 and u > 11

84. 2x − 3 < −5 and 4 − x < 9

2.10 Properties of Inequalities

For the following properties, a and b represent real numbers.

1. *Addition Property:* If a < b and c is *any* real number, then a + c < b + c. (Observe that the two inequalities are of the *same* sense.)

2. *Positive Multiplication Property:* If a < b, and c is a *positive* real number, then ac < bc. (Observe that the two inequalities are of the *same* sense.)

3. *Negative Multiplication Property:* If a < b and

c is a *negative* real number, then ac > bc. (Observe that the two inequalities are of the *opposite* sense.)

Note: Similar properties exist for the operations of subtraction and division. Also, the same properties are true for the other inequality symbols (>, ≤, and ≥).

Using the above properties, we now can solve linear inequalities in a single variable. For example, if

$$4u + 5 > 2,$$

then $4u > -3$ (Subtract 5 from *both* sides; *same* sense.)

and $u > \dfrac{-3}{4}$. (Divide *both* sides by 4, which is *positive*; 4 *same* sense.)

Hence, all real numbers that are greater than $\dfrac{-3}{4}$ are solutions for the given inequality.

As a second example, if

$$\dfrac{5 - 2u}{3} \le -6$$

then $5 - 2u \le -18$. (Multiply *both* sides by 3, which is *positive*; *same* sense.)

$-2u \le -23$. (Subtract 5 from *both* sides; *same* sense.)

and $u \ge \dfrac{23}{2}$. (Divide *both* sides by −2, which is *negative*; *opposite* sense.)

Hence, all real numbers that are greater than or equal to $\dfrac{23}{2}$ are solutions for the given inequality.

In Exercises 85-92, solve each of the given inequalities for the indicated variable.

85. $4t - 9 > 7$

86. $3 - 2y < 6$

87. $\dfrac{u - 5}{5} \le -4$

88. $\dfrac{2p - 7}{3} \ge \dfrac{2}{5}$

89. $7(s + 2) \ge 3(4 - 2s)$

90. $3(y - 1) - 4 \le 2 - 4(2 - y)$

91. $\dfrac{5(t - 1)}{2} < \dfrac{4(6 - t)}{-3}$

92. $\dfrac{-3(2m + 1)}{7} \ge \dfrac{-5(1 - 4m)}{5}$

✓ Check Yourself

1. The expressions 1.2x, −3x, 17x, and 0.5x are *like* terms. They are x–terms. (**Simplifying expressions**)

2. The expressions −4r, 5s, and 11r are *unlike* terms. The variable parts are different. (**Simplifying expressions**)

3. The expressions $\dfrac{1}{7}y^2$, $\dfrac{-2}{9}y^2$, $-6y^2$, and y^2 are *like* terms. They are y^2-terms. (**Simplifying expressions**)

4. The expressions $2x^4$, $3x^2$, and $-5x$ are *unlike* terms. The exponents are different. (**Simplifying expressions**)

5. The expressions -3, 14, $\sqrt{7}$, π, and 8.1 are like terms. They are constant terms. (**Simplifying expressions**)

6. $11x + 8x = (11 + 8)x$

    $= 19x$ **(Simplifying expressions)**

7. $-2y - 5y + 10y = (-2 - 5 + 10)y$

    $= 3y$ **(Simplifying expressions)**

8. $-5u^3 + 7u^3 - 21u^3 = (-5 + 7 - 21)u^3$

    $= -19u^3$ **(Simplifying expressions)**

9. $3a + 2b - 4a - 6b + 9a$

    $= (3a - 4a + 9a) + (2b - 6b)$ (Grouping the like terms)

    $= (3 - 4 + 9)a + (2b - 6b)$ (Combining the a–terms)

    $= (3 - 4 + 9)a + (2 - 6)b$ (Combining the b–terms)

    $= 8a - 4b$ **(Simplifying expressions)**

10. $10uv - 3uw + uv + 6uv - 7uw$

    $= (10uv + uv + 6uv) + (-3uw - 7uw)$ (Grouping the like terms)

    $= (10 + 1 + 6)uv + (-3uw - 7uw)$ (Combining the uv–terms)

    $= (10 + 1 + 6)uv + (-3 - 7)uw$ (Combining the uw–terms)

    $= 17uv - 10uw$ **(Simplifying expressions)**

11. If $x = 4$, then $x - 3 = 4 - 3 = 1$, which is not equal to 2. Hence, 4 is *not* a solution for the equation $x - 3 = 2$. **(Simplifying expressions)**

12. If $y = 2$, then $2y + 6 = 2(2) + 6 = 4 + 6 = 10$. Hence, 2 *is* a solution for the equation $2y + 6 = 10$. **(Simplifying expressions)**

13. If $r = 6$, then $3(2 - r) = 3(2 - 6) = 3(-4) = -12$. Hence, 6 *is* a solution for the equation $3(2 - r) = -12$. **(Simplifying expressions)**

14. If $u = -3$, then $\dfrac{3u - 5}{-2} = \dfrac{3(-3) - 5}{-2} = \dfrac{-9 - 14}{-2} = \dfrac{-23}{-2} = 11.5$, which is not equal to 5. Hence, -3 is *not* a

    solution for the equation $\dfrac{3u - 5}{-2} = 5$. **(Simplifying expressions)**

15. If $t = 0$, then $-3(t - 4) = -3(0 - 4) = -3(-4) = 12$,

    and
    $$3(2t - 1) + 15 = 3[2(0) - 1] + 15$$
    $$= 3(-1) + 15$$
    $$= -3 + 15$$
    $$= 12.$$

    Since $12 = 12$, 0 *is* a solution for the equation $-3(t - 4) = 3(2t - 1) + 15$. **(Simplifying expressions)**

16. If $p - 7 = 3$,

    then $(p - 7) + 7 = 3 + 7$

    or $p = 10$.

    Hence, the required solution is 10. **(Addition rule)**

17. If $\qquad x - 5 = -2,$

    then $\quad (x - 5) + 5 = -2 + 5$

    or $\qquad\qquad x = 3.$

    Hence, the required solution is 3. (**Addition rule**)

18. If $\qquad q - 1.2 = 0.1,$

    then $\quad (q - 1.2) + 1.2 = 0.1 + 1.2$

    or $\qquad\qquad q = 1.3.$

    Hence, the required solution is 1.3. (**Addition rule**)

19. If $\qquad m - \dfrac{1}{2} = \dfrac{2}{3},$

    then $\quad (m - \dfrac{1}{2}) + \dfrac{1}{2} = \dfrac{2}{3} + \dfrac{1}{2}$

    or $\qquad\qquad m = \dfrac{7}{6} \ (\text{or } 1\dfrac{1}{6}).$

    Hence, the required solution is $1\dfrac{1}{6}$. (**Addition rule**)

20. If $\qquad t - 5 = 3.9,$

    then $\quad (t - 5) + 5 = 3.9 + 5$

    or $\qquad\qquad t = 8.9.$

    Hence, the required solution is 8.9. (**Addition rule**)

21. If $\qquad q + 11 = -4,$

    then $\quad (q + 11) - 11 = -4 - 11$

    or $\qquad\qquad q = -15.$

    Hence, the required solution is −15. (**Subtraction rule**)

22. If $\qquad x + 1.7 = -3.9,$

    then $\quad (x + 1.7) - 1.7 = -3.9 - 1.7$

    or $\qquad\qquad x = -5.6.$

    Hence, the required solution is −5.6. (**Subtraction rule**)

23. If $\qquad y + \sqrt{3} = -4\sqrt{3},$

    then $\quad (y + \sqrt{3}) - \sqrt{3} = -4\sqrt{3} - \sqrt{3}$

    or $\qquad\qquad y = -5\sqrt{3}.$

    Hence, the required solution is $-5\sqrt{3}$. (**Subtraction rule**)

24. If $\qquad t + 5.6 = -9,$

    then $\quad (t + 5.6) - 5.6 = -9 - 5.6$

    or $\qquad\qquad t = -14.6.$

    Hence, the required solution is −14.6. (**Subtraction rule**)

25. If $w + \dfrac{2}{9} = \dfrac{-1}{4}$,

    then $\left(w + \dfrac{2}{9}\right) - \dfrac{2}{9} = \dfrac{-1}{4} - \dfrac{2}{9}$

    or $w = \dfrac{-17}{36}$.

    Hence, the required solution is $\dfrac{-17}{36}$. (**Subtraction rule**)

26. If $\dfrac{x}{5} = -2$,

    then $5\left(\dfrac{x}{5}\right) = 5(-2)$

    or $x = -10$.

    Hence, the required solution is -10. (**Multiplication rule**)

27. If $\dfrac{y}{0.3} = 1.2$,

    then $0.3\left(\dfrac{y}{0.3}\right) = 0.3(1.2)$

    or $y = 0.36$.

    Hence, the required solution is 0.36. (**Multiplication rule**)

28. If $\dfrac{q}{5} = \dfrac{-1}{4}$,

    then $5\left(\dfrac{q}{5}\right) = 5\left(\dfrac{-1}{4}\right)$

    or $q = \dfrac{-5}{4}$.

    Hence, the required solution is $\dfrac{-5}{4}$. (**Multiplication rule**)

29. If $\dfrac{u}{-5} = -2.6$,

    then $-5\left(\dfrac{u}{-5}\right) = -5(-2.6)$

    or $u = 13$.

    Hence, the required solution is 13. (**Multiplication rule**)

30. If $\dfrac{t}{-3.1} = \dfrac{2}{5}$,

    then $-3.1\left(\dfrac{t}{-3.1}\right) = -3.1\left(\dfrac{2}{5}\right)$

    or $t = -1.24$.

    Hence, the required solution is -1.24. (**Multiplication rule**)

31.   If $3p = -4$,

then $\dfrac{3p}{3} = \dfrac{-4}{3}$

or $p = \dfrac{-4}{3}$.

Hence, the required solution is $\dfrac{-4}{3}$. **(Division rule)**

32. If $-2t = 8$,

then $\dfrac{-2t}{-2} = \dfrac{8}{-2}$

or $t = -4$.

Hence, the required solution is -4. **(Division rule)**

33. If $1.2x = 0.36$,

then $\dfrac{1.2x}{1.2} = \dfrac{0.36}{1.2}$

or $x = 0.3$.

Hence, the required solution is 0.3. **(Division rule)**

34. If $-2.1q = 0.7$,

then $\dfrac{-2.1q}{-2.1} = \dfrac{0.7}{-2.1}$

or $q = \dfrac{-1}{3}$.

Hence, the required solution is $\dfrac{-1}{3}$. **(Division rule)**

35. If $\dfrac{-3}{5}y = \dfrac{-4}{7}$,

then $\left(\dfrac{-3}{5}y\right) \div \left(\dfrac{-3}{5}\right) = \left(\dfrac{-4}{7}\right) \div \left(\dfrac{-3}{5}\right)$

or $y = \left(\dfrac{-4}{7}\right)\left(\dfrac{-5}{3}\right)$

$y = y = \dfrac{20}{21}$.

Hence, the required solution is $\dfrac{20}{21}$. **(Division rule)**

36. $4x - 1 = 5$

$\dfrac{4x = 6}{4 \quad 4}$ (Add 1 to *both* sides.)

$x = \dfrac{6}{4}$ (Divide *both* sides by 4.)

$$x = \frac{3}{2}$$ (Simplify.)

Hence, the required solution is $\frac{3}{2}$. (**Solving linear equations**)

37. $\frac{2}{3}y + 3 = 1$

$\frac{2}{3}y = -2$ (Subtract 3 from both sides.)

$y = -2\left(\frac{3}{2}\right)$ (Divide both sides by $\frac{2}{3}$.)

$y = -3$ (Simplify.)

Hence, the required solution is -3. (**Solving linear equations**)

38. $\frac{q-5}{4} = -3$

$q - 5 = -12$ (Multiply *both* sides by 4.)

$q = -7$ (Add 5 to *both* sides.)

Hence, the required solution is -7. (**Solving linear equations**)

39. $4 - 3t = 5$

$-3t = 1$ (Subtract 4 from *both* sides.)

$t = \frac{-1}{3}$ (Divide *both* sides by -3.)

Hence, the required solution is $\frac{-1}{3}$. (**Solving linear equations**)

40. $5(p - 6) = 1$

$5p - 30 = 1$ (Remove parentheses.)

$5p = 31$ (Add 30 to *both* sides.)

$p = \frac{31}{5}$ (Divide *both* sides by 5.)

Hence, the required solution is $\frac{31}{5}$. (**Solving linear equations**)

41. $\frac{2x - 1}{2} = -9$

$2x - 1 = -18$ (Multiply *both* sides by 2.)

$2x = -17$ (Add 1 to *both* sides.)

$x = \frac{-17}{2}$. (Divide *both* sides by 2.)

Hence, the required solution is $\frac{-17}{2}$. (**Solving linear equations**)

42. $\dfrac{3-4u}{-5} = \dfrac{2}{3}$

$3 - 4u = \dfrac{-10}{3}$ (Multiply *both* sides by –5.)

$-4u = \dfrac{-19}{3}$ (Subtract 3 from *both* sides.)

$u = \dfrac{19}{12}$ (Divide *both* sides by –4.)

Hence, the required solution is $\dfrac{19}{12}$. (**Solving linear equations**)

43. $\dfrac{2}{5}m - 4\dfrac{1}{3} = -3\dfrac{1}{2}$

$\dfrac{2}{5}m = \dfrac{5}{6}$ (Add $4\dfrac{1}{3}$ to *both* sides.)

$m = \left(\dfrac{5}{6}\right)\left(\dfrac{5}{2}\right)$ (Divide *both* sides by $\dfrac{2}{5}$.)

$m = \dfrac{25}{12}$ (Simplify.)

Hence, the required solution is $\dfrac{25}{12}$. (**Solving linear equations**)

44. $2y - 3 = -3(2 + y)$

$2y - 3 = -6 - 3y$ (Remove parentheses.)

$5y - 3 = -6$ (Add 3y to *both* sides.)

$5y = -3$ (Add 3 to *both* sides.)

$y = \dfrac{-3}{5}$ (Divide *both* sides by 5.)

Hence, the required solution is $\dfrac{-3}{5}$. (**Solving linear equations**)

45. $-5(u + 1) = 4(1 - u)$

$-5u - 5 = 4 - 4u$ (Remove parentheses.)

$-5 = 4 + u$ (Add 5u to *both* sides.)

$-9 = u$ (Subtract 4 from *both* sides.)

Hence, the required solution is –9. (**Solving linear equations**)

46. $6(z - 4) + 5 = -2z$

$6z - 24 + 5 = -2z$ (Remove parentheses.)

$6z - 19 = -2z$ (Combine *like* terms.)

$8z - 19 = 0$ (Add 2z to *both* sides.)

$8z = 19$ (Add 19 to *both* sides.)

$$z = \frac{19}{8} \qquad \text{(Divide \textit{both} sides by 8.)}$$

Hence, the required solution is $\frac{19}{8}$. **(Solving linear equations)**

47. $\frac{1}{2}(t - 3) = \frac{2}{3}(4 - t)$

$$\frac{1}{2}t - \frac{3}{2} = \frac{8}{3} - \frac{2}{3}t \qquad \text{(Remove parentheses.)}$$

$$\frac{7}{6}t - \frac{3}{2} = \frac{8}{3} \qquad \text{(Add } \frac{2}{3}t \text{ to \textit{both} sides.)}$$

$$\frac{7}{6}t = \frac{25}{6} \qquad \text{(Add } \frac{3}{2} \text{ to \textit{both} sides.)}$$

$$t = (\frac{25}{6})(\frac{6}{7}) \qquad \text{(Divide \textit{both} sides by } \frac{7}{6}.)$$

$$t = \frac{25}{7} \qquad \text{(Simplify.)}$$

Hence, the required solution is $\frac{25}{7}$. **(Solving linear equations)**

48. $\frac{w + 1}{3} = 2(5 - w)$

$w + 1 = 6(5 - w)$ (Multiply *both* sides by 3.)

$w + 1 = 30 - 6w$ (Remove parentheses.)

$7w + 1 = 30$ (Add 6w to *both* sides.)

$7w = 29$ (Subtract 1 from *both* sides.)

$$w = \frac{29}{7} \qquad \text{(Divide \textit{both} sides by 7.)}$$

Hence, the required solution is $\frac{29}{7}$. **(Solving linear equations)**

49. $1 - 3(q - 5) = 4(2 - 3q)$

$1 - 3q + 15 = 8 - 12q$ (Remove parentheses.)

$-3q + 16 = 8 - 12q$ (Combine *like* terms.)

$9q + 16 = 8$ (Add 12q to *both* sides.)

$9q = -8$ (Subtract 16 from *both* sides.)

$$q = \frac{-8}{9} \qquad \text{(Divide \textit{both} sides by 9.)}$$

Hence, the required solution is $\frac{-8}{9}$. **(Solving linear equations)**

50. $-2(x - 3) + 5 = 3(1 - 4x) - 7$

    $-2x + 6 + 5 = 3 - 12x - 7$ (Remove parentheses.)

    $-2x + 11 = -12x - 4$ (Combine *like* terms.)

    $10x + 11 = -4$ (Add 12x to *both* sides.)

    $10x = -15$ (Subtract 11 from *both* sides.)

    $x = \dfrac{-3}{2}$ (Divide *both* sides by 10.)

Hence, the required solution is $\dfrac{-3}{2}$. **(Solving linear equations)**

51. $4(r - 5) - 2(3 - r) = 3 - 5(r + 4)$

    $4r - 20 - 6 + 2r = 3 - 5r - 20$ (Remove parentheses.)

    $6r - 26 = -5r - 17$ (Combine *like* terms.)

    $11r - 26 = -17$ (Add 5r to *both* sides.)

    $11r = 9$ (Add 26 to *both* sides.)

    $r = \dfrac{9}{11}$ (Divide *both* sides by 11.)

Hence, the required solution is $\dfrac{9}{11}$. **(Solving linear equations)**

52. Let n = the number.

    Then $21 + 2n = 45$

    and $2n = 24$

    or $n = 12.$

Therefore, the number is 12. **(Word problem)**

53. Let w = width of the region (in yd).

Since perimeter (P) of the rectangular region is equal to twice the length (L) plus twice the width (W), we have

    $P = 2L + 2W.$

Substituting 21 yd for L and 67 yd for P, we have

    $67 \text{ yd} = 2(21 \text{ yd}) + 2W$

    or $67 \text{ yd} = 42 \text{ yd} + 2W.$

    $25 \text{ yd} = 2W$

    $12.5 \text{ yd} = W$

Therefore, the width of the region is 12.5 yards. **(Word problem)**

54. Let S = the selling price.

    Then, $0.4S$ = the profit.

    Since profit (P) = selling price (S) − cost (C), we have

    $$P = S - C$$

    or $0.4S = S - \$14.60.$

    $$-0.6S = -\$14.60$$

    $$S = \frac{\$14.60}{-0.6}$$

    $$S = \$24.33$$

    Therefore, the selling price is approximately equal to $24.33. **(Word problem)**

55. Let n = the smallest whole number,

    $n + 1$ = the next larger whole number,

    and $n + 2$ = the largest whole number.

    Since the sum of the three whole numbers is 144, we have

    $$n + (n + 1) + (n + 2) = 144$$

    $$n + n + 1 + n + 2 = 144$$

    $$3n + 3 = 144$$

    $$3n = 141$$

    $$n = 47$$

    $$n + 1 = 48$$

    $$n + 2 = 49$$

    Therefore, the three consecutive whole numbers are 47, 48, and 49. **(Word problem)**

56. Let d = the number of degrees in the smallest angle.

    Then $3d$ = the number of degrees in the largest angle.

    and $d + 15$ = the number of degrees in the remaining angle.

    Since the sum of the three angles is 180 degrees, we have

    $$d + 3d + (d + 15) = 180 \text{ (in degrees)}$$

    or $d + 3d + d + 15 = 180.$

    $$5d + 15 = 180$$

    $$5d = 165$$

    $$d = 33$$

    $$3d = 99$$

    $$d + 15 = 48$$

    Therefore, the angles of the triangle are 33°, 99°, and 48°. **(Word problem)**

57. Let d = the number of dimes.

    Then $2d + 3$ = the number of nickels,

    and $2d$ = the number of quarters.

Since the *value* of the dimes, plus the *value* of the nickels, plus the *value* of the quarters is $14.85, we have

$$\$.10\,d + \$.05\,(2d + 3) + \$.25\,(2d) = \$14.85$$

or $10d + 5(2d + 3) + 25(2d) = 1485.$

$$10d + 10d + 15 + 50d = 1485$$
$$70d + 15 = 1485$$
$$70d = 1470$$
$$d = 21$$
$$2d + 3 = 45$$
$$2d = 42$$

Thus, Maria has 45 nickels, 21 dimes, and 42 quarters. (Verify that the value is $14.85).
(Word problem)

58. Let j = the number of juniors.

    Then $3j$ = the number of freshmen

    and $2j + 21$ = the number of sophomores.

Since the total enrollment is 357, we have

$$j + 3j + (2j + 21) = 357$$

or $j + 3j + 2j + 21 = 357.$

$$6j + 21 = 357$$
$$6j = 336$$
$$j = 56$$

Therefore, there are 56 juniors enrolled in the course. (Verify that there are also 168 freshmen and 133 sophomores for a total enrollment of 357.) **(Word problem)**

59. $d = rt$

$d = (55\text{ mph})(2.25\text{ hr})$

$d = 123.75\text{ mi}$ (mph $\times$ hr = mi) **(Formulas)**

60. $d = rt$

$300\text{ km} = r(150\text{ min})$

$300\text{ km} = r(2.5\text{ hr})$

$$\frac{300\text{ km}}{2.5\text{ hr}} = r$$

$120\text{ km/hr} = r$ **(Formulas)**

61. $P = 2L + 2W$ (in ft)

   $P = 2(33\ \text{ft}) + 2(9\ \text{yd})$

   $P = 2(33\ \text{ft}) + 2(27\ \text{ft})$

   $P = 66\ \text{ft} + 54\ \text{ft}$

   $P = 120\ \text{ft}$ **(Formulas)**

62. $P = 2L + 2W$ (in yd)

   $24\ \text{yd} = 2(27\ \text{ft}) + 2W$

   $24\ \text{yd} = 2(9\ \text{yd}) + 2W$

   $24\ \text{yd} = 18\ \text{yd} + 2W$

   $6\ \text{yd} = 2W$

   $3\ \text{yd} = W$ **(Formulas)**

63. $A = \dfrac{a + b + c}{3}$

   $A = \dfrac{63 + 72 + 59}{3}$

   $A = \dfrac{194}{3}$

   $A = 64\dfrac{2}{3}$ **(Formulas)**

64. $A = \dfrac{a + b + c}{3}$

   $242 = \dfrac{91 + 62 + c}{3}$

   $726 = 91 + 62 + c$

   $726 = 153 + c$

   $573 = c$ **(Formulas)**

65. Number of females = 13

   Number of males = 11

   Total number of members = 13 + 11 = 24

   a. The ratio

   $\dfrac{\text{Number of females}}{\text{Number of males}}$ is $\dfrac{13}{11}$, or 13:11.

   b. The ratio

   $\dfrac{\text{Number of females}}{\text{Total number of members}}$ is $\dfrac{13}{24}$, or 13:24.   **(Ratio)**

66.   Number of times at bat = 21

Number of hits = 8

Number of misses = 21 − 8 = 13

a. The ratio

$\dfrac{\text{Number of hits}}{\text{Number of misses}}$ is $\dfrac{8}{13}$, or 8:13.

b. The ratio

$\dfrac{\text{Number of times at bat}}{\text{Number of hits}}$ is $\dfrac{21}{8}$, or 21:8. **(Ratio)**

67.   Height of bookcase = 64 in.

Width of bookcase = 46 in.

Sum of width and height = 46 in. + 64 in. = 110 in.

a. The ratio

$\dfrac{\text{Height}}{\text{Width}}$ is $\dfrac{64 \text{ in.}}{46 \text{ in.}}$, or 64:46.

b. The ratio

$\dfrac{\text{Width}}{\text{Sum of width and height}}$ is $\dfrac{46 \text{ in.}}{110 \text{ in.}}$, or 46:110. **(Ratio)**

68.   Number of tenured faculty = 72

Number of nontenured faculty = 101

Total number of faculty = 72 + 101 = 173

a. The ratio

$\dfrac{\text{Number of tenured faculty}}{\text{Number of nontenured faculty}}$ is $\dfrac{72}{101}$, or 72:101.

b. The ratio

$\dfrac{\text{Number of tenured faculty}}{\text{Total number of faculty}}$ is $\dfrac{72}{173}$, or 72:173. **(Ratio)**

69. $\dfrac{3}{7} = \dfrac{9}{21}$

The extremes are 3 and 21. The means are 7 and 9. **(Proportion)**

70.   6:3::49:24.5

The extremes are 6 and 24.5. The means are 3 and 49. **(Proportion)**

71.   5:u::25:3

The extremes are 5 and 3. The means are u and 25. **(Proportion)**

72. $\dfrac{t + 4}{-3} = \dfrac{3 - t}{4}$

The extremes are (t + 4) and 4. The means are −3 and (3 − t). **(Proportion)**

73. $\dfrac{4}{8} ? \dfrac{15}{30}$

Does $(4)(30) = (8)(15)$? Yes, $(4)(30) = 120 = (8)(15)$. Therefore, the given ratios form a proportion. **(Proportion)**

74. $\dfrac{12}{9} ? \dfrac{8}{5}$

Does $(12)(5) = (9)(8)$? No, $(12)(5) = 60 \neq 72 = (9)(8)$. Therefore, the given ratios do *not* form a proportion. **(Proportion)**

75. $\dfrac{19}{7} ? \dfrac{51}{11}$

Does $(19)(11) = (51)(7)$? No, $(19)(11) = 209 \neq 357 = (51)(7)$.

Therefore, the given ratios do *not* form a proportion. **(Proportion)**

76. $\dfrac{101}{303} ? \dfrac{6}{18}$

Does $(101)(18) = (303)(6)$? Yes, $(101)(18) = 1818 = (303)(6)$.

Therefore, the given ratios form a proportion. **(Proportion)**

77. $\dfrac{x}{5} = \dfrac{15}{10}$

$(x)(10) = (5)(15)$

$\qquad 10x = 75$

$\qquad\quad x = 7.5 \quad$ **(Proportion)**

78. $\dfrac{-4}{t} = \dfrac{13}{21}$

$(-4)(21) = (t)(13)$

$\qquad -84 = 13t$

$\qquad \dfrac{-84}{13} = t \quad$ **(Proportion)**

79. $\dfrac{5}{12} = \dfrac{t}{1.2}$

$(5)(1.2) = (12)(t)$

$\qquad 6 = 12t$

$\qquad 0.5 = t \quad$ **(Proportion)**

80. $\dfrac{-7}{9} = \dfrac{11}{w}$

$(-7)(w) = (9)(11)$

$\qquad -7w = 99$

$\qquad\quad w = \dfrac{-99}{7} \quad$ **(Proportion)**

81. The linear inequalities x < 3 and x < −7 are of the *same* sense. (**Linear inequalities**)

82. The linear inequalities y < −9 and y > 2 are of the *opposite* sense. (**Linear inequalities**)

83. The linear inequalities u ≤ −5 and u > 11 are of the *opposite* sense. (**Linear inequalities**)

84. The linear inequalities 2x − 3 < −5 and 4 − x < 9 are of the *same* sense. (**Linear inequalities**)

85. $4t - 9 > 7$

$\qquad 4t > 16$ $\qquad$ (Add 9 to both sides; *same* sense)

$\qquad t > 4$ $\qquad$ (Divide *both* sides by 4, which is *positive* ; *same* sense)

The required solution is the set of all real numbers that are greater than 4. (**Linear inequalities**)

86. $3 - 2y < 6$

$\qquad -2y < 3$ $\qquad$ (Subtract 3 from *both* sides; *same* sense)

$\qquad y > \dfrac{3}{2}$ $\qquad$ (Divide *both* sides by −2, which is 2 *negative*; *opposite* sense)

The required solution is the set of all real numbers that are greater than −1.5. (**Linear inequalities**)

87. $\dfrac{u - 5}{5} \le -4$

$\qquad u - 5 \le -20$ $\qquad$ (Multiply *both* sides by 5, which is *positive*; *same* sense)

$\qquad u \le -15$ $\qquad$ (Add 5 to *both* sides; *same* sense)

The required solution is the set of all real numbers that are less than or equal to −15. (**Linear inequalities**)

88. $\dfrac{2p - 7}{-3} \ge \dfrac{2}{5}$

$\qquad 2p - 7 \le \dfrac{-6}{5}$ $\qquad$ (Multiply *both* sides by −3, which is *negative*; *opposite* sense)

$\qquad 2p \le \dfrac{29}{5}$ $\qquad$ (Add 7 to *both* sides; *same* sense)

$\qquad p \le \dfrac{29}{10}$ $\qquad$ (Divide *both* sides by 2, which is *positive*; same sense)

The required solution is the set of all real numbers that are less than or equal to 2.9. (**Linear inequalities**)

89. $7(s + 2) \ge 3(4 - 2s)$

$\qquad 7s + 14 \ge 12 - 6s$ $\qquad$ (Remove parentheses)

$\qquad 13s + 14 \ge 12$ $\qquad$ (Add 6s to *both* sides; *same* sense)

$\qquad 13s \ge -2$ $\qquad$ (Subtract 14 from *both* sides; *same* sense)

$\qquad s \ge \dfrac{-2}{13}$ $\qquad$ (Divide *both* sides by 13, which is *positive*; *same* sense)

The required solution is the set of all real numbers that are greater than or equal to $\dfrac{-2}{13}$. (**Linear inequalities**)

90. $3(y - 1) - 4 \leq 2 - 4(2 - y)$

    $3y - 3 - 4 \leq 2 - 8 + 4y$ (Remove parentheses)

       $3y - 7 \leq -6 + 4y$ (Combine *like* terms)

           $-7 \leq -6 + y$ (Subtract 3y from *both* sides; *same* sense)

              $-1 \leq y$ (Add 6 to *both* sides; *same* sense)

The required solution is the set of all real numbers that are greater than or equal to −1. (**Linear inequalities**)

91. $\dfrac{5(t - 1)}{2} < \dfrac{4(6 - t)}{-3}$

      $5(t - 1) < \dfrac{8(6 - t)}{-3}$ (Multiply *both* sides by 2, which is *positive*; *same* sense)

   $-15(t - 1) > 8(6 - t)$ (Multiply *both* sides by −3, which is *negative*; *opposite* sense)

   $-15t + 15 > 48 - 8t$ (Remove parentheses)

       $15 > 48 + 7t$ (Add 15t to *both* sides; *same* sense)

         $33 > 7t$ (Subtract 48 from *both* sides; *opposite* sense)

       $\dfrac{-33}{7} > t$ (Divide *both* sides by 7, which is *positive*; *same* sense)

The required solution is the set of all real numbers that are less than $\dfrac{-33}{7}$. (**Linear inequalities**)

92. $\dfrac{-3(2m + 1)}{7} \geq \dfrac{-5(1 - 4m)}{5}$

    $-3(2m + 1) \geq \dfrac{-35(1 - 4m)}{5}$ (Multiply *both* sides by 7, which is *positive*; *same* sense)

  $-15(2m + 1) \geq -35(1 - 4m)$ (Multiply *both* sides by 5; which is *positive*; *same* sense)

    $-30m - 15 \geq -35 + 140m$ (Remove parentheses)

        $-15 \geq -35 + 170m$ (Add 30m to *both* sides; *same* sense)

           $20 \geq 170m$ (Add 35 to *both* sides; *same* sense)

         $\dfrac{2}{17} \geq m$ (Divide *both* sides by 170, which is *positive*; *same* sense)

The required solution is the set of all real numbers that are less than or equal to $\dfrac{2}{17}$. (**Linear inequalities**)

Grade Yourself

Circle the numbers of the questions you missed, then fill in the total incorrect for each topic. If you answered more than three questions incorrectly, you need to focus on that topic. (If a topic has less than three questions and you had at least one wrong, we suggest you study that topic also. Read your textbook, a review book, or ask your teacher for help.)

Subject: Linear Equations and Inequalities

Topic	Question Numbers	Number Incorrect
Simplifying expressions	1, 2, 3, 4, 5, 6, 7, 8, 9, 10, 11, 12, 13, 14, 15	
Addition rule	16, 17, 18, 19, 20	
Subtraction rule	21, 22, 23, 24, 25	
Multiplication rule	26, 27, 28, 29, 30	
Division rule	31, 32, 33, 34, 35	
Solving linear equations	36, 37, 38, 39, 40, 41, 42, 43, 44, 45, 46, 47, 48, 49, 50, 51	
Word problems	52, 53, 54, 55, 56, 57, 58	
Formulas	59, 60, 61, 62, 63, 64	
Ratio	65, 66, 67, 68	
Proportion	69, 70, 71, 72, 73, 74, 75, 76, 77, 78, 79, 80	
Linear inequalities	81, 82, 83, 84, 85, 86, 87, 88, 89, 90, 91, 92	

Exponents and Scientific Notation

3

Test Yourself

3.1 Exponents

In Chapter 1, exponents were used to help write products containing repeated factors. For instance, in the expression 5^3, 5 is the factor that is repeated and is called the **base**. The **exponent** is 3 and indicates the number of times that the factor 5 occurs in the product. The exponential expression 5^3 is read as "the third power of 5," or, simply, as "5 cubed."

Definition: If x is a real number and n is a *positive integer* greater than 1, then

$$x^n = \underbrace{x \cdot x \cdot x \cdot \ldots \cdot x}_{n-times}.$$

If n = 1, then $x^n = x^1 = x$.

The following properties of exponents follow directly from the above definition.

Properties of Exponents

Let x be *any* real number and let m and n be *positive integers*. Then:

1. $x^m x^n = x^{m+n}$ (Product rule)

2. $(x^m)^n = x^{mn}$ (Power of a power rule)

3. a. $\dfrac{x^m}{x^n} = x^{n-m}$ (if m > n and x ≠ 0) (Quotient rules)

b. $\dfrac{x^m}{x^n} = \dfrac{1}{x^{n-m}}$ (if m < n and x ≠ 0)

c. $\dfrac{x^m}{x^n} = 1$ (if m = n, and x ≠ 0)

In Exercises 1-12, use the above rules to simplify each of the given expressions.

1. $(a^3)(a^6)$

2. $(-5)^2(-5)^3$

3. $(u^4)^5$

4. $(p^3) \div (p^7)$

5. $(8^6) \div (8^4)$

6. $(-2)^3(-2)^2(-2)$

7. $r^6 \div r^6$

8. $-4(-3)^2$

9. $3(a^2)^3(a^3)^4$

10. $5(q^3)^2 - 3q(q)^5$

11. $(1.7)^4(1.7)^7(1.7)^5(1.7)$

12. $\left(\dfrac{1}{s}\right)^4\left(\dfrac{1}{s}\right)^3 \div \left(\dfrac{1}{s}\right)^5$

13. Prove the Product Rule.

14. Prove the Power of a Power Rule.

Definition: If x is a *nonzero* real number, then $x^0 = 1$.

In Exercises 15-20, simplify each of the given expressions.

15. 6^0

16. $-2^0 - 2^0$

17. $5(a^0)$

18. $(5a)^0$

19. $2x^0 - 3y^0$

20. $2(u)^0(2u)^0$

Definition: If x is a *nonzero* real number and n is a *positive* integer, then,

$$x^{-n} = \frac{1}{x^n}.$$

Note: The rules given at the beginning of this section can now be used for any *integer* exponents—positive, negative, or zero.

In Exercises 21-26, simplify each of the given expressions and write the results without negative or zero exponents.

21. $(-2)^{-2}$

22. $(4)^{-1}(4)^3(4)^{-6}$

23. $(x^{-3})^2(x^{-2})^4$

24. $(-2a^{-1}b^2c)(3a^3b^{-5}c^0)$

25. $(-4x^2yz^0) \div (8x^{-2}y^3z)$

26. $(-5)^2(5)^{-3} \div [(5)^{-3}(-5)^4]$

3.2 Powers of Products and Quotients

The following are additional basic rules for working with integer exponents:

Powers of Product and Quotient Rules

Let x and y be *any* real numbers, and let m, n, and p be *positive integers*. Then:

1. a. $(xy)^m = x^m y^m$ (Power of Product Rule)

   b. $(x^m y^n)^p = x^{mp} y^{np}$

2. $\left(\dfrac{x}{y}\right)^m = \dfrac{x^m}{y^m}$ (if $y \neq 0$) (Power of Quotient Rule)

In Exercises 27-34, simplify each of the given expressions and write the results without negative or zero exponents.

27. $(x^2y)^3$

28. $(a^{-2}bc^3)^2$

29. $[p \div q]^4$

30. $[(-11)^{-3}(-11)^{-2}]^4 \div (-11)^{-5}$

31. $\dfrac{(x^{-2}y^{-3})^2(x^4y^5)^{-2}}{x^3y^5}$

32. $\left(\dfrac{p^3q^2}{p^3}\right)^{-1}\left(\dfrac{p^{-2}q^4}{q^{2^3}}\right)^3$

33. $(u^{-1}v^2)^3(uv)^{-2} \div [(u^2v)^0(u^{-2}v^0)]$

34. $(3a - 2b)^{-5}(3a - 2b)^2 \div (3a - 2b)^{-6}$

3.3 Scientific Notation

Using integer exponents, we can express very large or very small numbers in what is called *scientific notation* .

Definition: If N is a *positive* number, then to write N in **scientific notation** means to write it in the form

$$N = p \times 10^k$$

such that $1 \le p < 10$ and k is an integer.

Writing a Positive Number in Scientific Notation

To write a positive number, N, in scientific notation:

1. To determine the value of p, place a decimal

point in the number N after the first *nonzero* digit from the left.

2. To determine the integer k, count the number of digits that the decimal point must be moved to obtain the original number N.

    a. If the decimal point is moved to the *right* , then k will be *positive*.

    b. If the decimal point is moved to the *left*, then k will be *negative*.

    c. If the decimal point is not moved at all, then k = 0.

For instance, in scientific notation, we write 32096 as:

$$3.2096 \times 10^4 \text{ and } 0.008876 \text{ as } 8.876 \text{ x } 10^{-3}.$$

In Exercises 35-41, rewrite each of the given numbers in scientific notation.

35. 345

36. 909

37. 130.8

38. 21,768

39. 0.061

40. 0.000876

41. 461,000

In Exercises 42-47, rewrite each of the given numbers without exponents.

42. 3.82×10^3

43. 1.062×10^6

44. 809^0

45. 809×10^0

46. 72×10^{-5}

47. 0.06×10^{-4}

✔ Check Yourself

1. $(a^3)(a^6) = a^{3+6} = a^9$ (**Exponents**)

2. $(-5)^2(-5)^3 = (-5)^{2+3} = (-5)^5 = -3125$ (**Exponents**)

3. $(u^4)^5 = u^{4 \times 5} = u^{20}$ (**Exponents**)

4. $(p^3) \div (p^7) = \dfrac{1}{p^{7-3}} = \dfrac{1}{p^4}$ if $p \neq 0$ (**Exponents**)

5. $(8^6) \div (8^4) = 8^{6-4} = 8^2 = 64$ (**Exponents**)

6. $(-2)^3(-2)^2(-2) = (-2)^{3+2+1} = (-2)^6 = 64$ (**Exponents**)

7. $r^6 \div r^6 = 1$, if $r \neq 0$ (**Exponents**)

8. $-4(-3)^2 = (-4)(9) = -36$ (**Exponents**)

9. $3(a^2)^3(a^3)^4 = 3(a)^{2 \times 3}(a)^{3 \times 4} = 3(a)^6(a)^{12} = 3a^{6+12} = 3a^{18}$ (**Exponents**)

10. $5(q^3)^2 - 3q(q)^5 = 5q^{3 \times 2} - 3q^{1+5} = 5q^6 - 3q^6 = 2q^6$ (**Exponents**)

11. $(1.7)^4(1.7)^7(1.7)^5(1.7) = (1.7)^{4+7+5+1} = (1.7)^{17}$ **(Exponents)**

12. $\left(\dfrac{1}{s}\right)^4\left(\dfrac{1}{s}\right)^3 \div \left(\dfrac{1}{s}\right)^5 = \left(\dfrac{1}{s}\right)^{4+3} \div \left(\dfrac{1}{s}\right)^5 = \left(\dfrac{1}{s}\right)^7 : \left(\dfrac{1}{s}\right)^5 = \left(\dfrac{1}{s}\right)^{7-5} = \left(\dfrac{1}{s}\right)^2$, if $s \neq 0$ **(Exponents)**

13. If x is any real number and m and n are positive integers, then

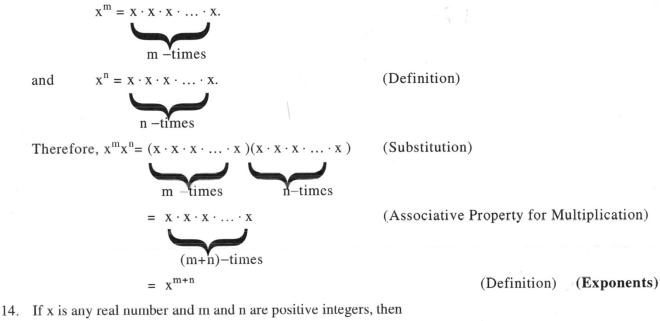

14. If x is any real number and m and n are positive integers, then

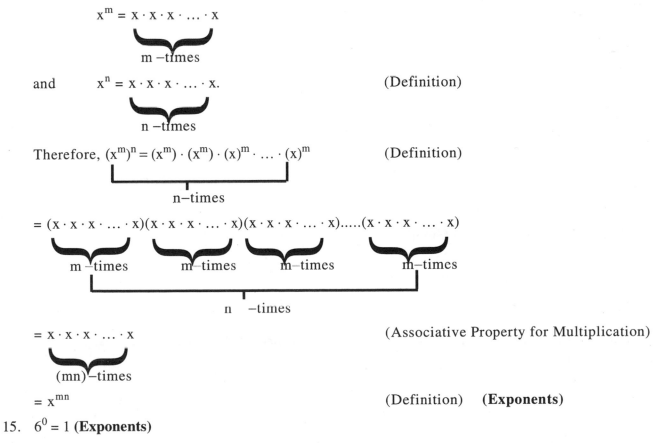

15. $6^0 = 1$ **(Exponents)**

16. $-2^0 - 2^0 = -1 - 1 = -2$ (**Exponents**)

17. $5(a^0) = 5(1) = 5$, if $a \neq 0$ (**Exponents**)

18. $(5a)^0 = 1$, if $a \neq 0$ (**Exponents**)

19. $2x^0 - 3y^0 = 2(1) - 3(1) = 2 - 3 = -1$, if $x \neq 0$ and $y \neq 0$ (**Exponents**)

20. $2(u)^0(2u)^0 = 2(1)(1) = 2$, if $u \neq 0$ (**Exponents**)

21. $(-2)^{-2} = \dfrac{1}{(-2)^2} = \dfrac{1}{4}$ (**Exponents**)

22. $(4)^{-1}(4)^3(4)^{-6} = (4)^{-1+3-6} = 4^{-4} = \dfrac{1}{4^4} = \dfrac{1}{256}$ (**Exponents**)

23. $(x^{-3})^2(x^{-2})^4 = (x)^{(-3)(2)}(x)^{(-2)(4)} = x^{-6}x^{-8} = x^{-6-8} = x^{-14} = \dfrac{1}{x^{14}}$, if $x \neq 0$ (**Exponents**)

24. $(-2a^{-1}b^2c)(3a^3b^{-5}c^0) = (-2)(3)(a)^{-1}(a)^3(b)^2(b)^{-5}(c)(c^0)$

    $= -6a^{-1+3}b^{2-5}c^{1+0} = -6a^2b^{-3}c = -6a^2\left(\dfrac{1}{b^3}\right)c = \dfrac{-6a^2c}{b^3}$, if $a \neq 0$, $b \neq 0$, and $c \neq 0$ (**Exponents**)

25. $(-4x^2yz^0) \div (8x^{-2}y^3z) = \left(\dfrac{-4}{8}\right)\left(\dfrac{x^2}{x^{-2}}\right)\left(\dfrac{y}{y^3}\right)\left(\dfrac{z^0}{z}\right)$

    $= \left(\dfrac{-1}{2}\right)x^{2-(-2)}\left(\dfrac{1}{y^{3-1}}\right)\left(\dfrac{1}{z}\right) = \left(\dfrac{-1}{2}\right)x^4\left(\dfrac{1}{y^2}\right)\left(\dfrac{1}{z}\right) = \dfrac{-x^4}{2y^2z}$, if $x \neq 0$, $y \neq 0$, and $z \neq 0$ (**Exponents**)

26. $(-5)^2(5)^{-3} \div [(5)^{-3}(-5)^4] = \left(\dfrac{(-5)^2}{(-5)^4}\right)\left(\dfrac{(-5)^{-3}}{(-5)^{-3}}\right) = \left(\dfrac{1}{(-5)^{4-2}}\right)(1) = \dfrac{1}{(-5)^2} = \dfrac{1}{25}$ (**Exponents**)

27. $(x^2y)^3 = (x)^{(2)(3)}(y)^{(1)(3)} = x^6y^3$ (**Power of product rule**)

28. $(a^{-2}bc^3)^2 = (a)^{(-2)(2)}(b)^{(1)(2)}(c)^{(3)(2)} = a^{-4}b^2c^6 = \left(\dfrac{1}{a^4}\right)b^2c^6 = \dfrac{b^2c^6}{a^4}$, if $a \neq 0$ (**Power of product rule**)

29. $[p \div q]4 = \dfrac{p^4}{q^4}$, if $q \neq 0$ (**Power of quotient rule**)

30. $[(-11)^{-3}(-11)^{-2}]^4 \div (-11)^{-5} = [(-11)^{-3-2}]^4 \div (-11)^{-5}$

    $= [(-11)^{-5}]^4 \div (-11)^{-5} = (-11)^{(-5)(4)} \div (-11)^{-5}$

    $= (-11)^{-20} \div (-11)^{-5} = \dfrac{1}{(-11)^{-5-(-20)}} = \dfrac{1}{(-11)^{15}}$ (**Power of product and quotient rules**)

31. $\dfrac{(x^{-2}y^{-3})^2(x^4y^5)^{-2}}{x^3y^5} = \dfrac{(x^{-4}y^{-6})(x^{-8}y^{-10})}{x^3y^5} = \dfrac{x^{-12}y^{-16}}{x^3y^5}$

$= \left(\dfrac{x^{-12}}{x^3}\right)\left(\dfrac{y^{-16}}{y^5}\right) = \left(\dfrac{1}{x^{15}}\right)\left(\dfrac{1}{y^{21}}\right) = \dfrac{1}{x^{15}y^{21}}$, if $x \neq 0$ and $y \neq 0$ (**Power of product and quotient rules**)

32. $\left(\dfrac{p^3q^2}{p^3}\right)^{-1}\left(\dfrac{p^{-2}q^4}{q^2}\right)^3 = \left(\dfrac{p^{-3}q^{-2}}{p^{-3}}\right)\left(\dfrac{p^{-6}q^{12}}{q^6}\right) = \left(\dfrac{p^{-9}q^{10}}{p^{-3}q^6}\right)$

$= \left(\dfrac{p^{-9}}{p^{-3}}\right)\left(\dfrac{q^{10}}{q^6}\right) = \left(\dfrac{1}{p^6}\right)q^4 = \dfrac{q^4}{p^6}$, $p \neq 0$ and $q \neq 0$ (**Power of product and quotient rules**)

33. $(u^{-1}v^2)^3(uv)^{-2} \div [(u^2v)^0(u^{-2}v^0)] = (u^{-3}v^6)(u^{-2}v^{-2}) \div [(1)(u)^{-2}(1)]$

$= (u^{-5}v^4) \div (u^{-2}) = \left(\dfrac{u^{-5}}{u^{-2}}\right)(v^4) = \left(\dfrac{1}{u^3}\right)(v^4) = \dfrac{v^4}{u^3}$, if $u \neq 0$ and $v \neq 0$ (**Power of product and quotient rules**)

34. $(3a - 2b)^{-5}(3a - 2b)^2 \div (3a - 2b)^{-6} = (3a - 2b)^{-3} \div (3a - 2b)^{-6} = (3a - 2b)^3$, if $3a \neq 2b$ (**Power of product and quotient rules**)

35. $345 = 3.45 \times 10^2$ (**Scientific notation**)

36. $909 = 9.09 \times 10^2$ (**Scientific notation**)

37. $130.8 = 1.308 \times 10^2$ (**Scientific notation**)

38. $21{,}768 = 2.1768 \times 10^4$ (**Scientific notation**)

39. $0.061 = 6.1 \times 10^{-2}$ (**Scientific notation**)

40. $0.000876 = 8.76 \times 10^{-4}$ (**Scientific notation**)

41. $461{,}000 = 4.61 \times 10^5$ (**Scientific notation**)

42. $3.82 \times 10^3 = 3820$ (**Scientific notation**)

43. $1.062 \times 10^6 = 1{,}062{,}000$ (**Scientific notation**)

44. $809° = 1$ (**Scientific notation**)

45. $809 \times 10^0 = 809 \times 1 = 809$ (**Scientific notation**)

46. $72 \times 10^{-5} = 0.00072$ (**Scientific notation**)

47. $0.06 \times 10^{-4} = 0.000006$ (**Scientific notation**)

Grade Yourself

Circle the numbers of the questions you missed, then fill in the total incorrect for each topic. If you answered more than three questions incorrectly, you need to focus on that topic. (If a topic has less than three questions and you had at least one wrong, we suggest you study that topic also. Read your textbook, a review book, or ask your teacher for help.)

Subject: Exponents and Scientific Notation

Topic	Question Numbers	Number Incorrect
Exponents	1, 2, 3, 4, 5, 6, 7, 8, 9, 10, 11, 12, 13, 14, 15, 16, 17, 18, 19, 20, 21, 22, 23, 24, 25, 26	
Power of product rule	27, 28	
Power of quotient rule	29	
Power of product and quotient rules	30, 31, 32, 33, 34	
Scientific notation	35, 36, 37, 38, 39, 40, 41, 42, 43, 44, 45, 46, 47	

Polynomials

Test Yourself

4.1 Polynomials

We now consider what are called *polynomials*.

Definitions:

1. A **polynomial**, in the variable x, is an algebraic expression that is a term or sum of terms of the form ax^n, where a is any *nonzero* number and n is a *nonnegative* integer.

2. A polynomial that contains exactly one term is called a **monomial**.

3. A polynomial that contains exactly two terms is called a **binomial**.

4. A polynomial that contains exactly three terms is called a **trinomial**.

It is to be emphasized that the exponent, n, in the expression ax^n, is a *nonnegative integer*.

In Exercises 1-6, determine whether the given expression is or is not a polynomial. If it is a polynomial, indicate in what variable. Also, if possible, classify it as being a monomial, binomial, or trinomial.

1. $3y - 5$

2. $-4x^2 + 5x - 11$

3. $\dfrac{2u}{u + 1}$

4. $2T^4 - 4T^2 + 5T - 7$

5. $z^5 - 5z^2 + 3z + 2z^{-1}$

6. $9s - 4s^5 + 2s^9 - 6$

Definitions:

1. If ax^n ($a \neq 0$) is a term of a polynomial, in the variable x, then a is called the **coefficient**, and n is called the **degree** of the term. (A constant term is of degree 0.)

2. The **degree of a polynomial** is the degree of the highest-degree term in the polynomial, after all like terms have been combined.

In Exercises 7-12, determine the degree for each term in the given polynomial. Then, determine the degree of the polynomial.

7. $3x^2 - 5x + 7$

8. $4 - 2y^3 + 3y$

9. $3u - u^3 + 7u^5 - 9u^2$

10. $t^3 - 4t^6 + 3t + 8t^2$

11. $2W^7 - 3W^5 + 9$

12. $5 - s + 2s^4 - 8s^6 + 9s^8$

Note: Polynomials are generally written in **descending powers** of the variable. That is, the *highest* degree term is written first, follwed in order by the decreasing degree terms.

In Exercises 13-16, rewrite each of the given polynomials in descending powers of the variable.

13. $3y - 4y^3 + 5 - y^4$

14. $p^2 - 3p^5 + 4p^3 - 6$

15. $7u^7 - 6 + 12u^3 - u^5$

16. $-3x^4 - 5x - 7x^2 + x^3 - 3$

4.2 Addition and Subtraction of Polynomials

Addition of Polynomials

To add polynomials, add their *like* terms.

Addition of polynomials can be done either horizontally or vertically. Adding the polynomials $3x^2 - 4x + 6$ and $3x - 7x^2 + 2$ horizontally, we have

$$(3x^2 - 4x + 6) + (3x - 7x^2 + 2)$$

$= 3x^2 - 4x + 6 + 3x - 7x^2 + 2$ (Remove parentheses.)

$= -4x^2 - 4x + 6 + 3x + 2$ (Add the 2nd-degree terms.)

$= -4x^2 - x + 6 + 2$ (Add the 1st-degree terms.)

$= -4x^2 - x + 8$ (Add the constant terms.)

To add the two polynomials vertically, write the like terms under each other and then add their numerical coefficients.

We now have

$$3x^2 - 4x + 6$$
$$\underline{-7x^2 + 3x + 2}$$
$$-4x^2 - x + 8$$

More than two polynomials can be added either horizontally or vertically. When adding vertically, leave a space for any missing terms.

In Exercises 17-20, add the indicated polynomials horizontally.

17. $2y^3 - 4y^2 + 5; 3y - 5y^3 + y^2 - 7$

18. $x^6 - 2x^4 + 4x^2 - 3; 4x^5 - 6x^2 + 9x;$
    $2x^4 - 3x^2 + x - 8$

19. $1.2t^5 - 2.3t^3 + 3.7; 0.9t^3 - 0.7t^2 + 1.7t;$
    $5.6t^5 - 4.9t^2 - 7.2$

20. $7b - 5b^2 + 9b^4 - 11; b^4 - 2b^3 + 6b - 1;$
    $8b^3 - 5b + 12$

In Exercises 21-24, add the indicated polynomials vertically.

21. $3m^3 - 5m^2 + m - 7; 4m^2 + 7m^3 + 13$

22. $x^6 - 1.9x^4 + 3.1x^3 - 5x; 2x^5 + 4.1x^4 - 5x^3 + 2$

23. $4u^5 - 6u^3 + u^2 - 8; 5u^4 - 7u^2 + 3u - 7;$
    $u^5 - 2u^3 + 7u - 14$

24. $-3s^5 + 8s + s^2 - 4s^4; 5s^4 - 7s^2 - s + 8;$
    $6s^5 - 4s^2 + 1; s^4 - s^2 + s$

Subtraction of Polynomials

To subtract one polynomial from another polynomial, subtract the *like* terms.

Subtraction of polynomials can be done either horizontally or vertically. Subtracting $2x^3 - 3x^2 + 5$ from $x^2 + 6x - x^3 + 3$ horizontally, we have

$$(x^2 + 6x - x^3 + 3) - (2x^3 - 3x^2 + 5)$$

$= x^2 + 6x - x^3 + 3 - 2x^3 + 3x^2 - 5$ (Remove parentheses.)

$= -3x^3 + x^2 + 6x + 3 + 3x^2 - 5$ (Add the 3rd-degree terms)

$= -3x^3 + 4x^2 + 6x + 3 - 5$ (Add the 2nd-degree terms.)

$= -3x^3 + 4x^2 + 6x - 2$ (Add the constant terms.)

To subtract polynomials vertically, write the polynomials with like terms under each other and subtract their numerical coefficients. To subtract $u - 6u^2 + 8u^3 - 1$ from $2u^4 - 5u^3 + u$, we have

$$2u^4 - 5u^3 + \quad u$$

$$-(\quad 8u^3 - 6u^2 + u - 1)$$

$$2u^4 - 13u^3 + 6u^2 \quad + 1 \text{ (Subtract } like \text{ terms.)}$$

In Exercises 25-28, subtract horizontally.

25. Subtract $3x^3 - x^2 + 5x - 7$ from $7x^3 - 3x^2 + 9x + 1$.

26. Subtract $2y^3 - 4y + 6$ from $y - 3y^2 + y^3 - 7$.

27. From $u^3 - 3u^2 + 6u + 2$, subtract $3u^3 - 8u + 7$.

28. From $2t^5 - 4t + t^3 - t^2 - 11$, subtract $5t^4 - 8t^3 + 3t^2 - t - 2$.

In Exercises 29-32, subtract vertically.

29. Subtract $3u^3 - 4u^2 + u - 7$ from $u^3 - 5u^2 + 7u + 3$.

30. Subtract $1.2t - 3.6t^3 - 7.2\,t^2$ from $t^3 - 4.1t^2 + 5.6t - 3$.

31. From $2r^3 - r^4 - 3r + 1$, subtract $2r^4 - 3r^2 + 2r - 4$.

32. From $3p^4 - p^3 + 5p - 2$, subtract $5 - 2p^2 + 7p^3 - 4p^4$.

4.3 Multiplication of Polynomials

We first consider the product of two monomials.

Multiplication of a Monomial by a Monomial

To multiply a monomial by a monomial:

1. Multiply the numerical coefficients.

2. Multiply the variable factors, using properties of exponents.

3. Form the product of the results obtained in Steps 1 and 2.

For example, to multiply $-4y^3$ by $5y^2$, proceed as follows:

$$(-4y^3)(5y^2)$$

$= -20(y^3)(y^2)$ (Multiply the numerical coefficients.)

$= -20y^5$ (Multiply the variable factors.)

Next, we multiply a polynomial by a monomial.

Multiplication of a Polynomial by a Monomial

To multiply a polynomial by a monomial, multiply each term of the polynomial by the monomial.

For instance, to multiply $3u^2 - 4u + 7$ by $-2u^3$, we proceed as follows:

$-2u^3(3u^2 - 4u + 7) = (-2u^3)(3u^2) + (-2u^3)(-4u) +$
$(-2u^3)(7) = -6u^5 + 8u^4 - 14u^3$

We now consider multiplying a polynomial by a polynomial.

Multiplication of a Polynomial by a Polynomial

To multiply a polynomial by a polynomial, multiply *each* term in one of the polynomials by *every* term in the other polynomial. Then, combine like terms.

For instance, to multiply the polynomial $4s^3 - s^2 + 2s - 7$ by $2s^2 - 5s + 2$, proceed as follows:

$$(2s^2 - 5s + 2)(4s^3 - s^2 + 2s - 7)$$

$$= (2s^2)(4s^3 - s^2 + 2s - 7) + (-5s)(4s^3 - s^2 + 2s - 7)$$
$$+ (2)(4s^3 - s^2 + 2s - 7)$$

$$= (2s^2)(4s^3) + (2s^2)(-s^2) + (2s^2)(2s) + (2s^2)(-7) +$$
$$(-5s)(4s^3) + (-5s)(-s^2) + (-5s)(2s) + (-5s)(-7)$$
$$+ (2)(4s^3) + (2)(-s^2) + (2)(2s) + (2)(-7)$$

$$= 8s^5 - 2s^4 + 4s^3 - 14s^2 - 20s^4 + 5s^3 - 10s^2 + 35s$$
$$+ 8s^3 - 2s^2 + 4s - 14$$

$$= -8s^5 - 22s^4 + 17s^3 - 26s^2 + 39s - 14$$

In Exercises 33-41, multiply as indicated and write the result in descending powers of the variable.

33. $(-3y^4)(5y^5)$

34. $(1.3t^3)(2.4t^4)$

35. $(4u^2)(-5u^3)(u^4)$

36. $(7t^2)(t^3 - 3t^4 + 5t^2)$

37. $(-3p^3)(5p^2 - p - 2)$

38. $(3s - 7)(-2 + 7s)$

39. $(5x - 3)(x^3 - 2x^2 + 5x - 9)$

40. $(3r^2 - 2r + 2)(2r^2 - 7r + 6)$

41. $(4m^3 - 5m^2 + m + 1)(-2m^3 - 3m^2 + 5m - 4)$

4.4 Multiplication of Binomials

Consider

$$(3t - 2)(2t - 5) = (3t)(2t) + (3t)(-5) + (-2)(2t) + (-2)(-5) = 6t^2 - 15t - 4t + 10.$$

The first term of the product, $6t^2$, is the product of the *first* terms of the two binomials.

The last term of the product, 10, is the product of the *last* terms of the two binomials.

The second term of the product, $-15t$, is the product of the *first* term of the first binomial and the *last* term of the *second* binomial. This term is called the **outer product**.

The third term of the product, $-4t$, is the product of the *second* term of the first binomial and the *first* term of the *second* binomial. This term is called the **inner product**.

Expressing the product of two binomials as the sum of the products of the **F**irst, **O**uter, **I**nner, and **L**ast terms is known as the **FOIL** Method. The product of the two linear binomials given above is a trinomial. The middle term of the trinomial is the sum of the outer and inner products. Hence,

$$(3t - 2)(2t - 5) = (3t)(2t) + (3t)(-5) + (-2)(2t) + (-2)(-5)$$

$$= 6t^2 - 15t - 4t + 10$$

$$= 6t^2 + (-15t - 4t) + 10$$

$$= 6t^2 - 19t + 10$$

FOIL *Method for Determining the Product of Two Linear Binomials*

To determine the product of two linear binomials in the same variable(s), do the following:

To determine the *first* term of the product, multiply the first terms of the two binomials.

To determine the *middle* term of the product, form the *sum* of the *outer* and *inner* products of the two binomials.

To determine the *last* term of the product, multiply the last terms of the two binomials.

For example,

$$(3r - 5)(2r + 3) = 6r^2 + 9r - 10r - 15$$

First Outer Inner Last

$$= 6r^2 - r - 15$$

Consider the following:

$$(3u - 1)(3u + 1) = 9u^2 + 3u - 3u - 1$$

First Outer Inner Last

$$= 9u^2 - 1$$

Here, we see a product of two binomials, which is a binomial.

Observe, however, that the two binomials are the *sum* and the *difference* of the same terms.

In Exercises 42-51, multiply using the FOIL method.

42. $(x - 3)(x + 4)$

43. $(y - 9)(2y + 3)$

44. $(3u - 5)(2u + 7)$

45. $(1.2t - 7)(2.1t + 1)$

46. $(w - 4)(w + 4)$

47. $(2y - 7)(2y - 3)$

48. $(3p - 1.2)(p + 3.1)$

49. $(4t - 5)(4t + 5)$

50. $\left(\frac{1}{3}t + 5\right)\left(\frac{2}{5}t - 7\right)$

51. $\left(\dfrac{3}{7}u - 1\right)\left(\dfrac{2}{9}u + 4\right)$

To square a binomial means to multiply the binomial by itself. Squaring the binomial $2u - 7$, we have

$$(2u - 7)^2 = (2u - 7)(2u - 7) = 4u^2 - 14u - 14u + 49$$

First Outer Inner Last

$$= 4u^2 - 28u + 49$$

Notice that the inner and outer products are the same. The square of a binomial is *always* a trinomial.

Rule for Squaring a Binomial

To square a binomial, do the following:

1. Form the *first* term of the product by *squaring* the *first* term of the binomial.

2. Form the *middle* term of the product by taking *twice* the product of the two terms of the binomial. Remember to take into account the signs of the coefficients of the two terms.

3. Form the *last* term of the product by *squaring* the *last* term of the binomial.

In Exercises 52-57, square the given binomial.

52. $p + q$

53. $2x - 3y$

54. $4m + 5n$

55. $1.5u - 2v$

56. $\dfrac{2}{7}s - \dfrac{1}{4}t$

57. $3y - 3.2$

4.5 Division of Polynomials

Rule for Dividing a Polynomial by a Monomial

To divide a polynomial by a *nonzero* monomial,

1. Divide *each* term of the polynomial by the monomial, and

2. Simplify the results.

Consider $\dfrac{6u^2 - 4u - 10}{2}$ (a polynomial divided by a monomial)

$$= \frac{6u^2}{2} - \frac{4u}{2} - \frac{10}{2}$$ (Divide each term of the polynomial by the monomial)

$$= 3u^2 - 2u - 5$$ (Simplify)

Consider the following division, if $p \neq 0$.

$$\frac{4p^3 - 5p^2 + p - 8}{2p^2}$$ (a polynomial divided by a nonzero monomial)

$$= \frac{4p^3}{2p^2} - \frac{5p^2}{2p^2} + \frac{p}{2p^2} - \frac{8}{2p^2}$$ (Divide each term of the polynomial by the monomial.)

$$= 2p - \frac{5}{2} + \frac{1}{2p} - \frac{4}{p^2}$$ $(p \neq 0)$ (Simplify.)

Dividing a polynomial by a polynomial is similar to dividing whole numbers when the divisor has two or more digits. We will limit our divisors to linear binomials, as in the following example.

Divide $y^2 + 5y + 6$ by $y + 2$, if $y \neq -2$. (If $y \neq -2$, then the divisor is not equal to zero.)

Step 1: Arrange both the dividend and the divisor in *descending* powers of y.

$$y + 2 \overline{)y^2 + 5y + 6}$$

Step 2: Divide the *first* term of the dividend, y^2, by the *first* term of the divisor, y, obtaining y. Write the result as the *first* term of the quotient above the y–term in the dividend.

$$\begin{array}{r} y \\ y + 2 \overline{)y^2 + 5y + 6} \end{array}$$

Step 3: Multiply the *first* term of the quotient, y, by the *entire* divisor, y + 2. Write the result below the dividend and subtract like terms.

$$\frac{y}{y+2 \overline{)y^2 + 5y + 6}}$$
$$\underline{y^2 + 2y}$$
$$3y + 6$$

Step 4: Divide the *first* term of the remainder, 3y, by the *first* term of the divisor, obtaining 3. Write the result as the *second* term of the quotient as indicated below.

$$\frac{y+3}{y+2 \overline{)y^2 + 5y + 6}}$$
$$\underline{y^2 + 2y}$$
$$3y + 6$$

Step 5: Multiply the *second* term of the quotient, 3, by the *entire* divisor. Write the result below 3y + 6, and subtract like terms.

$$\frac{y+3}{y+2 \overline{)y^2 + 5y + 6}}$$
$$\underline{y^2 + 2y}$$
$$3y + 6$$
$$\underline{3y + 6}$$
$$0$$

Since the remainder is 0, we are done. If the remainder had been different from 0, but greater than degree zero, we would keep dividing. Hence, $(y^2 + 5y + 6) \div (y + 2) = y + 3$, if $y \neq -2$. We can check this division, just as in arithmetic, by multiplying the quotient (y + 3) by the divisor (y + 2) and adding the remainder (0). The result should be the dividend. The check is left to you.

When dividing a polynomial by a polynomial, after you arrange both the dividend and the divisor in descending powers of the variable, you may notice that there are missing terms in the dividend. If there is a missing term in the dividend, leave a space for it. This is illustrated in the next example.

Divide $u^2 + 3 + 6u^3$ by $2u - 1$, if $u \neq \dfrac{1}{2}$.

Step 1: Rearrange the dividend and the divisor in descending powers of u, leaving a space in the dividend for the missing u-term.

$$2u - 1 \overline{)6u^3 + u^2 \quad + 3}$$

Step 2: Divide the *first* term of the dividend by the *first* term of the divisor, obtaining $3u^2$. Write this result as the *first* term of the quotient as indicated.

$$\frac{3u^2}{2u - 1 \overline{)6u^3 + u^2 \quad + 3}}$$

Step 3: Multiply $3u^2$ by $2u - 1$ and write the result below the dividend as indicated. Subtract like terms.

$$\frac{3u^2}{2u - 1 \overline{)6u^3 + u^2 \quad + 3}}$$
$$6u^2 - 3u^2$$
$$\underline{}$$
$$4u^2 \quad + 3$$

Step 4: Divide $4u^2$ by 2u, obtaining 2u. Write the result in the quotient as indicated.

$$\frac{3u^2 + 2u}{2u - 1 \overline{)6u^3 + u^2 \qquad + 3}}$$
$$6u^2 - 3u^2$$
$$\underline{}$$
$$4u^2 \qquad + 3$$

Step 5: Multiply the entire divisor by 2u and write the result below the remainder as indicated. Subtract like terms.

$$\frac{3u^2 + 2u}{2u - 1 \overline{)6u^3 + u^2 \qquad + 3}}$$
$$6u^2 - 3u^2$$
$$\underline{}$$
$$4u^2 \qquad + 3$$
$$4u^2 - 2u$$
$$\underline{}$$
$$2u + 3$$

Step 6: Divide 2u, the *first* term of the remainder, by 2u, the first term of the divisor, obtaining 1. Write the result in the quotient as indicated.

$$
\begin{array}{r}
3u^2 + 2u + 1 \\
2u-1 \overline{)\,6u^3 + u^2 \qquad + 3} \\
6u^2 - 3u^2 \\
\hline
4u^2 + \qquad 3 \\
4u^2 - 2u \\
\hline
2u + 3
\end{array}
$$

Step 7: Multiply the entire divisor by 1, and write the result below the remainder as indicated. Subtract like terms.

$$
\begin{array}{r}
3u^2 + 2u \quad + 1 \\
2u-1 \overline{)\,6u^3 + u^2 \qquad + 3} \\
6u^2 - 3u^2 \\
\hline
4u^2 + \qquad 3 \\
4u^2 - 2u \\
\hline
2u + 3 \\
2u - 1 \\
\hline
4
\end{array}
$$

The new remainder, 4, is of lesser degree than the divisor. Thus, the division is done. Hence, $(6u^3 + u^2 + 3) \div (2u - 1) = (3u^2 + 2u + 1)$, with a remainder of 4. (Verify that the division is correct.)

In Exercises 58-65, divide as indicated.

58. $(16u^2 - 8u + 12) \div 4$

59. $(18t^4 - 12t^3 + 6t - 15) \div 9$

60. $(9y^5 - 8y^4 + 6y^3 - 5y + 12) \div 3y$, if $y \neq 0$

61. $(s^7 - 4s^5 + 9s^3 - 7s^2 + s - 11) \div 2s^3$, if $s \neq 0$

62. $(t^2 - 5t - 6) \div (t + 1)$, if $t \neq -1$

63. $(2p^3 + 5p^2 + p - 3) \div (2p + 3)$, if $p \neq \dfrac{-3}{2}$

64. $(12 - 11r + 6r^2) \div (3r - 7)$, if $r \neq \dfrac{7}{3}$

65. $(5x - 6x^5 + x^6 - 2x^2 + 4x^3) \div (x - 4)$, if $x \neq 4$

✓ Check Yourself

1. $3y - 5$ is a polynomial in the variable y. It is a binomial.   **(Polynomials)**

2. $-4x^2 + 5x - 11$ is a polynomial in the variable x. It is a trinomial. **(Polynomials)**

3. $\dfrac{2u}{u + 1}$ is not a polynomial. There is a variable in the denominator. **(Polynomials)**

4. $2T^4 - 4T^2 + 5T - 7$ is a polynomial in the variable T. **(Polynomials)**

5. $z^5 - 5z^2 + 3z + 2z^{-1}$ is *not* a polynomial. There is a negative integer exponent. **(Polynomials)**

6. $9s - 4s^5 + 2s^9 - 6$ is a polynomial in the variable s. **(Polynomials)**

7. The terms of the polynomial $3x^2 - 5x + 7$ have degree 2, 1, and 0, respectively. The degree of the polynomial is 2. (**Polynomials**)

8. The terms of the polynomial $4 - 2y^3 + 3y$ have degree 0, 3, and 1, respectively. The degree of the polynomial is 3. (**Polynomials**)

9. The terms of the polynomial $3u - u^3 + 7u^5 - 9u^2$ have degree 1, 3, 5, and 2, respectively. The degree of the polynomial is 5. (**Polynomials**)

10. The terms of the polynomial $t^3 - 4t^6 + 3t + 8t^2$ have degree 3, 6, 1, and 2, repsectively. The degree of the polynomial is 6. (**Polynomials**)

11. The terms of the polynomial $2W^7 - 3W^5 + 9$ have degree 7, 5, and 0, respectively. The degree of the polynomial is 7. (**Polynomials**)

12. The terms of the polynomial $5 - s + 2s^4 - 8s^6 + 9s^8$ have degree 0, 1, 4, 6, and 8, respectively. The degree of the polynomial is 8. (**Polynomials**)

13. In descending powers of y, the polynomial $3y - 4y^3 + 5 - y4$ is written $-y^4 - 4y^3 + 3y + 5$. (**Polynomials**)

14. In descending powers of p, the polynomial $p^2 - 3p^5 + 4p^3 - 6$ is written $-3p^5 + 4p^3 + p^2 - 6$. (**Polynomials**)

15. In descending powers of u, the polynomial $7u^7 - 6 + 12u^3 - u^5$ is written $7u^7 - u^5 + 12u^3 - 6$. (**Polynomials**)

16. In descending powers of x, the polynomial $-3x^4 - 5x - 7x^2 + x^3 - 3$ is written $-3x^4 + x^3 - 7x^2 - 5x - 3$. (**Polynomials**)

17. $(2y^3 - 4y^2 + 5) + (3y - 5y^3 + y^2 - 7)$
$= 2y^3 - 4y^2 + 5 + 3y - 5y^3 + y^2 - 7$
$= (2y^3 - 5y^3) + (-4y^2 + y^2) + 3y + (5 - 7)$
$= -3y^3 - 3y^2 + 3y - 2$ (**Addition of polynomials**)

18. $(x^6 - 2x^4 + 4x^2 - 3) + (4x^5 - 6x^2 + 9x) + (2x^4 - 3x^2 + x - 8)$
$= x^6 - 2x^4 + 4x^2 - 3 + 4x^5 - 6x^2 + 9x + 2x^4 - 3x^2 + x - 8$
$= x^6 + 4x^5 + (-2x^4 + 2x^4) + (4x^2 - 6x^2 - 3x^2) + (9x + x) + (-3 - 8)$
$= x^6 + 4x^5 - 5x^2 + 10x - 11$ (**Addition of polynomials**)

19. $(1.2t^5 - 2.3t^3 + 3.7) + (0.9t^3 - 0.7t^2 + 1.7t) + (5.6t^5 - 4.9t^2 - 7.2)$
$= 1.2t^5 - 2.3t^3 + 3.7 + 0.9t^3 - 0.7t^2 + 1.7t + 5.6t^5 - 4.9t^2 - 7.2$
$= (1.2t^5 + 5.6t^5) + (-2.3t^3 + 0.9t^3) + (-0.7t^2 - 4.9t^2) + 1.7t + (3.7 - 7.2)$
$= 6.8t^5 - 1.4t^3 - 5.6t^2 + 1.7t - 3.5$ (**Addition of polynomials**)

20. $(7b - 5b^2 + 9b^4 - 11) + (b^4 - 2b^3 + 6b - 1) + (8b^3 - 5b + 12)$

$= (9b^4 + b^4) + (-2b^3 + 8b^3) - 5b^2 + (7b + 6b - 5b) + (-11 - 1 + 12)$

$= 10b^4 + 6b^3 - 5b^2 + 8b$ **(Addition of polynomials)**

21. $\quad 3m^3 - 5m^2 + m - 7$

$+ (7m^3 + 4m^2 \quad\quad + 13)$
$\overline{}$
$\quad 10m^3 - m^2 + m + 6$ **(Addition of polynomials)**

22. $\quad x^6 \quad\quad - 1.9x^4 + 3.1x^3 \quad - 5x$

$+ (\quad 2x^5 + 4.1x^4 - 5x^3 \quad\quad + 2)$
$\overline{}$
$\quad x^6 + 2x^5 + 2.2x^4 - 1.9x^3 - 5x \quad + 2$ **(Addition of polynomials)**

23. $\quad 4u^5 \quad\quad\quad - 6u^3 \quad + u^2 \quad\quad\quad\quad - 8$

$\quad\quad 5u^4 \quad\quad\quad\quad\quad - 7u^2 \quad + 3u \quad - 7$

$\quad u^5 \quad\quad\quad\quad - 2u^3 \quad\quad\quad\quad + 7u \quad - 14$
$\overline{}$
$\quad 5u^5 + 5u^4 \quad - 8u^3 \quad - 6u^2 \quad + 10u \quad - 29$ **(Addition of polynomials)**

24. $\quad -3s^5 - 4s^4 \quad\quad + s^2 \quad + 8s$

$\quad\quad 5s^4 \quad\quad - 7s^2 \quad - s \quad\quad + 8$

$\quad 6s^5 \quad\quad\quad - 4s^2 \quad\quad\quad\quad + 1$

$\quad\quad s^4 \quad\quad - s^2 \quad + s$
$\overline{}$
$\quad 3s^5 + 2s^4 \quad - 11s^2 \quad + 8s \quad\quad + 9$ **(Addition of polynomials)**

25. $(7x^3 - 3x^2 + 9x + 1) - (3x^3 - x^2 + 5x - 7)$

$= 7x^3 - 3x^2 + 9x + 1 - 3x^3 + x^2 - 5x + 7$

$= (7x^3 - 3x^3) + (-3x^2 + x^2) + (9x - 5x) + (1 + 7)$

$= 4x^3 - 2x^2 + 4x + 8$ **(Subtraction of polynomials)**

26. $(y - 3y^2 + y^3 - 7) - (2y^3 - 4y + 6)$

$= y - 3y^2 + y^3 - 7 - 2y^3 + 4y - 6$

$= (y^3 - 2y^3) - 3y^2 + (y + 4y) + (-7 - 6)$

$= -y^3 - 3y^2 + 5y - 13$ **(Subtraction of polynomials)**

27. $(u^3 - 3u^2 + 6u + 2) - (3u^3 - 8u + 7)$

$= u^3 - 3u^2 + 6u + 2 - 3u^3 + 8u - 7$

$= (u^3 - 3u^3) - 3u^2 + (6u + 8u) + (2 - 7)$

$= -2u^3 - 3u^2 + 14u - 5$ **(Subtraction of polynomials)**

28. $(2t^5 - 4t + t^3 - t^2 - 11) - (5t^4 - 8t^3 + 3t^2 - t - 2)$

    $= 2t^5 - 4t + t^3 - t^2 - 11 - 5t^4 + 8t^3 - 3t^2 + t + 2$

    $= 2t^5 - 5t^4 + (t^3 + 8t^3) + (-t^2 - 3t^2) + (-4t + t) + (-11 + 2)$

    $= 2t^5 - 5t^4 + 9t^3 - 4t^2 - 3t - 9$ **(Subtraction of polynomials)**

29.
$$
\begin{array}{rrrr}
u^3 & -5u^2 & +7u & +3 \\
-(3u^3 & -4u^2 & +u & -7) \\
\hline
-2u^3 & -u^2 & +6u & +10
\end{array}
$$
   (Subtraction of polynomials)

30.
$$
\begin{array}{rrrr}
t^3 & -4.1t^2 & +5.6t & -3 \\
-(-3.6t^3 & -7.2t^2 & +1.2t &) \\
\hline
4.6t^3 & +3.1t^2 & +4.4t & -3
\end{array}
$$
   (Subtraction of polynomials)

31.
$$
\begin{array}{rrrrr}
-r^4 & +2r^3 & & -3r & +1 \\
-(2r^4 & & -3r^2 & +2r & -4) \\
\hline
-3r^4 & +2r^3 & +3r^2 & -5r & +5
\end{array}
$$
   (Subtraction of polynomials)

32.
$$
\begin{array}{rrrrr}
3p^4 & -p^3 & & +5p & -2 \\
-(-4p^4 & +7p^3 & -2p^2 & & +5) \\
\hline
7p^4 & -8p^3 & +2p^2 & +5p & -7
\end{array}
$$
   (Subtraction of polynomials)

33. $(-3y^4)(5y^5) = (-3)(5)(y^4)(y^5) = -15y^9$ **(Multiplication of polynomials)**

34. $(1.3t^3)(2.4t^4) = (1.3)(2.4)(t^3)(t^4) = 3.12t^7$ **(Multiplication of polynomials)**

35. $(4u^2)(-5u^3)(u^4) = (4)(-5)(1)(u^2)(u^3)(u^4) = -20u^9$ **(Multiplication of polynomials)**

36. $(7t^2)(t^3 - 3t^4 + 5t^2) = (7t^2)(t^3) + (7t^2)(-3t^4) + (7t^2)(5t^2) = 7t^5 - 21t^6 + 35t^4$ **(Multiplication of polynomials)**

37. $(-3p^3)(5p^2 - p - 2) = (-3p^3)(5p^2) + (-3p^3)(-p) + (-3p^3)(-2) = -15p^5 + 3p^4 + 6p^3$ **(Multiplication of polynomials)**

38. $(3s - 7)(-2 + 7s) = (3s)(-2 + 7s) + (-7)(-2 + 7s)$

    $= -6s + 21s^2 + 14 - 49s$

    $= 21s^2 - 55s + 14$ **(Multiplication of polynomials)**

39. $(5x - 3)(x^3 - 2x^2 + 5x - 9)$

    $= (5x)(x^3 - 2x^2 + 5x - 9) + (-3)(x^3 - 2x^2 + 5x - 9)$

    $= 5x^4 - 10x^3 + 25x^2 - 45x - 3x^3 + 6x^2 - 15x + 27$

    $= 5x^4 - 13x^3 + 31x^2 - 60x + 27$ **(Multiplication of polynomials)**

40. $(3r^2 - 2r + 2)(2r^2 - 7r + 6)$

   $= (3r^2)(2r^2 - 7r + 6) + (-2r)(2r^2 - 7r + 6) + (2)(2r^2 - 7r + 6)$

   $= 6r^4 - 21r^3 + 18r^2 - 4r^3 + 14r^2 - 12r + 4r^2 - 14r + 12$

   $= 6r^4 - 25r^3 + 36r^2 - 26r + 12$ **(Multiplication of polynomials)**

41. $(4m^3 - 5m^2 + m + 1)(-2m^3 - 3m^2 + 5m - 4)$

   $= (4m^3)(-2m^3 - 3m^2 + 5m - 4) + (-5m^2)(-2m^3 - 3m^2 + 5m - 4) + (m)(-2m^3 - 3m^2 + 5m - 4) +$
   $(1)(-2m^3 - 3m^2 + 5m - 4)$

   $= -8m^6 - 12m^5 + 20m^4 - 16m^3 + 10m^5 + 15m^4 - 25m^3 + 20m^2 - 2m^4 - 3m^3 + 5m^2 - 4m -$
   $2m^3 - 3m^2 + 5m - 4$

   $= -8m^6 - 2m^5 + 33m^4 - 46m^3 + 22m^2 + m - 4$ **(Multiplication of polynomials)**

42. $(x - 3)(x + 4) = (x)(x) + (x)(4) + (-3)(x) + (-3)(4)$

   $= x^2 + 4x - 3x - 12$

   $= x^2 + x - 12$ **(Multiplication of binomials)**

43. $(y - 9)(2y + 3) = (y)(2y) + (y)(3) + (-9)(2y) + (-9)(3)$

   $= 2y^2 + 3y - 18y - 27$

   $= 2y^2 - 15y - 27$ **(Multiplication of binomials)**

44. $(3u - 5)(2u + 7) = (3u)(2u) + (3u)(7) + (-5)(2u) + (-5)(7)$

   $= 6u^2 + 21u - 10u - 35$

   $= 6u^2 + 11u - 35$ **(Multiplication of binomials)**

45. $(1.2t - 7)(2.1t + 1) = (1.2t)(2.1t) + (1.2t)(1) + (-7)(2.1t) + (-7)(1)$

   $= 2.52t^2 + 1.2t - 14.7t - 7$

   $= 2.52t^2 - 13.5t - 7$ **(Multiplication of binomials)**

46. $(w - 4)(w + 4) = (w)(w) + (w)(4) + (-4)(w) + (-4)(4)$

   $= w^2 + 4w - 4w - 16$

   $= w^2 - 16$ **(Multiplication of binomials)**

47. $(2y - 7)(2y - 3) = (2y)(2y) + (2y)(-3) + (-7)(2y) + (-7)(-3)$

   $= 4y^2 - 6y - 14y + 21$

   $= 4y^2 - 20y + 21$ **(Multiplication of binomials)**

48. $(3p - 1.2)(p + 3.1) = (3p)(p) + (3p)(3.1) + (-1.2)(p) + (-1.2)(+3.1)$

   $= 3p^2 + 9.3p - 1.2p - 3.72$

   $= 3p^2 + 8.1p - 3.72$ **(Multiplication of binomials)**

49. $(4t - 5)(4t + 5) = (4t)(4t) + (4t)(5) + (-5)(4t) + (-5)(5)$

   $= 16t^2 + 20t - 20t - 25$

   $= 16t^2 - 25$ **(Multiplication of binomials)**

50. $\left(\frac{1}{3}t + 5\right)\left(\frac{2}{5}t - 7\right) = \left(\frac{1}{3}t\right)\left(\frac{2}{5}t\right) + \left(\frac{1}{3}t\right)(-7) + (5)\left(\frac{2}{5}t\right) + (5)(-7)$

$= \frac{2}{15}t^2 - \frac{7}{3}t + 2t - 35$

$= \frac{2}{15}t^2 - \frac{1}{3}t - 35$ **(Multiplication of binomials)**

51. $\left(\frac{3}{7}u - 1\right)\left(\frac{2}{9}u + 4\right) = \left(\frac{3}{7}u\right)\left(\frac{2}{9}u\right) + \left(\frac{3}{7}u\right)(4) + (-1)\left(\frac{2}{9}u\right) + (-1)(4)$

$= \frac{2}{21}u^2 + \frac{12}{7}u - \frac{2}{9}u - 4$

$\frac{2}{21}u^2 + \frac{94}{63}u - 4$ **(Multiplication of binomials)**

52. $(p + q)^2 = (p)^2 + 2(p)(q) + (q)^2$

$= p^2 + 2pq + q^2$ **(Squaring a binomial)**

53. $(2x - 3y)^2 = (2x)^2 + 2(2x)(-3y) + (-3y)^2$

$= 4x^2 - 12xy + 9y^2$ **(Squaring a binomial)**

54. $(4m + 5n)^2 = (4m)^2 + 2(4m)(5n) + (5n)^2$

$= 16m^2 + 40mn + 25n^2$ **(Squaring a binomial)**

55. $(1.5u - 2v)^2 = (1.5u)^2 + 2(1.5u)(-2v) + (-2v)^2$

$= 2.25u^2 - 6uv + 4v^2$ **(Squaring a binomial)**

56. $(\frac{2}{7}s - \frac{1}{4}t)^2 = (\frac{2}{7}s)^2 + 2(\frac{2}{7}s)(\frac{-1}{4}t) + (\frac{-1}{4}t)^2$

$= \frac{4}{49}s^2 - \frac{1}{7}st + \frac{1}{16}t^2$ **(Squaring a binomial)**

57. $(3y - 3.2)^2 = (3y)^2 + 2(3y)(-3.2) + (-3.2)^2$

$= 9y^2 - 19.2y + 10.24$ **(Squaring a binomial)**

58. $\dfrac{16u^2 - 8u + 12}{4} = \dfrac{16u^2}{4} - \dfrac{8u}{4} + \dfrac{12}{4} = 4u^2 - 2u + 3$ **(Division of polynomials)**

59. $\dfrac{18t^4 - 12t^3 + 6t - 15}{9} = \dfrac{18t^4}{9} - \dfrac{12t^3}{9} + \dfrac{6t}{9} - \dfrac{15}{9} = 2t^4 - \dfrac{4}{3}t^3 + \dfrac{2}{3}t - \dfrac{5}{3}$ **(Division of polynomials)**

60. $\dfrac{9y^5 - 8y^4 + 6y^3 - 5y + 12}{3y} = \dfrac{9y^5}{3y} - \dfrac{8y^4}{3y} + \dfrac{6y^3}{3y} - \dfrac{5y}{3y} + \dfrac{12}{3y}$

$= 3y^4 - \dfrac{8}{3}y^3 + 2y^2 - \dfrac{5}{3} + \dfrac{4}{y}$ $(y \neq 0)$ **(Division of polynomials)**

61. $$\frac{s^7 - 4s^5 + 9s^3 - 7s^2 + s - 11}{2s^3}$$

$$= \frac{s^7}{2s^3} - \frac{4s^5}{2s^3} + \frac{9s^3}{2s^3} - \frac{7s^2}{2s^3} + \frac{s}{2s^3} - \frac{11}{2s^3}$$

$$= \frac{1}{2}s^4 - 2s^2 + \frac{9}{2} - \frac{7}{2s} + \frac{1}{2s^2} - \frac{11}{2s^3} \quad (s \neq 0) \quad \textbf{(Division of polynomials)}$$

62. If $t \neq -1$, then

$$
\begin{array}{r}
t - 6 \\
t + 1 \overline{) t^2 - 5t - 6} \\
t^2 + t \\
\hline
-6t - 6 \\
-6t - 6 \\
\hline
0
\end{array}
$$

Therefore, if $t \neq -1$, then $(t^2 - 5t - 6) \div (t + 1) = t - 6$.   **(Division of polynomials)**

63. If $p \neq \dfrac{-3}{2}$, then

$$
\begin{array}{r}
p^2 + p - 1 \\
2p + 3 \overline{) 2p^3 + 5p^2 + p - 3} \\
2p^3 + 3p^2 \\
\hline
2p^2 + p - 3 \\
2p^2 + 3p \\
\hline
-2p - 3 \\
-2p - 3 \\
\hline
0
\end{array}
$$

Therefore, if $p \neq \dfrac{-3}{2}$, then $(2p^3 + 5p^2 + p - 3) \div (2p + 3) = p^2 + p - 1$.   **(Division of polynomials)**

64. If $r \neq \dfrac{7}{3}$, then

$$
\begin{array}{r}
2r + 1 \\
3r - 7 \overline{) 6r^2 + 11r + 12} \\
6r^2 - 14r \\
\hline
3r + 12 \\
3r - 7 \\
\hline
19
\end{array}
$$

Therefore, if $r \neq \dfrac{7}{3}$, then $(12 - 11r + 6r^2) \div (3r - 7) = 2r + 1$, with a remainder of 19. **(Division of polynomials)**

65. If $x \neq 4$, then

$$
\begin{array}{r}
x^5 - 2x^4 - 8x^3 - 28x^2 - 114x - 451 \\
x - 4 \overline{)\, x^6 - 6x^5 \qquad + 4x^3 - 2x^2 + 5x} \\
\underline{x^6 - 4x^5} \\
-2x^5 \qquad + 4x^3 - 2x^2 + 5x \\
\underline{-2x^5 + 8x^4} \\
-8x^4 + 4x^3 - 2x^2 + 5x \\
\underline{-8x^4 + 2x^3} \\
-28x^3 - 2x^2 + 5x \\
\underline{-28x^3 + 12x^2} \\
-114x^2 + 5x \\
\underline{-114x^2 + 56x} \\
-451x \\
\underline{-451x + 804} \\
-804
\end{array}
$$

Therefore, if $x \neq 4$, then $(5x - 6x^5 + x^6 - 2x^2 + 4x^3) \div (x - 4) = x^5 - 2x^4 - 8x^3 - 28x^2 - 114x - 451$, with a remainder of -1804. **(Division of polynomials)**

Grade Yourself

Circle the numbers of the questions you missed, then fill in the total incorrect for each topic. If you answered more than three questions incorrectly, you need to focus on that topic. (If a topic has less than three questions and you had at least one wrong, we suggest you study that topic also. Read your textbook, a review book, or ask your teacher for help.)

Subject: Polynomials

Topic	Question Numbers	Number Incorrect
Polynomials	1, 2, 3, 4, 5, 6, 7, 8, 9, 10, 11, 12, 13, 14, 15, 16	
Addition of polynomials	17, 18, 19, 20, 21, 22, 23, 24	
Subtraction of polynomials	25, 26, 27, 28, 29, 30, 31, 32	
Multiplication of polynomials	33, 34, 35, 36, 37, 38, 39, 40, 41	
Multiplication of binomials	42, 43, 44, 45, 46, 47, 48, 49, 50, 51	
Squaring a binomial	52, 53, 54, 55, 56, 57	
Division of polynomials	58, 59, 60, 61, 62, 63, 64, 65	

Factoring

5

Test Yourself

5.1 The Greatest Common Factor

The Distributive Property can be stated as a(b + c) = ab + ac. The left-hand side of the equation is a product of the two factors *a* and (b + c). The right hand side of the equation is a sum of two terms. Each term in the sum has a factor of a.

Definition: To **factor** an expression means to write the expression as a product.

For instance, we can factor the natural number 42 by writing $42 = 2 \times 21$. We can also factor 42 by writing $42 = 6 \times 7$.

In the algebraic expression 4t – 8, the first term, 4t, can be written as (4)(t), and the second term, without its sign, can be written as 8 = (4)(2). We now have

$$4t - 8 = (4)(t) - (4)(2).$$

Note that 4 is a common monomial factor in the two terms. Factoring out this common factor, we have

$$4t - 8 = 4(t - 2).$$

Hence, the expression 4t – 8 can be written as a product of the two factors, 4 and (t – 2). The factors 4 and t – 2 have no factors in common.

The expression $6u^2 - 21u$ can be written as

$$6u^2 - 21u = (2)(3)(u)(u) - (3)(7)(u), \text{ or}$$

$$6u^2 - 21u = 3u(2u - 7).$$

Both 3 and u are common factors in the given expression, and 3u is the *greatest common factor*.

Definition: The **greatest common factor**, denoted

by **GCF**, of an expression is the greatest factor that is common to *all* of the terms of the expression.

Rule for Determining the Greatest Common Factor

To determine the greatest common factor, GCF, of an expression, proceed as follows:

1. Factor *each term* of the expression completely. Write repeated factors using exponents.

2. Form the product of all the *different* factors appearing in Step 1.

3. Raise each of the factors in the product to the *lowest* power that it is found in the factorizations in Step 1.

4. The GCF is the product of all of the factors raised to the powers determined in Step 3.

Factor $8x^4 - 12x^3 + 24x^2$.

Step 1: Determine the GCF of $8x^4$, $12x^3$, and $24x^2$:

a. $8x^4 = 2^3x^4$

$12x^3 = 2^2(3)x^3$

$24x^2 = 2^3(3)x^2$

b. $\text{GCF}(8x^4, 12x^3, 24x^2) = 2^2 3^0 x^2 = 4(1)x^2 = 4x^2$.

Step 2: Divide $8x^4 - 12x^3 + 24x^2$ by $4x^2$:

$$\frac{8x^4 - 12x^3 + 24x^2}{4x^2} = 2x^2 - 3x + 6$$

Step 3: Therefore,

$$8x^4 - 12x^3 + 24x^2 = 4x^2(2x^2 - 3x + 6).$$

In Exercises 1-8, factor each of the given expressions by first determining the greatest common factor.

1. $3x + 15$

2. $4y^2 - 8y$

3. $36u - 54$

4. $9r^2s^4 - 54r^5s^3$

5. $2z^3 - 6z^2 + 10z$

6. $22x^2y^3 - 55x^3y^2 + 88x^4y$

7. $-5a^2b^4 + 10a^3b - 25a^4b^5 - 20a^2$

8. $3x^3y^2z^4 - 12x^4y^3z - 6xy^5z^6 + 24x^2y^3z^4$

5.2 Factoring the Difference of Squares

In Section 3.7, we formed the product of the sum and the difference of two identical terms. The product was the difference of the squares of the terms. For instance,

$$(x + 5)(x - 5) = x^2 - 5x + 5x - 25 = x^2 - 25.$$

Since the product of the sum and the difference of two identical terms is the difference of the squares of the terms, we have a procedure for factoring the difference of two squares.

Factoring the Difference of Two Squares

$$x^2 - y^2 = (x)^2 - (y)^2 = (x + y)(x - y)$$

Factoring $16a^2 - 25b^2$, we have

$$16a^2 - 25b^2 = (4a)^2 - (5b)^2 = (4a + 5b)(4a - 5b).$$

Now, consider factoring $18p^2 - 8q^2$. First, observe that 2 is the GCF of $18p^2$ and $8q^2$. Hence, we have

$$18p^2 - 8q^2 = 2(9p^2 - 4q^2).$$

We next observe that $9p^2 - 4q^2$ is the difference of two squares. Hence,

$$18p^2 - 8q^2 = 2(9p^2 - 4q^2)$$

$$= 2[(3p)^2 - (2q)^2]$$

$$= 2(3p + 2q)(3p - 2q).$$

Whenever you have an expression that needs to be factored, **always look for the greatest common factor first.**

In Exercises 9-18, factor each of the given expressions as completely as possible.

9. $t^2 - 81$

10. $36a^2 - 121$

11. $4u^2 - 9v^2$

12. $144p^2 - 625q^2$

13. $2x^2 - 98$

14. $75 - 12y^2$

15. $a^2b^2 - c^2d^2$

16. $r^4 - s^4$

17. $mn^3 - m^3n$

18. $8u^2v^3 - 50u^4v$

5.3 Factoring Trinomials of the Form $x^2 + bx + c$

Definition: A **quadratic trinomial** is a *second-degree* polynomial containing *three* terms. The **leading coefficient** of a quadratic trinomial is the coefficient of the second-degree term.

The polynomial $4x^2 - 7x + 1$ is a quadratic trinomial in the variable x. Its leading coefficient is 4.

The polynomial $5 - y^2 - 4y$ is a quadratic trinomial in the variable y. Its leading coefficient is -1.

If a quadratic polynomial is factorable, then the factors will always be *two linear first-degree binomials.* Quadratic trinomials with leading coefficients of 1 are easier to factor than are quadratic trinomials with leading cofficients other than 1.

Procedure for Factoring Quadratic Trinomials with Leading Coefficients of 1

If the quadratic trinomial $y^2 + (a + b)y + ab$ is factorable, the two linear binomial factors will be $(y + a)$ and $(y + b)$. Hence,

$$y^2 + (a + b)y + ab = (y + a)(y + b)$$

such that:

1. If the constant term, ab, is *positive*, then the factors a and b will both have the *same* sign as the sign of the middle term of the trinomial.

2. If the constant term, ab, is *negative*, then the factors a and b will have *opposite* signs.

3. The sum of the inner product and the outer product of the two linear factors must equal the middle term of the trinomial.

To factor $u^2 - 5u + 6$, observe that the constant term, 6, is *positive*. The middle term has a negative coefficient, -5. Hence, the two linear factors will be of the form

$$(u -)(u -).$$

Next, determine that the negative factors of 6, such that their sum is -5, are -2 and -3. Therefore,

$$u^2 - 5x + 6 = (u - 2)(u - 3).$$

To factor $v^2 - v - 6$, observe that the constant term, -6, is *negative*. Hence, the two linear factors will be of the form

$$(v +)(v -).$$

Next, determine that the two factors of -6, with *opposite* signs and such that their sum is -1, are -3 and 2. Therefore,

$$v^2 - v - 6 = (v + 2)(v - 3).$$

In Exercises 19-28, factor each of the given expressions as completely as possible. If the expression is not factorable, so indicate.

19. $p^2 - 4p + 3$

20. $u^2 - 5u - 6$

21. $x^2 + 4x + 4$

22. $y^2 + 8y - 9$

23. $q^2 + 2q + 3$

24. $v^2 - v - 42$

25. $m^2 - 13m + 40$

26. $w^2 + 17w + 60$

27. $z^2 - 3z + 7$

28. $t^2 + 3t - 54$

5.4 Factoring Trinomials of the Form $ax^2 + bx + c$ $(a \neq 0)$

We now consider factoring quadratic trinomials with leading coefficients other than 1. Again, if such trinomials are factorable, the factors will be two linear binomials.

To factor $2x^2 + 5x - 3$, proceed as follows:

Determine the *first* terms of the binomial factors. These will be linear factors of $2x^2$. Here, the only linear factors of $2x^2$ are 2x and x. Hence, the linear binomial factors will be of the form

$$(2x \quad)(x \quad).$$

Determine the *last* terms of the binomial factors. These will be factors of -3. The only choices of such factors are 1 and -3, or -1 and 3. We now have

$$(2x + 1)(x - 3) \text{ or } (2x - 1)(x + 3).$$

Check the middle term. We want 5x.

For $(2x + 1)(x - 3)$, the middle term is $-5x$, which is wrong.

For $(2x - 1)(x + 3)$, the middle term is 5x, which is right.

Hence, $2x^2 + 5x - 3 = (2x - 1)(x + 3)$.

If the quadratic trinomial is not written in descending powers of the variable, rewrite it so that it is.

This makes it easier to factor the expression, if it is, in fact, factorable.

In Exercises 29-38, factor each of the expressions as completely as possible. If the expression is not factorable, so indicate.

29. $3y^2 - 8y - 3$

30. $5x^2 + 8x - 4$

31. $7t^2 - 4t - 3$

32. $3p^2 - p - 14$

33. $11q^2 - 53q - 10$

34. $49u - 12 + 13u^2$

35. $2v^2 - 63 + 5v$

36. $10m^2 - 3m - 4$

37. $6p^2 - 15 + p$

38. $6t^2 - 7t - 3$

5.5 Quadratic Equations and Factoring

A quadratic equation in the variable x is an equation of the form $ax^2 + bx + c = 0$ such that $a \neq 0$. Factoring is one method that can be used to solve quadratic equations. For instance, to solve the equation $x^2 - 25 = 0$, proceed as follows.

$$x^2 - 25 = 0$$

$$(x + 5)(x - 5) = 0 \text{ (Factor left-hand side.)}$$

$x + 5 = 0$ or $x - 5 = 0$ (If ab = 0, then either a = 0, or b = 0.)

$x = -5 \qquad x = 5$ (Solve the linear equations.)

Therefore, the two solutions for the given equation are −5 and 5.

Factoring can also be used to solve certain equations of higher degree. For example, to solve the equation $2y^3 + y^2 - y = 0$, first observe that y is a common factor for all three terms on the left-hand side of the equation. Hence,

$$2y^3 + y^2 - y = 0$$

$$y(2y^2 + y - 1) = 0 \text{ (Common factor)}$$

$$y(2y - 1)(y + 1) = 0 \text{ (Factor the trinomial.)}$$

$y = 0$ or $2y - 1 = 0$ or $y + 1 = 0$ (If a product of 3 factors is equal to 0, then at least one of the factors must be 0.)

$y = 0 \qquad y = \dfrac{1}{2} \quad y = -1$ (Solve the linear equations.)

Therefore, the solutions for the given equation are $-1, 0,$ and $\dfrac{1}{2}$.

In Exercises 39-46, solve each of the given equations.

39. $x^2 - 5x - 24 = 0$

40. $y^2 - 6y = 0$

41. $5u^3 + 8u^2 - 4u = 0$

42. $4v^3 - 9v = 0$

43. $x^4 + 10x^3 = -25x^2$

44. $72p^3 = 162p$

45. $q^3 = 48q + 13q^2$

46. $(4t^2 - 9)(9t^2 - 25) = 0$

5.6 Factoring by Grouping

We now consider another method of factoring that involves a common factor that is not a monomial. The expression

$$ax + ay + bx + by$$

is an expression consisting of four terms. Observe that there are no common factors for *all* of the terms. The expression cannot be factored as the difference of two squares, nor is it a quadratic trinomial. However, the expression can be factored by first grouping terms as follows:

ax + ay + bx + by

= (ax + ay) + (bx + by) (Group the terms.)

= a(x + y) + (bx + by) (Common factor, a)

= a(x + y) + b(x + y) (Common factor, b)

= (x + y)(a + b) (Common factor, x + y)

= (a + b)(x + y) (Commutative property for multiplication)

Therefore, ax + ay + bx + by = (a + b)(x + y).

This method of factoring is called *factoring by grouping*. The method can be used to factor certain polynomials, depending upon how the terms of the expression are grouped.

In Exercises 47–54, factor each of the given expressions by grouping.

47. ax + bx + ay + by

48. au − bu + av − bv

49. rs + r − s − 1

50. a + 1 + 2b + 2ab

51. $s^2 + 4s + 4t - t^2$

52. $y^2 - 5x - 25 + xy$

53. $r^2 + rs - 3s - 9$

54. $3p^2 - 12 - 6q + 3pq$

Check Yourself

1. a. Determine the GCF of 3x and 15:

    3x = (3)(x)

    15 = (3)(5)

    GCF(3x, 15) = $(3)(5)^0(x)^0 = (3)(1)(1) = 3$.

    b. Divide 3x + 15 by 3:

    $$\frac{3x + 15}{3} = x + 5$$

    c. Therefore, 3x + 15 = 3(x + 5). **(Greatest common factor)**

2. a. Determine the GCF of $4y^2$ and 8y:

    $4y^2 = (2)^2(y)^2$

    $8y = (2)^3(y)$

    GCF($4y^2$, 8y) = $(2)^2(y)^1 = 4y$.

    b. Divide $4y^2 - 8y$ by 4y.

    $$\frac{4y^2 - 8y}{4y} = y - 2$$

    c. Therefore, $4y^2 - 8y = 4y(y - 2)$. **(Greatest common factor)**

3. a. Determine the GCF of 36u and 54:

$$36u = (2)^2(3)^2(u)$$

$$54 = (2)(3)^3$$

$$GCF(36u, 54) = (2)(3)^2(u)^0 = (2)(9)(1) = 18.$$

b. Divide $36u - 54$ by 18:

$$\frac{36u - 54}{18} = 2u - 3$$

c. Therefore, $36u - 54 = 18(2u - 3)$. **(Greatest common factor)**

4. a. Determine the GCF of $9r^2s^4$ and $54r^5s^3$:

$$9r^2s^4 = (3)^2(r)^2(s)^4$$

$$54r^5s^3 = (2)(3)^3(r)^5(s)^3$$

$$GCF(9r^2s^4, 54r^5s^3) = (2)^0(3)^2(r)^2(s)^3 = (1)(9)(r^2)(s^3) = 9r^2s^3.$$

b. Divide $9r^2s^4 - 54r^5s^3$ by $9r^2s^3$:

$$\frac{9r^2s^4 - 54r^5s^3}{9r^2s^3} = s - 6r^3$$

c. Therefore, $9r^2s^4 - 54r^5s^3 = 9r^2s^3(s - 6r^3)$.   **(Greatest common factor)**

5. a. Determine the GCF of $2z^3$, $6z^2$, and $10z$:

$$2z^3 = (2)(z)^3$$

$$6z^2 = (2)(3)(z)^2$$

$$10z = (2)(5)(z)$$

$$GCF(2z^3, 6z^2, 10z) = (2)(3)^0(5)^0(z) = (2)(1)(1)(z) = 2z.$$

b. Divide $2z^3 - 6z^2 + 10z$ by $2z$:

$$\frac{2z^3 - 6z^2 + 10z}{2z} = z^2 - 3z + 5$$

c. Therefore, $2z^3 - 6z^2 + 10z = 2z(z^2 - 3z + 5)$. **(Greatest common factor)**

6. a. Determine the GCF of $22x^2y^3$, $55x^3y^2$, and $88x^4y$:

$$22x^2y^3 = (2)(11)(x)^2(y)^3$$

$$55x^3y^2 = (5)(11)(x)^3(y)^2$$

$$88x^4y = (2)^3(11)(x)^4(y)$$

$$GCF(22x^2y^3, 55x^3y^2, 88x^4y) = (2)^0(5)^0(11)(x)^2(y) = (1)(1)(11)(x^2)(y) = 11x^2y.$$

b. Divide $22x^2y^3 - 55x^3y^2 + 88x^4y$ by $11x^2y$:

$$\frac{22x^2y^3 - 55x^3y^2 + 88x^4y}{11x^2y} = 2y^2 - 5xy + 8x^2$$

c. Therefore, $22x^2y^3 - 55x^3y^2 + 88x^4y = 11x^2y(2y^2 - 5xy + 8x^2)$. **(Greatest common factor)**

7. a. Determine the GCF of $5a^2b^4$, $10a^3b$, $25a^4b^5$, and $20a^2$:

$5a^2b^4 = (5)(a)^2(b)^4$

$10a^3b = (2)(5)(a)^3(b)$

$25a^4b^5 = (5)^2(a)^4(b)^5$

$20a^2 = (2)^2(5)(a)^2$

$GCF(5a^2b^4, 10a^3b, 25a^4b^5, 20a^2) = (2)^0(5)(a)^2(b)^0 = (1)(5)(a)^2(1) = 5a^2$

b. Divide $-5a^2b^4 + 10a^3b - 25a^4b^5 - 20a^2$ by $5a^2$:

$$\frac{-5a^2b^4 + 10a^3b - 25a^4b^5 - 20a^2}{5a^2} = -b^4 + 2ab - 5a^2b^5 - 4$$

c. Therefore, $-5a^2b^4 + 10a^3b - 25a^4b^5 - 20a^2 = 5a^2(-b^4 + 2ab - 5a^2b^5 - 4)$ **(Greatest common factor)**

8. a. Determine the GCF of $3x^3y^2z^4$, $12x^4y^3z$, $6xy^5z^6$, and $24x^2y^3z^4$:

$3x^3y^2z^4 = (3)(x)^3(y)^2(z)^4$

$12x^4y^3z = (2)^2(3)(x)^4(y)^3(z)$

$6xy^5z^6 = (2)(3)(x)(y)^5(z)^6$

$24x^2y^3z^4 = (2)^3(3)(x)^2(y)^3(z)^4$

$GCF(3x^3y^2z^4, 12x^4y^3z, 6xy^5z^6, 24x^2y^3z^4) = (2)^0(3)(x)(y)^2(z) = (1)(3)(x)(y^2)z = 3xy^2z$

b. Divide $3x^3y^2z^4 - 12x^4y^3z - 6xy^5z^6 + 24x^2y^3z^4$ by $3xy^2z$:

$$\frac{3x^3y^2z^4 - 12x^4y^3z - 6xy^5z^6 + 24x^2y^3z^4}{3xy^2z} = x^2z^3 - 4x^3y - 2y^3z^5 + 8xyz^3$$

c. Therefore, $3x^3y^2z^4 - 12x^4y^3z - 6xy^5z^6 + 24x^2y^3z^4 = 3xy^2z(x^2z^3 - 4x^3y - 2y^3z^5 + 8xyz^3)$. **(Greatest common factor)**

9. $t^2 - 81 = (t)^2 - (9)^2$

$\qquad = (t + 9)(t - 9)$ **(Factoring the difference of two squares)**

10. $36a^2 - 121 = (6a)^2 - (11)^2$

$\qquad = (6a + 11)(6a - 11)$ **(Factoring the difference of two squares)**

11. $4u^2 - 9v^2 = (2u)^2 - (3v)^2$

$\qquad = (2u + 3v)(2u - 3v)$ **(Factoring the difference of two squares)**

12. $144p^2 - 625q^2 = (12p)^2 - (25q)2$

$\qquad = (12p + 25q)(12p - 25q)$ **(Factoring the difference of two squares)**

13. $2x^2 - 98 = 2(x^2 - 49)$ $\qquad$ (Common Factor, 2)

$\qquad = 2[(x)^2 - (7)^2]$

$\qquad = 2(x + 7)(x - 7)$ **(Factoring the difference of two squares)**

14. $75 - 12y^2 = 3(25 - 4y^2)$ (Common Factor, 3)

$\qquad = 3[(5)^2 - (2y)^2]$

$\qquad = 3(5 + 2y)(5 - 2y)$ **(Factoring the difference of two squares)**

15. $a^2b^2 - c^2d^2 = (ab)^2 - (cd)^2$

    $= (ab + cd)(ab - cd)$ **(Factoring the difference of two squares)**

16. $r^4 - s^4 = (r^2)^2 - (s^2)^2$

    $= (r^2 + s^2)(r^2 - s^2)$

    $= (r^2 + s^2)[(r)^2 - (s)^2]$

    $= (r^2 + s^2)(r + s)(r - s)$ **(Factoring the difference of two squares)**

17. $mn^3 - m^3n = mn(n^2 - m^2)$ (Common Factor, mn)

    $= mn[(n)^2 - (m)^2]$

    $= mn(n + m)(n - m)$ **(Factoring the difference of two squares)**

18. $8u^2v^3 - 50u^4v = 2u^2v(4v^2 - 25u^2)$ (Common Factor, $2u^2v$)

    $= 2u^2v[(2v)^2 - (5u)^2]$

    $= 2u^2v(2v + 5u)(2v - 5u)$ **(Factoring the difference of two squares)**

19. The constant term in the expression $p^2 - 4p + 3$ is 3, which is positive. The middle term has a negative coefficient, −4. Hence, the two linear factors will be of the form $(p - \ )(p - \ )$.

    The negative factors of 3, such that their sum is −4, are −3 and −1. Therefore, $p^2 - 4p + 3 = (p - 3)(p - 1)$. **(Factoring quadratic trinomials)**

20. The constant term in the expression $u^2 - 5u - 6$ is −6, which is negative. Hence, the two linear factors will be of the form $(u + \ )(u - \ )$.

    The two factors of −6, with opposite signs, and such that their sum is −5, are −6 and 1. Therefore, $u^2 - 5u - 6 = (u + 1)(u - 6)$. **(Factoring quadratic trinomials)**

21. The constant term in the expression $x^2 + 4x + 4$ is 4, which is positive. The middle term has a positive coefficient, 4. Hence, the two linear factors will be of the form $(x + \ )(x + \ )$.

    The positive factors of 4, such that their sum is 4, are 2 and 2. Therefore, $(x^2 + 4x + 4) = (x + 2)(x + 2)$. **(Factoring quadratic trinomials)**

22. The constant term in the expression $y^2 + 8y - 9$ is −9, which is negative. Hence, the two linear factors will be of the form $(y + \ )(y - \ )$.

    The two factors of −9, with opposite signs and such that their sum is 8, are −1 and 9. Therefore, $y^2 + 8y - 9 = (y + 9)(y - 1)$. **(Factoring quadratic trinomials)**

23. The constant term in the expression $q^2 + 2q + 3$ is 3, which is positive. The middle term has a positive coefficient, 2. Hence, the two linear factors will be of the form $(q + \ )(q + \ )$.

    There are no positive factors of 3 such that their sum is 2. Hence, the given expression is *not* factorable. **(Factoring quadratic trinomials)**

24. The constant term in the expression $v^2 - v - 42$ is −42, which is negative. Hence, the two linear factors will be of the form $(v + \ )(v - \ )$.

    The factors of −42, with opposite signs and such that their sum is −1, are −7 and 6. Therefore, $v^2 - v - 42 = (v + 6)(v - 7)$. **(Factoring quadratic trinomials)**

25. The constant term in the expression $m^2 - 13m + 40$ is 40, which is positive. The middle term has a negative coefficient, −13. Hence, the two linear factors will be of the form $(m - \ )(m - \ )$.

    The negative factors of 40, such that their sum is −13, are −8 and −5. Therefore, $m^2 - 13m + 40 = (m - 8)(m - 5)$. **(Factoring quadratic trinomials)**

26. The constant term in the expression $w^2 + 17w + 60$ is 60, which is positive. The middle term has a positive coefficient, 17. Hence, the two linear factors will be of the form $(w + \ )(w + \ )$.

    The positive factors of 60, such that their sum is 17, are 5 and 12. Therefore, $w^2 + 17w + 60 = (w + 5)(w + 12)$. **(Factoring quadratic trinomials)**

27. The constant term in the expression $z^2 - 3z + 7$ is 7, which is positive. The middle term has a negative coefficient, −3. Hence, the two linear factors will be of the form $(z - \ )(z - \ )$.

    There are no negative factors of 7, such that their sum is −3. Therefore, the given expression is *not* factorable. **(Factoring quadratic trinomials)**

28. The constant term in the expression $t^2 + 3t - 54$ is −54, which is negative. Hence, the two linear factors will be of the form $(t + \ )(t - \ )$.

    The factors of −54, with opposite signs and such that their sum is 3, are −6 and 9. Therefore, $t^2 + 3t - 54 = (t + 9)(t - 6)$. **(Factoring quadratic trinomials)**

29. The linear factors of the first term, $3y^2$, in the expression $3y^2 - 8y - 3$, are 3y and y. Hence, we have $(3y \ )(y \ )$.

    The choices for factors of the last term, −3, of the expression, are −1 and 3, or −3 and 1. We now have $3y -1)(y + 3)$, $(3y + 3)(y - 1)$, $(3y + 1)(y - 3)$, $(3y - 3)(y + 1)$.

    Since we want the middle term to be −8y, we select the third choice. Therefore, $3y^2 - 8y - 3 = (3y + 1)(y - 3)$.

    Note: In this exercise, it was not necessary to consider the second and fourth choices of factors. In both cases, these factorizations contain factors that have a common factor of 3. Since there is no common factor in the original expression, we cannot have a common factor in either of the two linear factors of the correct factorization.   **(Factoring quadratic trinomials)**

30. The linear factors of the first term, $5x^2$, in the expression $5x^2 + 8x - 4$, are 5x and x. Hence, we have $(5x \ )(x \ )$.

    The factors of the last term, −4, are −1 and 4, −2 and 2, and −4 and 1. We now consider the following possibilities:

    $(5x - 4)(x + 1)$, $(5x - 1)(x + 4)$, $(5x - 2)(x + 2)$, and

    $(5x + 1)(x - 4)$, $(5x + 4)(x - 1)$, $(5x + 2)(x - 2)$.

    Checking for the correct middle term, determine that $5x^2 + 8x - 4 = (5x - 2)(x + 2)$. **(Factoring quadratic trinomials)**

31. The linear factors of the first term, $7t^2$, in the expression $7t^2 - 4t - 3$, are 7t and t. Hence, we have $(7t \ )(t \ )$.

    The factors of the last term, −3, are −1 and 3, and −3 and 1. We now consider the following possiblities:

    $(7t - 3)(t + 1)$, $(7t + 3)(t - 1)$, and

    $(7t + 1)(t - 3)$, $(7t - 1)(t + 3)$.

    Checking for the correct middle term, determine that $7t^2 - 4t - 3 = (7t + 3)(t - 1)$. **(Factoring quadratic trinomials)**

32. The linear factors of the first term, $3p^2$, in the expression $3p^2 - p - 14$, are 3p and p. Hence, we have (3p   )(p   ).

    The factors of the last term, -14, are -1 and 14, -2 and 7, -7 and 2, and -14 and 1. We now consider the following possibilites:

    $(3p - 1)(p + 14)$, $(3p - 2)(p + 7)$, $(3p - 7)(p + 2)$,

    $(3p - 14)(p + 1)$, $(3p + 14)(p - 1)$, $(3p + 7)(p - 2)$, and

    $(3p + 2)(p - 7)$, $(3p + 1)(p - 14)$.

    Checking for the correct middle term, determine that

    $3p^2 - p - 14 = (3p - 7)(p + 2)$.

    Note: After the correct choice is determined, it is, of course, not necessary to consider the remaining possibilities. With practice, you will be able to notice that some choices clearly cannot be correct, so these don't need to be checked, either. (**Factoring quadratic trinomials**)

33. The linear factors of the first term, $11q^2$, in the expression $11q^2 - 53q - 10$, are 11q and q. Hence, we have (11q   )(q   ).

    The factors of the last term, -10, are -1 and 10, -2 and 5, -5 and 2, and -10 and 1. Considering these possible factors, together with the factors of $11q^2$, and checking for the correct middle term, determine that $11q^2 - 53q - 10 = (11q + 2)(q - 5)$. (**Factoring quadratic trinomials**)

34. Rearranging the polynomial $49u - 12 + 13u^2$ in descending powers of u, we have $13u^2 + 49u - 12$. The linear factors of the first term, $13u^2$, are 13u and u. Hence, we have (13u   )(u   ).

    The factors of the last term, -12, are -1 and 12, -2 and 6, -3 and 4, -4 and 3, -6 and 2, and -12 and 1. Considering these possibilities, together with the factors of $13u^2$, and checking for the correct middle term, determine that $13u^2 + 49u - 12 = (13u - 3)(u + 4)$. (**Factoring quadratic trinomials**)

35. Rearranging the polynomial $2v^2 - 63 + 5v$ in descending powers of v, we have $2v^2 + 5v - 63$. The linear factors of the first term, $2v^2$, are 2v and v. Hence, we have (2v   )(v   ).

    The factors of the last term, -63, are -1 and 63, -3 and 21, -7 and 9, -9 and 7, -21 and 3, and -63 and 1. Considering these possibilities, together with the factors of $2v^2$, and checking for the correct middle term, determine that $2v^2 + 5v - 63 = (2v - 9)(v + 7)$. (**Factoring quadratic trinomials**)

36. The linear factors of the first term, $10m^2$, in the expression $10m^2 - 3m - 4$, are 2m and 5m. Hence, we have (2m   )(5m   ) or (10m   )(m   ).

    The factors of the last term, -4, are -1 and 4, -2 and 2, and -4 and 1. Considering these possibilities, together with the factors of $10m^2$, and checking for the correct middle term, determine that $10m^2 - 3m - 4 = (2m + 1)(5m - 4)$. (**Factoring quadratic trinomials**)

37. Rearranging the polynomial $6p^2 - 15 + p$ in descending powers of p, we have $6p^2 + p - 15$. The linear factors of the first term, $6p^2$, are 2p and 3p. We have (2p   )(3p   ) or (−6p   )(p   ).

    The factors of the last term, -15, are -1 and 15, -3 and 5, -5 and 3, and -15 and 1. Considering these possibilities, together with the factors of $6p^2$, and checking for the correct middle term, determine that $6p^2 + p - 15 = (2p - 3)(3p + 5)$. (**Factoring quadratic trinomials**)

38. The linear factors of the first term, $6t^2$, of the expression $6t^2 - 7t - 3$, are 2t and 3t. Hence, we have (2t   )(3t   ) or (6t   )(t   ).

    The factors of the last term, -3, are -1 and 3, and -3 and 1. Considering these possibilities, together with the factors of $6t^2$, and checking for the correct middle term, determine that $6t^2 - 7t - 3 = (2t - 3)(3t + 1)$. (**Factoring quadratic trinomials**)

39. $x^2 - 5x - 24 = 0$

    $(x - 8)(x + 3) = 0$

    $x - 8 = 0$ or $x + 3 = 0$

    $x = 8$ $x = -3$

    Therefore, the required solutions are −3 and 8. (**Quadratic equations and factoring**)

40. $y^2 - 6y = 0$

    $y(y - 6) = 0$

    $y = 0$ or $y - 6 = 0$

                  $y = 6$

    Therefore, the required solutions are 0 and 6. (**Quadratic equations and factoring**)

41. $5u^3 + 8u^2 - 4u = 0$

     $u(5u^2 + 8u - 4) = 0$

     $u(5u - 2)(u + 2) = 0$

    $u = 0$ or $5u - 2 = 0$ or $u + 2 = 0$

                  $u = \dfrac{2}{5}$ $u = -2$

    Therefore, the required solutions are $= -2, 0,$ and $\dfrac{2}{5}.$ (**Quadratic equations and factoring**)

42. $4v^3 - 9v = 0$

               $v(4v^2 - 9) = 0$

    $v(2v + 3)(2v - 3) = 0$

    $v = 0$ or $2v + 3 = 0$ or $2v - 3 = 0$

                  $v = \dfrac{-3}{2}$ $v = \dfrac{3}{2}$

    Therefore, the required solutions are $\dfrac{-3}{2}, 0,$ and $\dfrac{3}{2}.$ (**Quadratic equations and factoring**)

43. $x^4 + 10x^3 = -25x^2$

    $x^4 + 10x^3 + 25x^2 = 0$ Rewriting the equation so that one side is equal to 0.

    $x^2(x^2 + 10x + 25) = 0$

     $x^2(x + 5)(x + 5) = 0$

    $x^2 = 0$ or $x + 5 = 0$ or $x + 5 = 0$

    $x = 0$ $x = -5$ $x = -5$

    Therefore, the required solutions are −5 and 0. (**Quadratic equations and factoring**)

44.
$$72p^3 = 162p$$
$$72p^3 - 162p = 0$$
$$18p(4p^2 - 9) = 0$$
$$18p(2p + 3)(2p - 3) = 0$$
$$18p = 0 \quad \text{or} \quad 2p + 3 = 0 \quad \text{or} \quad 2p - 3 = 0$$
$$p = 0 \qquad\qquad p = \frac{-3}{2} \qquad\qquad p = \frac{3}{2}$$

Therefore, the required solutions are $\frac{-3}{2}$, 0, and $\frac{3}{2}$. **(Quadratic equations and factoring)**

45.
$$q^3 = 48q + 13q^2$$
$$q^3 - 13q^2 - 48q = 0$$
$$q(q^2 - 13q - 48) = 0$$
$$q(q - 16)(q + 3) = 0$$
$$q = 0 \quad \text{or} \quad q - 16 = 0 \quad \text{or} \quad q + 3 = 0$$
$$q = 16 \qquad\qquad q = -3$$

Therefore, the required solutions are −3, 0, and 16. **(Quadratic equations and factoring)**

46.
$$(4t^2 - 9)(9t^2 - 25) = 0$$
$$(2t + 3)(2t - 3)(3t + 5)(3t - 5) = 0$$
$$2t + 3 = 0 \quad \text{or} \quad 2t - 3 = 0 \quad \text{or} \quad 3t + 5 = 0 \quad \text{or} \quad 3t - 5 = 0$$
$$t = \frac{-3}{2} \qquad t = \frac{3}{2} \qquad t = \frac{-5}{3} \qquad t = \frac{5}{3}$$

Therefore, the required solutions are $\frac{-5}{3}$, $\frac{-3}{2}$, $\frac{3}{2}$, and $\frac{5}{3}$. **(Quadratic equations and factoring)**

47. $ax + bx + ay + by$
$$= (ax + bx) + (ay + by)$$
$$= x(a + b) + (ay + by)$$
$$= x(a + b) + y(a + b)$$
$$= (a + b)(x + y) \quad \textbf{(Factoring by grouping)}$$

48. $au - bu + av - bv$
$$= (au - bu) + (av - bv)$$
$$= u(a - b) + (av - bv)$$
$$= u(a - b) + v(a - b)$$
$$= (a - b)(u + v) \quad \textbf{(Factoring by grouping)}$$

49. $rs + r - s - 1$

$= (rs + r) - (s + 1)$

$= r(s + 1) - (s + 1)$

$= r(s + 1) - 1(s + 1)$

$= (s + 1)(r - 1)$ **(Factoring by grouping)**

50. $a + 1 + 2b + 2ab$

$= (a + 1) + (2b + 2ab)$

$= (a + 1) + 2b(1 + a)$

$= (a + 1) + 2b(a + 1)$

$= (a + 1)(1 + 2b)$ **(Factoring by grouping)**

51. $s^2 + 4s + 4t - t^2$

$= (s^2 - t^2) + (4s + 4t)$

$= (s + t)(s - t) + (4s + 4t)$

$= (s + t)(s - t) + 4(s + t)$

$= (s + t)[(s - t) + 4)]$

$= (s + t)(s - t + 4)$ **(Factoring by grouping)**

52. $y^2 - 5x - 25 + xy$

$= (y^2 - 25) + (-5x + xy)$

$= (y + 5)(y - 5) + (-5x + xy)$

$= (y + 5)(y - 5) + x(-5 + y)$

$= (y + 5)(y - 5) + x(y - 5)$

$= (y - 5)[(y + 5) + x)]$

$= (y - 5)(y + 5 + x)$

$= (y - 5)(x + y + 5)$ **(Factoring by grouping)**

53. $r^2 + rs - 3s - 9$

$= (r^2 - 9) + (rs - 3s)$

$= (r + 3)(r - 3) + (rs - 3s)$

$= (r + 3)(r - 3) + s(r - 3)$

$= (r - 3)[(r + 3) + s]$

$= (r - 3)(r + 3 + s)$

$= (r - 3)(r + s + 3)$ **(Factoring by grouping)**

54. $3p^2 - 12 - 6q + 3pq$

     $= (3p^2 - 12) + (-6q + 3pq)$

     $= 3(p^2 - 4) + 3q(-2 + p)$

     $= 3(p + 2)(p - 2) + 3q(p - 2)$

     $= 3(p - 2)[(p + 2) + q]$

     $= 3(p - 2)(p + 2 + q)$

     $= 3(p - 2)(p + q + 2)$ **(Factoring by grouping)**

Grade Yourself

Circle the numbers of the questions you missed, then fill in the total incorrect for each topic. If you answered more than three questions incorrectly, you need to focus on that topic. (If a topic has less than three questions and you had at least one wrong, we suggest you study that topic also. Read your textbook, a review book, or ask your teacher for help.)

Subject: Factoring

Topic	Question Numbers	Number Incorrect
Greatest common factor	1, 2, 3, 4, 5, 6, 7, 8	
Factoring the difference of two squares	9, 10, 11, 12, 13, 14, 15, 16, 17, 18	
Factoring quadratic trinomials	19, 20, 21, 22, 23, 24, 25, 26, 27, 28, 29, 30, 31, 32, 33, 34, 35, 36, 37, 38	
Quadratic equations and factoring	39, 40, 41, 42, 43, 44, 45, 46	
Factoring by grouping	47, 48, 49, 50, 51, 52, 53, 54	

Rational Expressions

Test Yourself

6.1 The Fundamental Principle of Fractions

Definition: A rational expression is the quotient of two polynomials in the same variable(s).

$\dfrac{2u+5}{u^2+1}$ is a rational expression in the variable u.

$\dfrac{3t^2-4t+2}{1-t+4t^2}$ is a rational expression in the variable t.

The denominator of a rational expression cannot be zero.

Definition: Any value of the variable(s) in the denominator that makes the denominator zero is called an **excluded value**.

The excluded value for $\dfrac{y}{y+1}$ is –1.

The excluded values for $\dfrac{u^5-7}{u^2+5u+6}$ are –3 and –2.

In Exercises 1-6, determine all excluded values for the given rational expressions.

1. $\dfrac{9}{x-5}$

2. $\dfrac{2t-7}{t(3t-1)}$

3. $\dfrac{(3y-5)(6y+5)}{2y^2-9y-5}$

4. $\dfrac{-4a^2b^4}{3a^3b}$

5. $\dfrac{5u}{(u-4)(u^2-4)}$

6. $\dfrac{2s-1}{s^2+7}$

Rational expressions can be simplified by using what is called the *Fundamental Principle of Fractions*.

Fundamental Principle of Fractions

If a, b, and c are real numbers, such that $b \neq 0$ and $c \neq 0$, then

$$\frac{ac}{bc}=\frac{a}{b}.$$

A rational expression can be simplified as follows:

To simplify a rational expression,

1. Factor the numerator and the denominator completely.

2. Divide *both* the numerator and the denominator by *all nonzero* common factors.

To simplify the rational expression $\dfrac{x^2-4}{x^2+x-6}$, proceed as follows:

$$\frac{x^2-4}{x^2+x-6}=\frac{(x+2)(x-2)}{(x-2)(x+3)} \quad \text{(Factor.)}$$

$= \dfrac{x+2}{x+3}$, $(x \neq -3$, $x \neq 2)$ (Divide numerator and

denominator by common nonzero

factor, $x - 2$.)

In Exercises 7-12, simplify each of the given expressions.

7. $\dfrac{-16p^5}{8p^3}$

8. $\dfrac{5a^2b^6}{25a^3b^2}$

9. $\dfrac{3t-15}{2t-10}$

10. $\dfrac{2s-8}{s^2-16}$

11. $\dfrac{2q^2+5q-3}{2q^2-9q+4}$

12. $\dfrac{6x^2-5x+1}{3x^2+5x-2}$

6.2 Multiplication and Division of Rational Expressions

Rule for Multiplying Rational Expressions

To multiply rational expressions:

1. Factor all numerators and denominators completely.

2. Write as a single product all of the factored numerators, to form the numerator of the new expression.

3. Write as a single product all of the factored denominators, to form the denominator of the new expression.

4. Divide the numerator and denominator of the new expression by *all* of the *nonzero* factors common to both.

As an example of the above rule, consider the following:

Multiply $\dfrac{6}{x+3} \cdot \dfrac{x^2-9}{x}$, if $x \neq -3, 0$.

$\dfrac{6}{x+3} \cdot \dfrac{x^2-9}{x} = \dfrac{6}{x+3} \cdot \dfrac{(x+3)(x-3)}{x}$ (Factor the numerators and the denominators.)

$= \dfrac{6(x+3)(x-3)}{x(x+3)}$ (Form the new numerator and the new denominator.)

$= \dfrac{6(x-3)}{x}$ (Divide numerator and denominator by common nonzero factor, $x + 3$.)

Therefore, $\dfrac{6}{x+3} \cdot \dfrac{x^2-9}{x} = \dfrac{6(x-3)}{x}$, if $x \neq -3, 0$.

In Exercises 13-18, multiply as indicated. Simplify the results.

13. $\dfrac{8s}{9t} \cdot \dfrac{3t}{2s}$

14. $\dfrac{y^3}{6x} \cdot \dfrac{4x^2}{y}$

15. $\dfrac{p+2}{2p-4} \cdot \dfrac{8}{p^2-4}$

16. $\dfrac{2u^2+u-1}{2u^2-7u+3} \cdot \dfrac{u^2-u-6}{u^2-3u-4}$

17. $\dfrac{r-3}{r+1} \cdot \dfrac{r^2-1}{r^2-r-6} \cdot \dfrac{r^2+6r+8}{r^2-6r+5}$

18. $\dfrac{2v^2+7v+3}{v^2+v-2} \cdot \dfrac{v^2-v-2}{v^2-9} \cdot \dfrac{v^2-3v}{2v+1}$

Rule for Dividing Rational Expressions

To divide a rational expression by a rational expression, multiply the first expression by the *reciprocal* of the second expression.

As an example of the above rule, consider the following:

Divide $\dfrac{s}{s^2-9}$ by $\dfrac{2}{s+3}$, if $s \neq -3, 3$.

$$\dfrac{s}{s^2-9} \div \dfrac{2}{s+3}, \text{ if } s \neq -3, 3$$

$$= \dfrac{s}{s^2-9} \cdot \dfrac{s+3}{2} \text{ (Multiply by the reciprocal of}$$

$$\dfrac{2}{s+3}.)$$

$$= \dfrac{s}{(s+3)(s-3)} \cdot \dfrac{s+3}{2} \text{ (Factor.)}$$

$$= \dfrac{s}{s-3} \cdot \dfrac{1}{2} \text{ (Common factor, } s+3)$$

$$= \dfrac{s}{2(s-3)}$$

Therefore, $\dfrac{s}{s^2-9} \div \dfrac{2}{s+3} = \dfrac{s}{2s-6}$, if $s \neq -3, 3$.

In Exercises 19-24, divide as indicated. Simplify the results.

19. $\dfrac{2a^2b}{3c^2d^3} \div \dfrac{-4ab^3}{9cd^4}$

20. $\dfrac{3x-4}{x^2-9} \div \dfrac{3x-6}{2x+6}$

21. $\dfrac{3y}{y+4} \div \dfrac{2y^3}{y^2-16}$

22. $\dfrac{u^2+u-2}{u^2+5u+4} \div \dfrac{u^2-u-6}{u^2-u-2}$

23. $\dfrac{6t^2-7t-3}{2t^2-7t+6} \div \dfrac{3t^2+5t+2}{t^2-4t+4}$

24. $\dfrac{3p^2+13p+4}{p^2+2p-15} \div \dfrac{6p^2-7p-3}{p^2+4p-5}$

6.3 The Least Common Denominator

Definitions: Rational expressions that have the *same* denominators are called **like** rational expressions.

Rational expressions that have *different* denominators are called **unlike** rational expressions.

In the next section, we will add rational expressions. If the expressions are unlike rational expressions, we use a procedure involving what is called the *least common denominator* (LCD).

Rule for Determining the Least Common Denominator (LCD)

To determine the LCD of the denominators of two or more unlike rational expressions:

1. Factor each denominator completely, writing repeated factors using exponents.

2. Form the product of *all* the *different* factors determined in Step 1.

3. Raise each of these factors to the *highest* power in which it is found in the factorizations in Step 1.

4. The resulting product is the LCD.

Determine the least common denominator for the rational expressions $\dfrac{3s-7}{s^2-9}$, $\dfrac{s^3+1}{2s+6}$, and $\dfrac{2s^2-4s+10}{s^2-6s+9}$.

Step 1: Factor each of the denominators completely:

$s^2-9 = (s+3)(s-3)$

$2s+6 = 2(s+3)$

$s^2-6s+9 = (s-3)^2$

Step 2: Form the product of all the different factors obtained in Step 1:

$2(s+3)(s-3)$

Step 3: Raise each of these factors to the highest power in which it is found in Step 1:

$2(s+3)(s-3)^2$

Therefore, the LCD$(s^2-9, 2s+6, s^2-6s+9) = 2(s+3)(s-3)^2$.

In Exercises 25-30, determine the least common denominator for the given rational expressions.

25. $\dfrac{-3}{2x^3y}$, $\dfrac{4x}{6x^3y^5}$

26. $\dfrac{s-5}{(s^2-1)^2}$, $\dfrac{s^3-17s+23}{2(s+1)^3(s^2+3s-4)}$

27. $\dfrac{3}{7x^2y^4}$, $\dfrac{-2xy}{5x^3y}$, $\dfrac{x-y}{10x^4y^3}$

28. $\dfrac{-7x}{x^2-16}$, $\dfrac{x+19}{4(x+4)^2}$, $\dfrac{x^2+1}{12(x-4)}$

29. $\dfrac{-5}{y^3-9y}$, $\dfrac{y}{6y^3-18y^2}$, $\dfrac{y-9}{y^2-6y+9}$

30. $\dfrac{3pq}{(2p-q)^3}$, $\dfrac{p^4-7pq+q}{4p^2-q^2}$, $\dfrac{7p-9q}{(2p+q)^2}$

In Exercises 31-36, add or subtract as indicated. Simplify the results and indicate the excluded values.

31. $\dfrac{2a}{t+7}+\dfrac{3b}{t+7}$

32. $\dfrac{2x}{x^2-25}-\dfrac{3}{x^2-25}$

33. $\dfrac{3x-2y}{4x^2-y^2}-\dfrac{x+4y}{4x^2-y^2}$

34. $\dfrac{7ab}{(r+s)^3}+\dfrac{bc-cd}{(r+s)^3}$

35. $\dfrac{x-2y}{x(x^2-4)}-\dfrac{3x+4y}{x(x^2-4)}+\dfrac{x-y}{x(x^2-4)}$

36. $\dfrac{p-4q^2}{p^2-9q^2}-\dfrac{2p^2+q}{p^2-9q^2}-\dfrac{p^2-q^2}{p^2-9q^2}$

6.4 Addition and Subtraction of Rational Expressions

Rule for Adding or Subtracting Like Rational Expressions

To add (or subtract) like rational expressions:

1. Add (or subtract) their numerators.

2. Write the sum (or difference) over the common denominator.

3. Simplify the result.

For example, $\dfrac{4}{x-2}-\dfrac{x}{x-2}+\dfrac{8}{x-2}$

$$=\dfrac{4-x+8}{x-2}$$

$$=\dfrac{12-x}{x-2}$$

The excluded value is 2.

Rule for Adding or Subtracting Unlike Rational Expressions

To add (or subtract) unlike rational expressions:

1. Determine the LCD for all of the denominators involved.

2. (Re)write each of the expressions in equivalent form, with the LCD as the common denominator.

3. Add (or subtact) the resulting *like* rational expressions.

4. Simplify the results.

The above rule will be illustrated with the following example:

To add $\dfrac{4}{b-5}+\dfrac{-7}{b+7}$, proceed as follows:

1. Determine that the LCD($b-5$, $b+7$) is $(b-5)(b+7)$.

2. Rewrite the rational expressions as like rational expressions with the LCD:

$$\frac{4(b+7)}{(b-5)(b+7)} + \frac{-7(b-5)}{(b-5)(b+7)}$$

3. Add the like rational expressions:

$$\frac{4(b+7)}{(b-5)(b+7)} + \frac{-7(b-5)}{(b-5)(b+7)} = \frac{4(b+7)+(-7)(b-5)}{(b-5)(b+7)}$$

4. Simplify the results:

$$\frac{4(b+7)+(-7)(b-5)}{(b-5)(b+7)} = \frac{4b+28-7b+35}{(b-5)(b+7)}$$

$$= \frac{-3b+63}{(b-5)(b+7)}$$

Therefore, $\dfrac{4}{b-5} + \dfrac{-7}{b+7} = \dfrac{-3b+63}{(b-5)(b+7)}$. The excluded values are −7 and 5.

In Exercises 37–42, add or subtract as indicated. Simplify the results and indicate the excluded values.

37. $\dfrac{5}{3x^2y^3} + \dfrac{-2}{6xy^2}$

38. $\dfrac{p}{2p^3q^2} - \dfrac{2q}{6p^2q^5}$

39. $\dfrac{2t}{t+2} + \dfrac{7}{t-5}$

40. $\dfrac{3r}{r^2-s^2} - \dfrac{r-2s}{2(r+s)}$

41. $\dfrac{a^2-2b}{2a^2-ab-3b^2} + \dfrac{a-3b}{a^2-ab-2b^2}$

42. $\dfrac{2t-3}{(t-2)^2(t+3)} - \dfrac{5-4t}{(t+3)^3(t-2)}$

6.5 Equations Involving Rational Expressions

Rule for Solving Equations Involving Rational Expressions

To solve an equation involving rational expressions:

1. Multiply *every* term on *both* sides of the

---

equation by the LCD of *all* denominators involved. This will remove fractions.

2. Solve the resulting equation.

3. Check the results in the original equation.

The above rule will be illustrated in the following example:

Solve the equation $\dfrac{2}{t+3} + 1 = \dfrac{t}{t-3}$ for t, if t ≠ -3, 3.

1. The LCD (t + 3, t - 3) is (t + 3)(t - 3). Multiply *both* sides of the equation by the LCD:

$$(t+3)(t-3)\left(\frac{2}{t+3}+1\right) = (t+3)(t-3)\left(\frac{t}{t-3}\right)$$

2. Solve the resulting equation:

$$(t+3)(t-3)\left(\frac{2}{t+3}+1\right) = (t+3)(t-3)\left(\frac{t}{t-3}\right)$$

$$(t+3)(t-3)\left(\frac{2}{t+3}\right) + (t+3)(t-3)(1)$$

$$= (t+3)(t-3)\left(\frac{t}{t-3}\right)$$

$$(t-3)(2) + (t+3)(t-3) = (t+3)(t)$$

$$2t - 6 + t^2 - 9 = t^2 + 3t$$

$$2t - 6 - 9 = 3t$$

$$2t - 15 = 3t$$

$$-15 = t$$

3. Check the result in the *original* equation:

$$\frac{2}{t+3} + 1 = \frac{t}{t-3}$$

$$\frac{2}{-15+3} + 1 \; ? \; \frac{-15}{-15-3}$$

$$\frac{2}{-12} + 1 \; ? \; \frac{-15}{-18}$$

$$\frac{-1}{6} + 1 \; ? \; \frac{5}{6}$$

$$\frac{5}{6} = \frac{5}{6} \checkmark$$

4. Therefore, the required solution is −15.

In Exercises 43-48, solve each of the given equations for the indicated variable. Check the results in the original equation.

43. $\dfrac{4x}{x+2} - 4 = \dfrac{1}{x-2}$

44. $\dfrac{5y}{y+3} = 5 + \dfrac{4}{y-2}$

45. $\dfrac{2u}{u-1} + \dfrac{4}{u+1} = 2$

46. $\dfrac{8}{t+5} + \dfrac{t}{t-5} = 1$

47. $\dfrac{3r}{r^2-25} + \dfrac{2}{r+5} = \dfrac{4}{r-5}$

48. $\dfrac{5}{3p-6} - \dfrac{3}{p+2} = \dfrac{8p}{2p^2-8}$

6.6 Complex Rational Expressions

Definition: A **complex rational expression** is an expression having a rational expression in its numerator or in its denominator, or in both.

$\dfrac{3}{\dfrac{1}{u+1}}$ is a complex rational expression with a

rational expression in the denominator.

$\dfrac{\dfrac{u-7}{u+1}}{u^2-7u+9}$ is a complex rational expression with a

rational expression in the numerator.

$\dfrac{\dfrac{t^2-5}{t+2}}{\dfrac{17t+31}{t-11}}$ is a complex rational expression with a

rational expression in the numerator and in the denominator.

Rule for Simplifying Complex Rational Expressions

To simplify a complex rational expression:

1. Simplify the numerator and simplify the denominator.

2. Divide the simplified numerator by the simplified denominator.

3. Simplify the result.

The above rule will be illustrated in the following example:

Simplify: $\dfrac{\dfrac{2}{x-1} + \dfrac{3}{x+1}}{\dfrac{x}{x^2-1}}$

$$\frac{\dfrac{2}{x-1} + \dfrac{3}{x+1}}{\dfrac{x}{x^2-1}} = \frac{\dfrac{2(x+1)+3(x-1)}{(x+1)(x-1)}}{\dfrac{x}{x^2-1}} = \frac{\dfrac{5x-1}{(x+1)(x-1)}}{\dfrac{x}{x^2-1}}$$

$$= \frac{5x-1}{x^2-1} \cdot \frac{x^2-1}{x} = \frac{5x-1}{x},$$

provided that $x \neq -1, 0,$ or 1.

In Exercises 49-54, simplfy each of the given complex rational expressions. Indicate all excluded values.

49. $\dfrac{5p^4q^5}{\dfrac{p}{2p^3q^2}}$

50. $\dfrac{\dfrac{2a^2b^3}{xy}}{\dfrac{4ab}{3x^4y^3}}$

51. $\dfrac{x - \dfrac{x}{y}}{x^3y}$

52. $\dfrac{\dfrac{p}{q}+\dfrac{q}{p}}{\dfrac{p}{q}-\dfrac{q}{p}}$

54. $\dfrac{\dfrac{s}{s-t}-\dfrac{t}{s+t}}{\dfrac{st}{s^2-t^2}}$

53. $\dfrac{\dfrac{x}{x-y}}{\dfrac{y}{x^2-y^2}}$

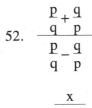

Check Yourself

1. $x - 5 = 0$, if $x = 5$. Therefore, the excluded value for $\dfrac{9}{x-5}$ is $x = 5$. (**Excluded values**)

2. $t(3t - 1) = 0$, if $t = 0$ or $\dfrac{1}{3}$. Therefore, the excluded values for $\dfrac{2t-7}{t(3t-1)}$ are $t = 0$ and $t = \dfrac{1}{3}$. (**Excluded values**)

3. $2y^2 - 9y - 5 = 0$, if $(2y + 1)(y - 5) = 0$, or $y = \dfrac{-1}{2}$ or 5. Therefore, the excluded values for $\dfrac{(3y-5)(6y+5)}{2y^2-9y-5}$ are $y = \dfrac{-1}{2}$ and $y = 5$. (**Excluded values**)

4. $3a^3b = 0$, if $a = 0$ or $b = 0$. Therefore, the excluded values of $\dfrac{-4a^2b^4}{3a^3b}$ are $a = 0$ and $b = 0$. (**Excluded values**)

5. $(u - 4)(u^2 - 4) = 0$, if $u = -2$, 2 or 4. Therefore, the excluded values for $\dfrac{5u}{(u-4)(u^2-4)}$ are $u = -2$, $u = 2$, and $u = 4$. (**Excluded values**)

6. There are no real values of s for which $s^2 + 7 = 0$. Therefore, there are *no* excluded values for $\dfrac{2s-1}{s^2+7}$. (**Excluded values**)

7. $\dfrac{-16p^5}{8p^3} = \left(\dfrac{-16}{8}\right)\left(\dfrac{p^5}{p^3}\right) = -2p^2$, provided that $p \neq 0$. (**Fundamental principle of fractions**)

8. $\dfrac{5a^2b^6}{25a^3b^2} = \left(\dfrac{5}{25}\right)\left(\dfrac{a^2}{a^3}\right)\left(\dfrac{b^6}{b^2}\right) = \left(\dfrac{1}{5}\right)\left(\dfrac{1}{a}\right)b^4 = \dfrac{b^4}{5a}$, provided that $a \neq 0$ and $b \neq 0$. (**Fundamental principle of fractions**)

9. $\dfrac{3t-15}{2t-10} = \dfrac{3(t-5)}{2(t-5)} = \dfrac{3}{2}$, provided that $t \neq 5$. (**Fundamental principle of fractions**)

10. $\dfrac{2s-8}{s^2-16} = \dfrac{2(s-4)}{(s+4)(s-4)} = \dfrac{2}{s+4}$, provided that s ≠ −4 or 4. (**Fundamental principle of fractions**)

11. $\dfrac{2q^2+5q-3}{2q^2-9q+4} = \dfrac{(2q-1)(q+3)}{(2q-1)(q-4)} = \dfrac{q+3}{q-4}$, provided that q ≠ $\dfrac{1}{2}$, 4. (**Fundamental principle of fractions**)

12. $\dfrac{6x^2-5x+1}{3x^2+5x-2} = \dfrac{(2x-1)(3x-1)}{(3x-1)(x+2)} = \dfrac{2x-1}{x+2}$, provided that x ≠ −2, $\dfrac{1}{3}$. (**Fundamental principle of fractions**)

13. $\dfrac{8s}{9t} \cdot \dfrac{3t}{2s} = \dfrac{(8s)(3t)}{(9t)(2s)} = \dfrac{24st}{18st} = \dfrac{(6)(4)st}{(6)(3)st} = \dfrac{4}{3}$, provided that s ≠ 0 and t ≠ 0. (**Multiplication of rational expressions**)

14. $\dfrac{y^3}{6x} \cdot \dfrac{4x^2}{y} = \dfrac{(y^3)(4x^2)}{(6x)(y)} = \dfrac{4x^2y^3}{6xy} = \dfrac{2}{3}xy^2$, provided that x ≠ 0 and y ≠ 0. (**Multiplication of rational expressions**)

15. $\dfrac{p+2}{2p-4} \cdot \dfrac{8}{p^2-4} = \dfrac{8(p+2)}{(2p-4)(p^2-4)} = \dfrac{8(p+2)}{2(p-2)((p+2)(p-2)} = \dfrac{4}{(p-2)(p-2)} = \dfrac{4}{(p-2)^2}$, provided that p ≠ −2, 2. (**Multiplication of rational expressions**)

16. $\dfrac{2u^2+u-1}{2u^2-7u+3} \cdot \dfrac{u^2-u-6}{u^2-3u-4} = \dfrac{(2u^2+u-1)(u^2-u-6)}{(2u^2-7u+3)(u^2-3u-4)}$

$= \dfrac{(2u-1)(u+1)(u-3)(u+2)}{(2u-1)(u-3)(u-4)(u+1)} = \dfrac{u+2}{u-4}$, provided that u ≠ −1, $\dfrac{1}{2}$, 3, 4. (**Multiplication of rational expressions**)

17. $\dfrac{r-3}{r+1} \cdot \dfrac{r^2-1}{r^2-r-6} \cdot \dfrac{r^2+6r+8}{r^2-6r+5} = \dfrac{(r-3)(r^2-1)(r^2+6r+8)}{(r+1)(r^2-r-6)(r^2-6r+5)}$

$= \dfrac{(r-3)(r+1)(r-1)(r+4)(r+2)}{(r+1)(r-3)(r+2)(r-5)(r-1)} = \dfrac{r+4}{r-5}$, provided that t ≠ −2, −1, 1, 3, 5. (**Multiplication of rational expressions**)

18. $\dfrac{2v^2+7v+3}{v^2+v-2} \cdot \dfrac{v^2-v-2}{v^2-9} \cdot \dfrac{v^2-3v}{2v+1} = \dfrac{(2v^2+7v+3)(v^2-v-2)(v^2-3v)}{(v^2+v-2)(v^2-9)(2v+1)}$

$= \dfrac{(2v+1)(v+3)(v-2)(v+1)(v)(v-3)}{(v+2)(v-1)(v+3)(v-3)(2v+1)}$

$= \dfrac{v(v-2)(v+1)}{(v+2)(v-1)} = \dfrac{v(v^2-v-2)}{v^2+v-2} = \dfrac{v^3-v^2-2v}{v^2+v-2}$, provided that v ≠ −3, −2, $\dfrac{-1}{2}$, 3, 1. (**Multiplication of rational expressions**)

19. $\dfrac{2a^2b}{3c^2d^3} \div \dfrac{-4ab^3}{9cd^4} = \dfrac{2a^2b}{3c^2d^3} \cdot \dfrac{9cd^4}{-4ab^3} = \dfrac{(2a^2b)(9cd^4)}{(3c^2d^3)(-4ab^3)}$

$= \dfrac{18a^2bcd^4}{-12ab^3c^2d^3} = \dfrac{-3ad}{2b^2c}$, provided that a ≠ 0, b ≠ 0, c ≠ 0, and d ≠ 0. (**Division of rational expressions**)

20. $\dfrac{3x-4}{x^2-9} \div \dfrac{3x-6}{2x+6} = \dfrac{3x-4}{x^2-9} \cdot \dfrac{2x+6}{3x-6} = \dfrac{(3x-4)(2x+6)}{(x^2-9)(3x-6)}$

$= \dfrac{(3x-4)(2)(x+3)}{(x+3)(x-3)(3)(x-2)} = \dfrac{(3x-4)(2)}{(x-3)(3)(x-2)}$

$= \dfrac{6x-8}{3(x^2-5x+6)}$, provided that $x \neq -3, 2, 3$. **(Division of rational expressions)**

21. $\dfrac{3y}{y+4} \div \dfrac{2y^3}{y^2-16} = \dfrac{3y}{y+4} \cdot \dfrac{y^2-16}{2y^3} = \dfrac{3y(y^2-16)}{2y^3(y+4)}$

$= \dfrac{3y(y+4)(y-4)}{2y^3(y+4)} = \dfrac{3(y-4)}{2y^2}$, provided that $y \neq -4, 0, 4$. **(Division of rational expressions)**

22. $\dfrac{u^2+u-2}{u^2+5u+4} \div \dfrac{u^2-u-6}{u^2-u-2} = \dfrac{u^2+u-2}{u^2+5u+4} \cdot \dfrac{u^2-u-2}{u^2-u-6}$

$\dfrac{(u^2+u-2)(u^2-u-2)}{(u^2+5u+4)(u^2-u-6)} = \dfrac{(u+2)(u-1)(u-2)(u+1)}{(u+4)(u+1)(u-3)(u+2)}$

$= \dfrac{(u-1)(u-2)}{(u+4)(u-3)} = \dfrac{u^2-3u+2}{u^2+u-12}$, provided that $u \neq -4, -2, -1, 2, 3$. **(Division of rational expressions)**

23. $\dfrac{6t^2-7t-3}{2t^2-7t+6} \div \dfrac{3t^2+5t+2}{t^2-4t+4} = \dfrac{6t^2-7t-3}{2t^2-7t+6} \cdot \dfrac{t^2-4t+4}{3t^2+5t+2}$

$\dfrac{(6t^2-7t-3)(t^2-4t+4)}{(2t^2-7t+6)(3t^2+5t+2)} = \dfrac{(2t-3)(3t+1)(t-2)(t-2)}{(2t-3)(t-2)(3t+2)(t+1)}$

$= \dfrac{(3t+1)(t-2)}{(3t+2)(t+1)} = \dfrac{3t^2-5t-2}{3t^2+5t+2}$, provided that $t \neq -1, \dfrac{-2}{3}, \dfrac{3}{2}, 2$. **(Division of rational expressions)**

24. $\dfrac{3p^2+13p+4}{p^2+2p-15} \div \dfrac{6p^2-7p-3}{p^2+4p-5} = \dfrac{3p^2+13p+4}{p^2+2p-15} \cdot \dfrac{p^2+4p-5}{6p^2-7p-3}$

$= \dfrac{(2p^2+13p+4)(p^2+4p-5)}{(p^2+2p-15)(6p^2-7p-3)} = \dfrac{(3p+1)(p+4)(p+5)(p-1)}{(p+5)(p-3)(3p+1)(2p-3)}$

$= \dfrac{(p+4)(p-1)}{(p-3)(2p-3)} = \dfrac{p^2+3p-4}{2p^2-9p+9}$, provided that $p \neq -5, \dfrac{-1}{3}, 1, \dfrac{3}{2}, 3$. **(Division of rational expressions)**

25. $2x^3y = 2(x)^3(y)$

$6x^3y^5 = (2)(3)(x)^3(y)^5$

Therefore, $\text{LCD}(2x^3y, 6x^3y^5) = (2)^1(3)^1(x)^3(y)^5 = (2)(3)(x^3)(y^5) = 6x^3y^5$. **(Least common denominator)**

26. $(s^2-1)^2 = [(s+1)(s-1)]^2 = (s+1)^2(s-1)^2$

$2(s+1)^3(s^2+3s-4) = 2(s+1)^3(s+4)(s-1)$

Therefore, $\text{LCD}[(s^2-1)^2, 2(s+1)^3(s^2+3s-4)]$

$= (2)^1(s+1)^3(s-1)^2(s+4)^1 = 2(s+1)^3(s-1)^2(s+4)$. **(Least common denominator)**

27. $7x^2y^4 = (7)(x)^2(y)^4$

    $5x^3y = (5)(x)^3(y)$

    $10x^4y^3 = (2)(5)(x)^4(y)^3$.

    Therefore, $\text{LCD}(7x^2y^4, 5x^3y, 10x^4y^3) = (2)^1(5)^1(7)^1(x)^4(y)^4$

    $= (2)(5)(7)(x^4)(y^4) = 70x^4y^4$. (**Least common denominator**)

28. $x^2 - 16 = (x + 4)(x - 4)$

    $4(x + 4)^2 = (2)^2(x + 4)^2$

    $12(x - 4) = (2)^2(3)(x - 4)$.

    Therefore, $\text{LCD}[x^2 - 16, 4(x + 4)^2, 12(x - 4)]$

    $= (2)^2(3)^1(x + 4)^2(x - 4)^1 = (4)(3)(x + 4)^2(x - 4)$

    $= 12(x + 4)^2(x - 4)$ (**Least common denominator**)

29. $y^3 - 9y = y(y^2 - 9) = y(y + 3)(y - 3)$

    $6y^3 - 18y^2 = 6y^2(y - 3) = (2)(3)(y)^2(y - 3)$

    $y^2 - 6y + 9 = (y - 3)^2$.

    Therefore, $\text{LCD}(y^3 - 9y, 6y^3 - 18y^2, y^2 - 6y + 9)$

    $= (2)^1(3)^1(y)^2(y - 3)^2(y + 3)^1 = (2)(3)(y)^2(y - 3)^2(y + 3)$

    $= 6y^2(y - 3)^2(y + 3)$. (**Least common denominator**)

30. $(2p - q)^3$

    $4p^2 - q^2 = (2p + q)(2p - q)$

    $(2p + q)^2$.

    Therefore, $\text{LCD}[(2p - q)^3, 4p^2 - q^2, (2p + q)^2]$

    $= (2p - q)^3(2p + q)^2$. (**Least common denominator**)

31. $\dfrac{2a}{t + 7} + \dfrac{3b}{t + 7} = \dfrac{2a + 3b}{t + 7}$, $(t \neq -7)$ (**Addition of rational expressions**)

32. $\dfrac{2x}{x^2 - 25} - \dfrac{3}{x^2 - 25} = \dfrac{2x - 3}{x^2 - 25}$, $(x \neq -5, 5)$ (**Subtraction of rational expressions**)

33. $\dfrac{3x - 2y}{4x^2 - y^2} - \dfrac{x + 4y}{4x^2 - y^2} = \dfrac{(3x - 2y) - (x + 4y)}{4x^2 - y^2} = \dfrac{3x - 2y - x - 4y}{4x^2 - y^2} = \dfrac{2x - 6y}{4x^2 - y^2}$, $(y \neq -2x, 2x)$.   (**Subtraction of rational expressions**)

34. $\dfrac{7ab}{(r + s)^3} + \dfrac{bc - cd}{(r + s)^3} = \dfrac{7ab + (bc - cd)}{(r + s)^3} = \dfrac{7ab + bc - cd}{(r + s)^3}$, $(r \neq -s)$.   (**Addition of rational expressions**)

35. $\dfrac{x - 2y}{x(x^2 - 4)} - \dfrac{3x + 4y}{x(x^2 - 4)} + \dfrac{x - y}{x(x^2 - 4)} = \dfrac{(x - 2y) - (3x + 4y) + (x - y)}{x(x^2 - 4)}$

$$= \frac{x - 2y - 3x - 4y + x - y}{x(x^2 - 4)} = \frac{-x - 7y}{x(x^2 - 4)}, (x \neq -2, 0, 2). \quad \textbf{(Addition and subtraction of rational}$$

expressions)

36. $\dfrac{p - 4q^2}{p^2 - 9q^2} - \dfrac{2p^2 + q}{p^2 - 9q^2} - \dfrac{p^2 - q^2}{p^2 - 9q^2} = \dfrac{(p - 4q^2) - (2p^2 + q) - (p^2 - q^2)}{p^2 - 9q^2}$

$$= \frac{p - 4q^2 - 2p^2 - q - p^2 + q^2}{p^2 - 9q^2} = \frac{p - 3q^2 - 3p^2 - q}{p^2 - 9q^2}, (p \neq -3q, 3q). \quad \textbf{(Subtraction of rational expressions)}$$

37. $\text{LCD}(3x^2y^3, 6xy^2) = 6x^2y^3$. Therefore,

$$\frac{5}{3x^2y^3} + \frac{-2}{6xy^2} = \frac{10}{6x^2y^3} + \frac{-2xy}{6x^2y^3} = \frac{10 - 2xy}{6x^2y^3}, (x \neq 0, y \neq 0). \quad \textbf{(Addition of rational expressions)}$$

38. $\text{LCD}(2p^3q^2, 6p^2q^5) = 6p^3q^5.$ Therefore,

$$\frac{p}{2p^3q^2} - \frac{2q}{6p^2q^5} = \frac{3pq^3}{6p^3q^5} - \frac{2pq}{6p^3q^5} = \frac{3pq^3 - 2pq}{6p^3q^5}, (p \neq 0, q \neq 0) \quad \textbf{(Subtraction of rational expressions)}$$

39. $\text{LCD}(t + 2, t - 5) = (t + 2)(t - 5)$. Therefore,

$$\frac{2t}{t + 2} + \frac{7}{t - 5} = \frac{2t(t - 5)}{(t + 2)(t - 5)} + \frac{7(t + 2)}{(t + 2)(t - 5)}$$

$$= \frac{2t(t - 5) + 7(t + 2)}{(t + 2)(t - 5)} = \frac{2t^2 - 10t + 7t + 14}{(t + 2)(t - 5)} = \frac{2t^2 - 3t + 14}{t^2 - 3t - 10}, (t \neq -2, 5). \quad \textbf{(Addition of rational expressions)}$$

40. $\text{LCD}[r^2 - s^2, 2(r + s)] = 2(r + s)(r - s)$. Therefore,

$$\frac{3r}{r^2 - s^2} - \frac{r - 2s}{2(r + s)} = \frac{6r}{2(r + s)(r - s)} - \frac{(r - 2s)(r - s)}{2(r + s)(r - s)}$$

$$= \frac{6r - (r - 2s)(r - s)}{2(r + s)(r - s)} = \frac{6r - (r^2 - 3rs + 2s^2)}{2(r + s)(r - s)}$$

$$= \frac{6r - r^2 + 3rs - 2s^2}{2(r^2 - s^2)}, (r \neq -s, s). \ \textbf{(Subtraction of rational expressions)}$$

41. $2a^2 - ab - 3b^2 = (2a - 3b)(a + b)$

$a^2 - ab - 2b^2 = (a - 2b)(a + b)$

$\text{LCD}(2a^2 - ab - 3b^2, a^2 - ab - 2b^2) = (a + b)(a - 2b)(2a - 3b)$. Therefore,

$$\frac{a^2 - 2b}{2a^2 - ab - 3b^2} + \frac{a - 3b}{a^2 - ab - 2b^2}$$

$$= \frac{(a^2 - 2b)(a - 2b)}{(a + b)(a - 2b)(2a - 3b)} + \frac{(a - 3b)(2a - 3b)}{(a + b)(a - 2b)(2a - 3b)}$$

$$= \frac{(a^2 - 2b)(a - 2b) + (a - 3b)(2a - 3b)}{(a + b)(a - 2b)(2a - 3b)}$$

$$= \frac{a^3 - 2ab - 2a^2b + 4b^2 + 2a^2 - 9ab + 9b^2}{(a + b)(a - 2b)(2a - 3b)}$$

$$= \frac{a^3 - 2a^2b - 11ab + 2a^2 + 13b^2}{(a+b)(a-2b)(2a-3b)}, \ (a \neq -b, \frac{3}{2}b, 2b). \ \textbf{(Addition of rational expressions)}$$

42. $LCD[(t-2)^2(t+3), (t+3)^3(t-2)] = (t-2)^2(t+3)^3$. Therefore,

$$\frac{2t-3}{(t-2)^2(t+3)} - \frac{5-4t}{(t+3)^3(t-2)} = \frac{(2t-3)(t+3)^2}{(t-2)^2(t+3)^3} - \frac{(5-4t)(t-2)}{(t-2)^2(t+3)^3}$$

$$= \frac{(2t-3)(t+3)^2 - (5-4t)(t-2)}{(t-2)^2(t+3)^3}, \ (t \neq -3, 2). \quad \textbf{(Subtraction of rational expressions)}$$

43. $\dfrac{4x}{x+2} - 4 = \dfrac{1}{x-2} \ (x \neq -2, 2)$

Multiply both sides by $LCD(x+2, 1, x-2) = (x+2)(x-2)$:

$$(x+2)(x-2)\left(\frac{4x}{x+2} - 4\right) = (x+2)(x-2)\left(\frac{1}{x-2}\right)$$

$$\overset{1}{(\cancel{x+2})}(x-2)\left(\frac{4x}{\underset{1}{\cancel{x+2}}}\right) - (x+2)(x-2)(4) = (x+2)(x\cancel{-2})\left(\frac{1}{\underset{1}{\cancel{x-2}}}\right)$$

$$(x-2)(4x) - (x+2)(x-2)(4) = (x+2)(1)$$

$$4x^2 - 8x - 4(x^2 - 4) = x + 2$$

$$4x^2 - 8x - 4x^2 + 16 = x + 2$$

$$-8x + 16 = x + 2$$

$$16 = 9x + 2$$

$$14 = 9x$$

$$\frac{14}{9} = x$$

Check: $\dfrac{4x}{x+2} - 4 = \dfrac{1}{x-2}$

$$\frac{4\left(\frac{14}{9}\right)}{\frac{14}{9} + 2} - 4 \ ? \ \frac{1}{\frac{14}{9} - 2}$$

$$\frac{\frac{56}{9}}{\frac{32}{9}} - 4 \ ? \ \frac{1}{\frac{-4}{9}}$$

$$\frac{56}{32} - 4 \ ? \ \frac{-9}{4}$$

$$\frac{7}{4} - 4 \ ? \ \frac{-9}{4}$$

$$\frac{-18}{8} \ ? \ \frac{-9}{4}$$

$\dfrac{-9}{4} = \dfrac{-9}{4}$ ✓   Therefore, $\dfrac{14}{9}$ is the required solution.   (**Equations involving rational expressions**)

Note: For the remaining equations in this section, the check will be left to the student. **Remember to check your results in the original equation.**

44. $\dfrac{5y}{y+3} = 5 + \dfrac{4}{y-2}$, $(y \neq -3, 2)$

Multiply both sides by LCD$(y + 3, y - 2) = (y + 3)(y - 2)$:

$$(y+3)(y-2)\left(\dfrac{5y}{y+3}\right) = (y+3)(y-2)\left(5 + \dfrac{4}{y-2}\right)$$

$$(y+3)^{1}(y-2)\left(\dfrac{5y}{y+3_{1}}\right) = (y+3)(y-2)(5) + (y+3)(y-2)^{1}\left(\dfrac{4}{y-2_{1}}\right)$$

$$(y-2)(5y) = (y+3)(y-2)(5) + (y+3)(4)$$

$$5y^2 - 10y = 5y^2 + 5y - 30 + 4y + 12$$

$$-10y = 9y - 18$$

$$-19y = -18$$

$$y = \dfrac{18}{19}$$

Therefore, the required solution is $\dfrac{18}{19}$.   (**Equations involving rational expressions**)

45. $\dfrac{2u}{u-1} + \dfrac{4}{u+1} = 2$, $(u \neq -1, 1)$

Multiply both sides by LCD$(u - 1, u + 1) = (u - 1)(u + 1)$:

$$(u-1)(u+1)\left(\dfrac{2u}{u-1} + \dfrac{4}{u+1}\right) = (u-1)(u+1)(2)$$

$$(u-1)^{1}(u+1)\left(\dfrac{2u}{u-1_{1}}\right) + (u-1)(u+1)^{1}\left(\dfrac{4}{u+1_{1}}\right) = (u-1)(u+1)(2)$$

$$(u+1)(2u) + (u-1)(4) = 2(u-1)(u+1)$$

$$2u^2 + 2u + 4u - 4 = 2u^2 - 2$$

$$6u - 4 = -2$$

$$6u = 2$$

$$u = \dfrac{1}{3}$$

Therefore, the required solution is $\dfrac{1}{3}$.   (**Equations involving rational expressions**)

46. $\dfrac{8}{t+5} + \dfrac{t}{t-5} = 1$, $(t \neq -5, 5)$

Multiply both sides by LCD$(t + 5, t - 5) = (t + 5)(t - 5)$:

$$(t+5)(t-5)\left(\dfrac{8}{t+5} + \dfrac{t}{t-5}\right) = (t+5)(t-5)(1)$$

$$\overset{1}{\cancel{(t+5)}}(t-5)\left(\dfrac{8}{\underset{1}{\cancel{t+5}}}\right) + (t+5)\overset{1}{\cancel{(t-5)}}\left(\dfrac{t}{\underset{1}{\cancel{t-5}}}\right) = (t+5)(t-5)(1)$$

$$(t-5)(8) + (t+5)(t) = (t+5)(t-5)$$

$$8t - 40 + t^2 + 5t = t^2 - 25$$

$$13t - 40 = -25$$

$$13t = 15$$

$$t = \dfrac{15}{13}$$

Therefore, the required solution is $\dfrac{15}{13}$. **(Equations involving rational expressions)**

47. $\dfrac{3r}{r^2 - 25} + \dfrac{2}{r+5} = \dfrac{4}{r-5}$, $(r \neq -5, 5)$

Multiply both sides by LCD$(r^2 - 25, r + 5, r - 5) = r^2 - 25$:

$$(r^2 - 25)\left(\dfrac{3r}{r^2-25} + \dfrac{2}{r+5}\right) = (r^2 - 25)\left(\dfrac{4}{r-5}\right)$$

$$\overset{1}{\cancel{(r^2-25)}}\left(\dfrac{3r}{\underset{1}{\cancel{r^2-25}}}\right) + \overset{r-5}{\cancel{(r^2-25)}}\left(\dfrac{2}{\underset{1}{\cancel{r+5}}}\right) = \overset{r+5}{\cancel{(r^2-25)}}\left(\dfrac{4}{\underset{1}{\cancel{r-5}}}\right)$$

$$3r + (r-5)(2) = (r+5)(4)$$

$$3r + 2r - 10 = 4r + 20$$

$$5r - 10 = 4r + 20$$

$$r - 10 = 20$$

$$r = 30$$

Therefore, the required solution is 30. **(Equations involving rational expressions)**

48. $\dfrac{5}{3p-6} - \dfrac{3}{p+2} = \dfrac{8p}{2p^2 - 8}$, $(p \neq -2, 2)$

Multiply both sides by LCD$(3p - 6, p + 2, 2p^2 - 8) = 6(p^2 - 4)$:

$$6(p^2 - 4)\left(\dfrac{5}{3p-6} - \dfrac{3}{p+2}\right) = 6(p^2 - 4)\left(\dfrac{8p}{2p^2-8}\right)$$

$$\overset{2(p+2)}{\cancel{6(p^2-4)}}\left(\dfrac{5}{3\cancel{(p-2)}}\right) - \overset{6(p-2)}{\cancel{6(p^2-4)}}\left(\dfrac{3}{\underset{1}{\cancel{p+2}}}\right) = \overset{3}{\cancel{6(p^2-4)}}\left(\dfrac{8p}{2\underset{1}{\cancel{(p^2-4)}}}\right)$$

$$2(p + 2)(5) - 6(p - 2)(3) = 3(8p)$$

$$10p + 20 - 18p + 36 = 24p$$

$$56 - 8p = 24p$$

$$56 = 32p$$

$$\frac{7}{4} = p$$

Therefore, the required solution is $\frac{7}{4}$. (**Equations involving rational expressions**)

49. $\dfrac{5p^4q^5}{\dfrac{p}{2p^3q^2}} = \dfrac{5p^4q^5}{1} \cdot \dfrac{2p^2q^2}{1} = \dfrac{10p^7q^7}{p} = 10p^6q^7$, $(p \neq 0, q \neq 0)$. (**Complex rational expressions**)

50. $\dfrac{\dfrac{2a^2b^3}{xy}}{\dfrac{4ab}{3x^4y^3}} = \dfrac{2a^2b^3}{xy} \cdot \dfrac{3x^4y^3}{4ab} = \dfrac{2a^2b^3}{4ab} \cdot \dfrac{3x^4y^3}{xy}$

$= \dfrac{ab^2}{2} \cdot \dfrac{3x^3y^2}{1} = \dfrac{3}{2}ab^2x^3y^2$, $(a \neq 0, b \neq 0, x \neq 0, y \neq 0)$. (**Complex rational expressions**)

51. $\dfrac{x - \dfrac{x}{y}}{x^3y} = \dfrac{\dfrac{xy - x}{y}}{x^3y} = \dfrac{xy - x}{y} \cdot \dfrac{1}{x^3y} = \dfrac{xy - x}{y(x^3y)} = \dfrac{x(y - 1)}{x^3y^2} = \dfrac{y - 1}{x^2y^2}$, $(x \neq 0, y \neq 0)$. (**Complex rational**
expressions)

52. $\dfrac{\dfrac{p}{q} + \dfrac{q}{p}}{\dfrac{p}{q} - \dfrac{q}{p}} = \dfrac{\dfrac{p^2 + q^2}{pq}}{\dfrac{p^2 - q^2}{pq}} = \dfrac{p^2 + q^2}{pq} \cdot \dfrac{pq}{p^2 - q^2} = \dfrac{pq(p^2 + q^2)}{pq(p^2 - q^2)} = \dfrac{p^2 + q^2}{p^2 - q^2}$, $(p \neq 0, q \neq 0, p \neq -q, p \neq q)$. (**Complex**
rational expressions)

53. $\dfrac{\dfrac{x}{x - y}}{\dfrac{y}{x^2 - y^2}} = \dfrac{x}{x - y} \cdot \dfrac{x^2 - y^2}{y} = \dfrac{x(x^2 - y^2)}{y(x - y)} = \dfrac{x(x + y)(x - y)}{y(x - y)} = \dfrac{x(x + y)}{y}$, $(y \neq -x, y \neq x, y \neq 0)$. (**Complex**
rational expressions)

54. $\dfrac{\dfrac{s}{s - t} - \dfrac{t}{s + t}}{\dfrac{st}{s^2 - t^2}} = \dfrac{\dfrac{s(s + t) - t(s - t)}{(s - t)(s + t)}}{\dfrac{st}{s^2 - t^2}} = \dfrac{s^2 + st - st + t^2}{(s - t)(s + t)} \cdot \dfrac{s^2 - t^2}{st} = \dfrac{s^2 + t^2}{(s - t)(s + t)} \cdot \dfrac{s^2 - t^2}{st}$

$\dfrac{(s^2 + t^2)(s + t)(s - t)}{st(s - t)(s + t)} = \dfrac{s^2 + t^2}{st}$, $(s \neq -t, s \neq 0, s \neq t; t \neq 0)$. (**Complex rational expressions**)

Grade Yourself

Circle the numbers of the questions you missed, then fill in the total incorrect for each topic. If you answered more than three questions incorrectly, you need to focus on that topic. (If a topic has less than three questions and you had at least one wrong, we suggest you study that topic also. Read your textbook, a review book, or ask your teacher for help.)

Subject: Rational Expressions

Topic	Question Numbers	Number Incorrect
Excluded values	1, 2, 3, 4, 5, 6	
Fundamental principle of fractions	7, 8, 9, 10, 11, 12	
Multiplication of rational expressions	13, 14, 15, 16, 17, 18	
Division of rational expressions	19, 20, 21, 22, 23, 24	
Least common denominator	25, 26, 27, 28, 29, 30	
Addition of rational expressions	31, 34, 35, 37, 39, 41	
Subtraction of rational expressions	32, 33, 35, 36, 38, 40, 42	
Equations involving rational expressions	43, 44, 45, 46, 47, 48	
Complex rational expressions	49, 50, 51, 52, 53, 54	

Linear Equations and Inequalities in Two Variables

7.1 Rectangular Coordinate System

We use a number line to represent real numbers. To do so, we position the number 0 on the line and then locate the number 1 to its right. A *scale* is now determined, and the remaining real numbers can be located on the line. The point where the number 0 is positioned is called the *origin*.

If we take two such number lines, one horizontal and the other vertical, and join them at their origins, then we determine a **plane**. The horizontal number line is called the **horizontal axis**, and the vertical number line is called the **vertical axis**. It is customary, but not necessary, to label the horizontal axis the *x-axis* and the vertical axis the *y-axis*. The point of intersection of the two axes (plural of axis) is called the *origin* of the plane. (See Fig. 7.1.)

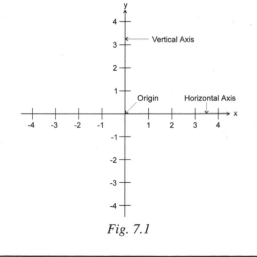

Fig. 7.1

In Fig. 7.2, we show the xy-plane with the points A, B, C, and D. To get to the point A, start at the origin, move 3 units to the right, and stop. To get to the point B, start at the origin, move 1 unit to the *right*, then 2 units *up*, and stop. To get to the point C, start at the origin, move 4 units to the *left*, and stop. To get to the point D, start at the origin, move 2 units to the *left*, then 3 units *down*, and stop.

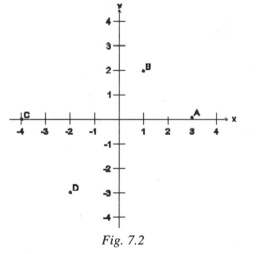

Fig. 7.2

On a horizontal number line, numbers to the right of 0 are *positive*, and numbers to the left of 0 are *negative*. Similarly, on a vertical number line, numbers above 0 are *positive* and numbers below 0 are *negative*. We represent a point in the plane by a pair of numbers called an **ordered pair**. In Fig. 7.2, the point A is represented by the ordered pair (3, 0), which means that the point A is located 3 units to the *right* of the y-axis and *on* the x-axis. The point B is represented by the ordered pair (1, 2), which means that the point B is located 1 unit to the *right* of the y-axis and 2 units *above* the x-axis. The point C is represented by the ordered pair (−4, 0), which means that the point C is located 4 units to the *left* of the y-axis and *on* the x-axis. Point D is represented by the ordered pair (−2,−3), which means that the point D is located 2 units to the *left* of the y-axis and 3 units *below* the x-axis.

The order in which we write the numbers in an ordered pair is important. For instance, the ordered pair (3, 2) is different from the ordered pair (2, 3). Each number is called a **coordinate**. The first coordinate is called the **abscissa** and indicates the horizontal distance that the point is right or left of the vertical axis. The second coordinate is called the **ordinate** and indicates the vertical distance that the point is above or below the horizontal axis. For the point with coordinates (−4, 7), the abscissa is −4 and the ordinate is 7.

We have now described what is called a **rectangular coordinate system**. In such a system, the two axes divide the plane into four regions, called **quadrants**, and are labeled Quadrants I, II, III, and IV, as indicated in Fig. 7.3 below.

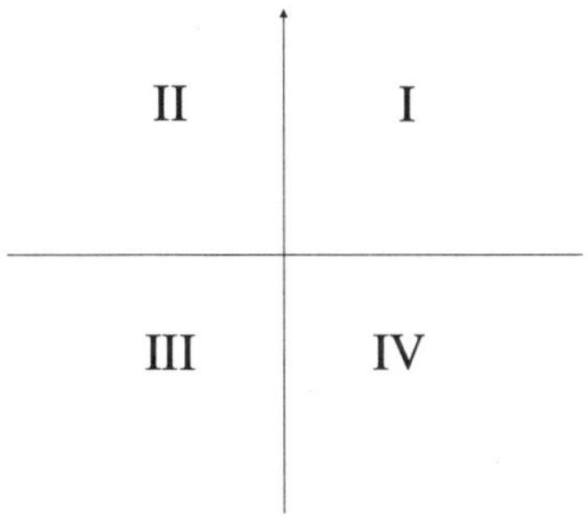

Fig. 7.3

We make the following observations:

In Quadrant I, the abscissa is *positive* and the ordinate is *positive*.

In Quadrant II, the abscissa is *negative* and the ordinate is *positive*.

In Quadrant III, the abscissa is *negative* and the ordinate is *negative*.

In Quadrant IV, the abscissa is *positive* and the ordinate is *negative*.

On the horizontal axis, the ordinate is 0. (The abscissa may be positive, negative, or 0.)

On the vertical axis, the abscissa is 0. (The ordinate may be positive, negative, or 0.)

The point (2, −3) lies in Quadrant IV since the abscissa, 2, is positive and the ordinate, −3, is negative. The point (−6, −1) lies in Quadrant III since both the abscissa and the ordinate are negative.

In Exercises 1-8, indicate in which quadrant the given point lies, and name its abscissa and the ordinate.

1. (2, −3)

2. (−6, 0)

3. (−8, −9)

4. (10, 23)

5. (0, −4)

6. (−8, 6)

7. (1.3, −5.8)

8. (−5.9, 0)

7.2 Linear Equations in Two Variables

Definition: A **linear equation in the two variables** x and y is an equation of the form $Ax + By + C = 0$, provided that $A \neq 0$ or $B \neq 0$.

A solution for a linear equation in two variables consists of two numbers, one for each variable, and is written as an ordered pair. For instance, (1, −3) is a solution for the equation $x - y = 4$ since, when x = 1 and y = −3, we have $1 - (-3) = 1 + 3 = 4$.

Is (−3, 4) a solution for the equation $2x - 3y = 5$? Substituting, −3 for x and 4 for y, we have

$$2x - 3y = 5$$

$$2(-3) - 3(4) \ ? \ 5$$

$$-6 - 12 \;?\; 5$$

$$-18 \neq 5$$

and, hence, $(-3, 4)$ is *not* a solution for the given equation.

Now, consider the equation $3x - y = 5$. Solving for y, in terms of x, we have

$$3x - y = 5$$

$$-y = 5 - 3x$$

or, $y = 3x - 5$.

If $x = 2$, then $y = 3(2) - 5 = 6 - 5 = 1$. Hence, the ordered pair $(2, 1)$ is a solution for the given equation.

If $x = -3$, then $y = 3(-3) - 5 = -9 - 5 = -14$. Hence, the ordered pair $(-3, -14)$ is a solution for the given equation.

How many solutions does the given equation have? Clearly, if x is *any* real number, then 3x is a unique real number, and $3x - 5$ is a unique real number. Hence, no matter what real number is chosen as a value for x, there will always be a corresponding real number value for y. Since there are infinitely many real numbers that can be chosen for values of x, there will be *infinitely many solutions* for the given equation. Of course, it would be impossible to list all of these solutions.

To solve the equation $4x + 5y = 7$, we solve for y in terms of x as follows:

$$4x + 5y = 7$$

$$5y = 7 - 4x$$

$$y = \frac{7 - 4x}{5}$$

Hence, $y = \frac{7 - 4x}{5}$ is the required solution.

To obtain particular solutions for the above equation, choose particular values for x and then solve for the corresponding y values.

In Exercises 9-16, solve each of the given equations for y.

9. $x + y = 10$

10. $3x = 4y - 7$

11. $2x - 6y + 7 = 0$

12. $5 - 2x = 4y - 5$

13. $1.2x - 4.5y = 6.1$

14. $7.2x = 5 - 8.4y$

15. $3(x - 1) - 4(y + 5) = 12$

16. $-4(y - 5) = 11 - 5(2 - 3x)$

7.3 Graphs of Linear Equations in Two Variables

As was noted in the previous section, every linear equation in two variables has infinitely many solutions. Each solution can be represented as an ordered pair. To graph a linear equation in two variables, we graph the ordered pairs which are the solutions of the equation. The graph will be a straight line. How many ordered pairs must we graph to determine the line?

Graphing Linear Equations in Two Variables

To graph a linear equation in two variables:

1. Determine at least two ordered pairs (solutions) for the equation.

2. Plot the solutions as points in the plane.

3. Draw a straight line through these points.

4. Label the line.

When graphing a linear equation in two variables, it is necessary to determine two points through which the required line passes. However, it is recommended that a third point also be determined, to be used as a check point.

To graph the equation $2x - 3y = 6$, determine three solutions for the equation. For instance:

if x = 0, then y = −2,

if x = 3, then y = 0, and

if x = 6, then y = 2.

We now have the ordered pairs (0, −2), (3, 0), and (6, 2). Plotting these ordered pairs, in the xy-plane, and passing a straight line through them, we have the graph of the equation. (See Fig. 7.4.)

To determine the y-intercept, set x = 0 and solve the resulting equation.

If the x-intercept is *a*, then the line passes through the point (a, 0). If the y-intercept is *b*, then the line passes through the point (0, b). (See Fig. 7.5 .)

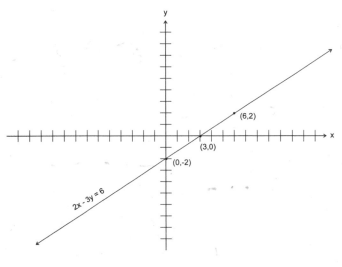

Fig. 7.4

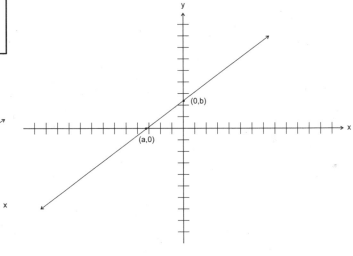

Fig. 7.5

In the above example, we chose 0 for a value of x. We also chose 3 for a value of x, and that gave a corresponding value of 0 for y. This makes our computations and graphing of points easier.

Definitions: Given the linear equation
Ax + By + C = 0, such that A ≠ 0 or B ≠ 0, then, the **x-intercept** is the *abscissa* of the point where the graph of the equation crosses the x-axis (that is, where y = 0). The **y-intercept** is the *ordinate* of the point where the graph crosses the y-axis (that is, where x = 0).

For the equation 2x − 3y = 6, the x-intercept is 3; that is, the line crosses the x-axis at the point (3, 0). The y-intercept is −2; that is, the line crosses the y-axis at the point (0, −2). From the above defintions, we observe that:

To determine the x-intercept, set y = 0 and solve the resulting equation.

The intercept method should be used whenever possible to graph an equation. For some lines, however, there is only one intercept. This occurs when the line is either horizontal or vertical, or when the line passes through the origin. For some lines, the points associated with the two intercepts may be too close together to draw the graph accurately. In these cases, use another point.

In Exercises 17-20, determine the x-intercept and the y-intercept for the graph of each of the given equations.

17. x + y = 7

18. y − 4 = 0

19. 3x − 5y = 1

20. 4x = 1 − 7y

In Exercises 21-26, graph each of the given equations, using at least three points through which the line passes.

21. x − y = 5

22. x − 4 = 0

23. $y = 3x + 7$

24. $3x - 4y = 12$

25. $2y - 6 = 0$

26. $2y = x - 5$

7.4 Slope of a Line

Definition: Consider the line, in the xy–plane, that passes through the two points (x_1, y_1) and (x_2, y_2). Then, the **slope**, m, of the line is given by

$$m = \frac{\text{Change in } y}{\text{Change in } x} = \frac{y_1 - y_2}{x_1 - x_2} \quad (x_1 \neq x_2)$$

In the above defintion, you may start with the y-value of *either* point and subtract the y-value of the other point, to form the numerator. Then, to form the denominator, you *must* start with the x-value of the point used first (when you formed the numerator) and subtract the x-value of the other point. Hence,

$$m = \frac{y_1 - y_2}{x_1 - x_2} \quad \text{or} \quad m = \frac{y_2 - y_1}{x_2 - x_1} \quad (x_1 \neq x_2)$$

In Exercises 27-30, determine the slope of the line passing through the indicated points.

27. $(2, -5)$ and $(-3, 8)$

28. $(0, 4)$ and $(-5, 0)$

29. $(-3, 8)$ and $(3, -2)$

30. $(1.2, -3.1)$ and $(-4.8, -6.3)$

If the equation of a line is given, we can determine the slope of the line by determining two points through which the line passes. It is generally convenient to use intercepts to determine the points.

In Exercises 31-34, determine the slope of the line with the indicated equation.

31. $2x + 4y = 6$

32. $3y - 5 = 0$

33. $3y = 8 - 5x$

34. $x - 5y = 0$

Consider the line with equation $Ax + By + C = 0$ ($A \neq 0$ or $B \neq 0$). Let m be the slope of the line. Then:

If $A = 0$ and $B \neq 0$, then the equation becomes $By + C = 0$, or $y = \dfrac{-C}{B}$. The line is *horizontal* and $m = 0$.

If $A \neq 0$ and $B = 0$, then the equation becomes $Ax + C = 0$, or $x = \dfrac{-C}{A}$. The line is *vertical* and m is undefined.

If $A \neq 0$ and $B \neq 0$, then the line is *oblique*; that is, the line is neither horizontal nor vertical. Then, m is either positive or negative.

1. If A and B both have the *same* sign, then $m < 0$. The line will have a downward direction as you move from left to right along it.

2. If A and B have *opposite* signs, then $m > 0$. The line will have an upward direction as you move from left to right along it.

In Exercises 35-40, determine, by inspection of the given equation, whether the slope of the line is positive, negative, zero, or undefined.

35. $2x - 7y + 5 = 0$

36. $3x = 5y - 1$

37. $4x - 9 = 0$

38. $6y = 3 - 7x$

39. $2 + 5x = 6y$

40. $2.3y - 4.9 = 1.2$

7.5 Equations of Lines

Slope-intercept Form of Equation of a Line

Let m = the slope of a line and let b = the y-intercept of the line, in the xy-plane. Then the equation

$$y = mx + b$$

is called the **slope-intercept** form of the line.

Rewriting the equation $5x - y = 3$ as $y = 5x - 3$, we determine that the slope of the line, m, is 5 and that the y-intercept = -3. The equation $y = 5$ is in the slope–intercept form, with $m = 0$ and $b = 5$. The equation $x = 5$ cannot be written in the slope-intercept form since the slope is undefined.

In Exercises 41-46, write each equation in the slope-intercept form and determine the slope and y-intercept of the line.

41. $2x + y = 4$

42. $3x - 5y = 15$

43. $7y - 2 = 0$

44. $6x = 1 - y$

45. $3 = 2x - 7y$

46. $2y = 4 - 8x$

In Exercises 47-50, write an equation for each line given its slope and y-intercept.

47. $m = 2$, y-intercept = -4

48. $m = -5$, y-intercept = 11

49. $m = 0$, y-intercept = -9

50. $m = -13$, y-intercept = 23

If we know the slope of a line and a point through which the line passes, then we can determine the equation of the line.

Point-slope Form of Equation of a Line

Let m = the slope of a line and let (x_1, y_1) be a point, in the xy-plane, through which the line passes. Then the equation

$$y - y_1 = m(x - x_1)$$

is called the **point-slope** form of the line.

To determine the equation of the line, in the xy-plane, that has a slope of -4 and passes through the point $(-2, 5)$, use the point-slope form of the equation with $m = -4$, $x_1 = -2$, and $y_1 = 5$.

$$y - y_1 = m(x - x_1)$$
$$y - 5 = -4[x - (-2)]$$
$$y - 5 = -4(x + 2)$$
$$y - 5 = -4x - 8$$
$$y = -4x - 3$$

Hence, the required equation is $y = -4x - 3$, which has been written in the slope–intercept form.

Of course, if we know two points through which a line passes, we can determine its slope. Then, we can use the point–slope form for the equation of a line, with either of the given points, and determine the equation of the line.

In Exercises 51-54, determine an equation of the line passing through the given point and having the indicated slope.

51. Point = $(-3, 6)$; $m = 2$

52. Point = $(-7, -6)$; $m = -8$

53. Point = $(5, -9)$; $m = 11$

54. Point = $(-2.3, -3.7)$; $m = -4.1$

In Exercises 55-56, determine an equation of the line that passes through the given pair of points.

55. $(3, -7)$ and $(-4, 9)$

56. $(-1, 0)$ and $(6, -8)$

7.6 Linear Inequalities in Two Variables

A linear equation in the two variables x and y is of the form $Ax + By + C = 0$ such that $A \neq 0$ or $B \neq 0$. If the symbol = is replaced by one of the symbols $<$, $\leq$, $>$, or $\geq$, then we have a **linear inequality in the two variables** x and y.

The properties used to solve linear inequalities in a single variable are also used to solve linear inequalities in two variables.

The equation

$$y = x - 7$$

is a linear equation in the two variables x and y. There are infinitely many values that can be chosen for x. For each value of x, there is only one value corresponding to y. For instance, if x = 4, then y = −3.

The inequality

$$y > x - 7$$

is a linear inequality in the two variables x and y. Again, there are infinitely many values that can be chosen for x. However, for *each* value of x, there are infinitely many values corresponding to y. For instance, if x = 4, then x − 7 = −3. Hence,

$$y > x - 7$$

becomes y > −3.

Therefore, when x = 4, y can be *any* real number that is *greater than* −3. The ordered pairs $(4, -2)$, $(4, 0)$, $(4, 2)$, and $(4, 12)$ are a few of the infinitely many solutions for the inequality y > x − 7 when x = 4. There are, similarly, infinitely many solutions when x is equal to any other number.

To solve the inequality 2x − 3y ≤ 5 for y, we proceed as follows:

$$2x - 3y \leq 5$$

$-3y \leq 5 - 2x$ (Subtract 2x from *both* sides; *same* sense.)

$y \geq \dfrac{2x - 5}{3}$ (Divide *both* sides by −3, which is *negative*; *opposite* sense.)

which is the required solution. Now, if x = 3, then

$$y \geq \frac{2(3) - 5}{3}$$

$$y \geq \frac{6 - 5}{3}$$

$$y \geq \frac{1}{3}$$

Hence, if x = 3, then *any* real number value that is greater than or equal to $\dfrac{1}{3}$ will satisfy the inequality 2x − 3y ≤ 5.

In Exercises 57-62, solve each of the given inequalities for y.

57. $2x + y < 5$

58. $x - 3y > 2$

59. $3x - 5y \leq -2$

60. $4x \geq 5 - 3y$

61. $2x - 3(y - 2) < 7$

62. $-3(x + 2) - 4(y - 5) \geq y - 3$

63. Is the ordered pair $(-3, 5)$ a solution for the inequality x + y > 1? Why (not)?

64. Is the ordered pair $(4, -6)$ a solution for the inequality 2x − 3y ≤ 5? Why (not)?

65. Given the inequality 3x + 2y < −2, determine four different values for y, if x = −1.

7.7 Graphs of Linear Inequalities in Two Variables

A line separates the plane containing it into two **half-planes**, one on one side of the line and the other on the other side of the line. The line is the **boundary** of the half-planes. The line is described by a linear *equation* whereas each of the half-planes is described by a linear *inequality*.

To graph a linear inequality in two variables, we must first determine the line that separates the plane and, then, determine the appropriate half-plane. This is illustrated as follows:

Graph the inequality $y > 3x + 6$ in the xy-plane.

1. Determine the line that separates the plane. This will be the graph of the corresponding equation, $y = 3x + 6$. The line passes through the points $(0, 6)$ and $(-2, 0)$. This line is the boundary of two half-planes but is not included as part of the graph. Hence, the line is graphed in *dashed* form. (See Fig. 7.6.)

$0 ? 3(0) + 6$

$0 ? 0 + 6$

$0 > 6$ is false.

Since $(0, 0)$ is *not* a solution for the inequality $y > 3x + 6$, the half-plane will be the one that does *not* contain the point $(0, 0)$. The required half-plane is shaded in Fig. 7.7.

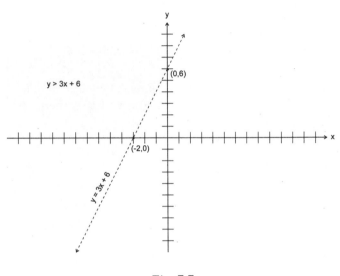

Fig. 7.7

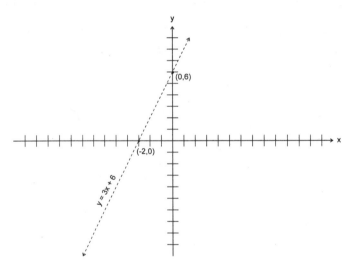

Fig. 7.6

2. Determine the appropriate half–plane. To do so, we can select any point in the plane and test to see if it satisfies the inequality. For convenience, we will use the point $(0, 0)$.

$$y > 3x + 6$$

In Exercises 66-71, graph each of the following inequalities in the xy-plane.

66. $y > 2x - 4$

67. $2x - 3y < 6$

68. $4x - 4y \geq 8$

69. $y \leq 4x$

70. $1.2x - 2.4y > 4.8$

71. $2(x - 3) < -3(y + 1)$

✔ Check Yourself

1. The point (2, −3) lies in Quadrant IV since the abscissa, 2, is positive, and the ordinate, −3, is negative. **(Rectangular coordinate system)**

2. The point (−6, 0) lies on the horizontal axis since the ordinate is 0 and the abscissa is −6. **(Rectangular coordinate system)**

3. The point (−8, −9) lies in Quadrant III since both the abscissa, −8, and the ordinate, −9, are negative. **(Rectangular coordinate system)**

4. The point (10, 23) lies in Quadrant I since both the abscissa, 10, and the ordinate, 23, are positive. **(Rectangular coordinate system)**

5. The point (0, −4) lies on the vertical axis since the abscissa is 0 and the ordinate is −4. **(Rectangular coordinate system)**

6. The point (−8, 6) lies in Quadrant II since the abscissa, −8, is negative, and the ordinate, 6, is positive. **(Rectangular coordinate system)**

7. The point (1.3, −5.8) lies in Quadrant IV since the abscissa, 1.3, is positive, and the ordinate, −5.8, is negative. **(Rectangular coordinate system)**

8. The point (−5.9, 0) lies on the horizontal axis since the ordinate is 0. **(Rectangular coordinate system)**

9. $x + y = 10$

   $y = 10 - x$

   Hence, the required solution is $y = 10 - x$. **(Linear equations in two variables)**

10. $3x = 4y - 7$

    $3x + 7 = 4y$

    $\dfrac{3x + 7}{4} - y$

    Hence, the required solution is $y = \dfrac{3x + 7}{4}$. **(Linear equations in two variables)**

11. $2x - 6y + 7 = 0$

    $2x + 7 = 6y$

    $\dfrac{2x + 7}{y} = 6$

    Hence, the required solution is $y = \dfrac{2x + 7}{6}$. **(Linear equations in two variables)**

12.　$5 - 2x = 4y - 5$

　　　$10 - 2x = 4y$

　　　$\dfrac{10 - 2x}{4} = y$

　　　$\dfrac{5 - x}{2} = y$

　　Hence, the required solution is $y = \dfrac{5 - x}{2}$.　**(Linear equations in two variables)**

13.　$1.2x - 4.5y = 6.1$

　　　$-4.5y = 6.1 - 1.2x$

　　　$y = \dfrac{1.2x - 6.1}{4.5}$

　　　$y = \dfrac{12x - 61}{45}$

　　Hence, the required solution is $y = \dfrac{12x - 61}{45}$.　**(Linear equations in two variables)**

14.　$7.2x = 5 - 8.4y$

　　　$72x = 50 - 84y$

　　　$72x - 50 = -84y$

　　　$\dfrac{50 - 72x}{84} = y$

　　　$\dfrac{25 - 36x}{42} = y$

　　Hence, the required solution is $y = \dfrac{25 - 36x}{42}$.　**(Linear equations in two variables)**

15.　$3(x - 1) - 4(y + 5) = 12$

　　　$3x - 3 - 4y - 20 = 12$

　　　$3x - 4y - 23 = 12$

　　　$3x - 4y = 35$

　　　$-4y = 35 - 3x$

　　　$y = \dfrac{3x - 35}{4}$

　　Hence, the required solution is $y = \dfrac{3x - 35}{4}$.　**(Linear equations in two variables)**

16.　$-4(y - 5) = 11 - 5(2 - 3x)$

　　　$-4y + 20 = 11 - 10 + 15x$

　　　$-4y + 20 = 1 + 15x$

　　　$-4y = -19 + 15x$

$$y = \frac{19 - 15x}{4}$$

Hence, the required solution is $y = \frac{19 - 15x}{4}$. **(Linear equations in two variables)**

17. $x + y = 7$

x-intercept: Set $y = 0$: $x + 0 = 7$

$$x = 7 \text{ (x-intercept)}$$

y-intercept: Set $x = 0$: $0 + y = 7$

$$y = 7 \text{ (y-intercept)} \quad \textbf{(Graphs of linear equations in two variables)}$$

18. $y - 4 = 0$

x-intercept: Set $y = 0$: $0 - 4 = 0$

$$-4 = 0, \text{ which is not true.}$$

Hence, there is *no* x-intercept.

y-intercept: Set $x = 0$: $y - 4 = 0$

$$y = 4 \text{ for all real values of x.}$$

Hence, y-intercept = 4.   **(Graphs of linear equations in two variables)**

19. $3x - 5y = 1$

x-intercept: Set $y = 0$: $3x - 5(0) = 1$

$$3x - 0 = 1$$

$$3x = 1$$

$$x = \frac{1}{3} \text{ (x-intercept)}$$

y-intercept: Set $x = 0$: $3(0) - 5y = 1$

$$0 - 5y = 1$$

$$-5y = 1$$

$$y = \frac{-1}{5} \text{ (y-intercept)} \quad \textbf{(Graphs of linear equations in two variables)}$$

20. $4x = 1 - 7y$

x-intercept: Set $y = 0$: $4x = 1 - 7(0)$

$$4x = 1 - 0$$

$$4x = 1$$

$$x = \frac{1}{4} \text{ (x-intercept)}$$

y-intercept: Set $x = 0$: $4(0) = 1 - 7y$

$$0 = 1 - 7y$$

$$7y = 1$$

$$y = \frac{1}{7} \text{ (y-intercept)} \quad \textbf{(Graphs of linear equations in two variables)}$$

21. x − y = 5

 If x = 0, then y = −5. If y = 0, then x = 5. If x = 2, then y = −3. Hence, the line passes through the points (0, −5), (5, 0), and (2, −3). Graphing these points in the xy-plane and drawing a straight line through them, we have the graph of x − y = 5. (See Fig. 7.8.) **(Graphs of linear equations in two variables)**

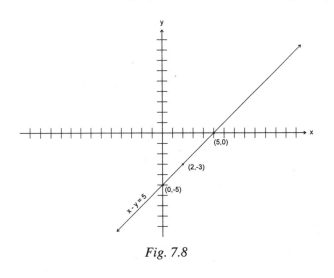

Fig. 7.8

22. x − 4 = 0

 x − 4 = 0, or x = 4, is true for all real values of y. Hence, we can take the points (4, 0), (4, −3), and (4, 4) as points through which the line passes. Graphing these points in the xy-plane and drawing a straight line through them, we have the graph of x − 4 = 0. (See Fig. 7.9.) **(Graphs of linear equations in two variables)**

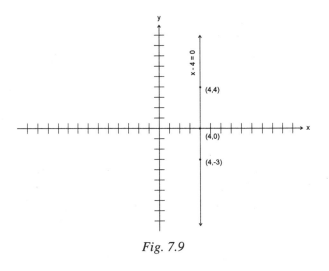

Fig. 7.9

23. y = 3x + 7

If x = 0, then y = 7. If y = 0, then x = $\frac{-7}{3}$. If x = –2, then y = 1. Hence, we have the points (0, 7), $\left(\frac{-7}{3}, 0\right)$, and (–2, 1) through which the line passes. Graphing these points in the xy-plane and drawing a straight line through them, we have the graph of y = 3x + 7. (See Fig. 7.10.) **(Graphs of linear equations in two variables)**

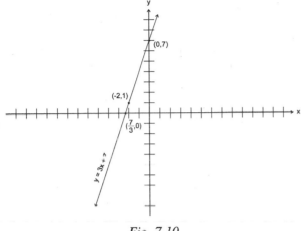

Fig. 7.10

24. 3x – 4y = 12

If x = 0, then y = –3. If y = 0, then x = 4. If x = –4, then y = –6. Hence, we have the points (0, –3), (4, 0), and (–4, –6) through which the line passes. Graphing these points in the xy-plane and drawing a straight line through them, we have the graph of 3x – 4y = 12. (See Fig. 7.11.) **(Graphs of linear equations in two variables)**

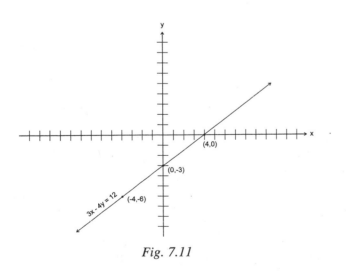

Fig. 7.11

25. $2y - 6 = 0$

$2y - 6 = 0$, or $y = 3$, is true for all real values of x. Hence, we can take the points $(-3, 3)$, $(0, 3)$, and $(4, 3)$ as points through which the line passes. Graphing these points in the xy-plane and drawing a straight line through them, we have the graph of $2y - 6 = 0$. (See Fig. 7.12.) **(Graphs of linear equations in two variables)**

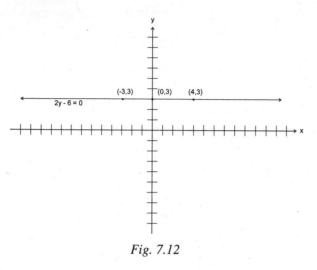

Fig. 7.12

26. $2y = x - 5$

If $x = 0$, then $y = -2.5$. If $y = 0$, then $x = 5$. If $x = 3$, then $y = -1$. Hence, we have the points $(0, -2.5)$, $(5, 0)$, and $(3, -1)$ through which the line passes. Graphing these points in the xy-plane and drawing a straight line through them, we have the graph of $2y = x - 5$. (See Fig. 7.13.) **(Graphs of linear equations in two variables)**

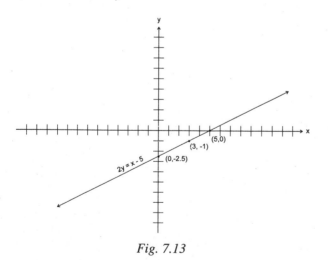

Fig. 7.13

27. $(2, -5)$ and $(-3, 8)$

$$m = \frac{-5 - 8}{2 - (-3)} = \frac{-13}{5}. \quad \textbf{(Slope of a line)}$$

28. (0, 4) and (−5, 0)

$$m = \frac{4-0}{0-(-5)} = \frac{4}{5}.$$ **(Slope of a line)**

29. (−3, 8) and (3, −2)

$$m = \frac{8-(-2)}{-3-3} = \frac{10}{-6} = \frac{-5}{3}.$$ **(Slope of a line)**

30. (1.2, −3.1) and (−4.8, −6.3)

$$m = \frac{-6.3-(-3.1)}{-4.8-1.2} = \frac{-3.2}{-6} = \frac{8}{15}.$$ **(Slope of a line)**

31. $2x + 4y = 6$

If x = 0, then y = 1.5. If y = 0, then x = 3. Hence, the line passes through the two points (0, 1.5) and (3, 0). Therefore, $m = \frac{1.5-0}{0-3} = \frac{1.5}{-3} = \frac{-1}{2}.$ **(Slope of a line)**

32. $3y - 5 = 0$ or, $y = \frac{5}{3}$ for all real values of x. Hence, the line passes through the two points $\left(0, \frac{5}{3}\right)$ and $\left(5, \frac{5}{3}\right)$. Therefore, $m = \frac{\frac{5}{3} - \frac{5}{3}}{5-0} = \frac{0}{5} = 0$ **(Slope of a line)**

33. $3y = 8 - 5x$

If x = 0, then $y = \frac{8}{3}$. If y = 0, then $x = \frac{8}{5}$. Hence, the line passes through the two points $\left(0, \frac{8}{3}\right)$ and $\left(\frac{8}{5}, 0\right)$. Therefore, $m = \frac{\frac{8}{3} - 0}{0 - \frac{8}{5}} = \frac{\frac{8}{3}}{\frac{-8}{5}} = \frac{-5}{3}.$ **(Slope of a line)**

34. $x - 5y = 0$

If x = 0, then y = 0. If x = 5, then y = 1. Hence, the line passes through the two points (0, 0) and (5, 1). Therefore, $m = \frac{0-1}{0-5} = \frac{-1}{-5} = \frac{1}{5}.$ **(Slope of a line)**

35. $2x - 7y + 5 = 0$ is of the form Ax + By + C = 0, with A = 2 and B = −7. Since A and B have *opposite* signs, the slope is positive. **(Slope of a line)**

36. $3x = 5y - 1$, rewritten as $3x - 5y + 1 = 0$, is of the form Ax + By + C = 0, with A = 3 and B = −5. Since A and B have *opposite* signs, the slope is positive. **(Slope of a line)**

37. $4x - 9 = 0$ is of the form Ax + By + C = 0, with A = 4 and B = 0. Hence, the slope is undefined. **(Slope of a line)**

38. $6y = 3 - 7x$, rewritten as $7x + 6y - 3 = 0$, is of the form Ax + By + C = 0, with A = 7 and B = 6. Since A and B have the *same* signs, the slope is negative. **(Slope of a line)**

39. $2 + 5x = 6y$, rewritten as $5x - 6y + 2 = 0$, is of the form Ax + By + C = 0, with A = 5 and B = −6. Since A and B have *opposite* signs, the slope is positive. **(Slope of a line)**

40. $2.3y - 4.9 = 1.2$, rewritten as $2.3y - 6.1 = 0$, is of the form $Ax + By + C = 0$, with $A = 0$ and $B = 2.3$. Therefore, the slope is 0. (**Slope of a line**)

41. $2x + y = 4$

$$y = -2x + 4$$

Hence, the slope-intercept form of the equation of the line is $y = -2x + 4$. $m = -2$ and $b = 4$. (**Equations of lines**)

42. $3x - 5y = 15$

$$-5y = -3x + 15$$

$$y = \frac{3}{5}x - 3$$

Hence, the slope-intercept form of the equation of the line is $y = \frac{3}{5}x - 3$. $m = \frac{3}{5}$ and $b = -3$. (**Equations of lines**)

43. $7y - 2 = 0$

$$7y = 2$$

$$y = \frac{2}{7}$$

Hence, the slope-intercept form of the equation of the line is $y = \frac{2}{7}$. $m = 0$ and $b = \frac{2}{7}$. (**Equations of lines**)

44. $6x = 1 - y$

$$6x - 1 = -y$$

$$-6x + 1 = y$$

Hence, the slope-intercept form of the equation of the line is $y = -6x + 1$. $m = -6$ and $b = 1$. (**Equations of lines**)

45. $3 = 2x - 7y$

$$-2x + 3 = -7y$$

$$\frac{2}{7}x - \frac{3}{7} = y$$

Hence, the slope-intercept form of the equation of the line is $y = \frac{2}{7}x - \frac{3}{7}$. $m = \frac{2}{7}$ and $b = \frac{-3}{7}$. (**Equations of lines**)

46. $2y = 4 - 8x$

$$2y = -8x + 4$$

$$y = -4x + 2$$

Hence, the slope-intercept form of the equation of the line is $y = -4x + 2$. $m = -4$ and $b = 2$. (**Equations of lines**)

47. m = 2, y-intercept = −4

   The required equation is y = 2x − 4. (**Equations of lines**)

48. m = −5, y-intercept = 11

   The required equation is y = −5x + 11. (**Equations of lines**)

49. m = 0, y-intercept = −9

   The required equation is y = −9. (**Equations of lines**)

50. m = −13, y-intercept = 23

   The required equation is y = −13x + 23. (**Equations of lines**)

51. Point = (−3, 6); m = 2

   $y - y_1 = m(x - x1)$

   $y - 6 = 2[x - (-3)]$

   $y - 6 = 2(x + 3)$

   $y - 6 = 2x + 6$

   $y = 2x + 12$

   Hence, a simplified equation is y = 2x + 12. (**Equations of lines**)

52. Point = (−7, −6); m = −8

   $y - y_1 = m(x - x_1)$

   $y - (-6) = -8[x - (-7)]$

   $y + 6 = -8(x + 7)$

   $y + 6 = -8x - 56$

   $8x + y + 62 = 0$

   Hence, a simplified equation is 8x + y + 62 = 0. (**Equations of lines**)

53. Point = (5, −9); m = 11

   $y - y_1 = m(x - x_1)$

   $y - (-9) = 11(x - 5)$

   $y + 9 = 11x - 55$

   $y = 11x - 64$

   Hence, a simplified equation is y = 11x − 64. (**Equations of lines**)

54. Point = (−2.3, −3.7); m = −4.1

   $y - y_1 = m(x - x_1)$

   $y - (-3.7) = -4.1[x - (-2.3)]$

   $y + 3.7 = -4.1(x + 2.3)$

   $y + 3.7 = -4.1x - 9.43$

   $4.1x + y + 13.13 = 0$

   Hence, a simplified equation is 4.1x + y + 13.13 = 0. (**Equations of lines**)

55. Using the points $(3, -7)$ and $(-4, 9)$, determine the slope.

$$m = \frac{-7 - 9}{3 - (-4)} = \frac{-16}{7}$$

Using the point $(3, -7)$, $m = \frac{-16}{7}$, and the point-slope form of the equation of the line, we have

$$y - y_1 = m(x - x_1)$$

$$y - (-7) = \frac{-16}{7}(x - 3)$$

$$y + 7 = \frac{-16}{7}(x - 3)$$

$$7(y + 7) = -16(x - 3)$$

$$7y + 49 = -16x + 48$$

$$16x + 7y + 1 = 0$$

Hence, a simplified form for the equation of the line is $16x + 7y + 1 = 0$. **(Equations of lines)**

56. Using the points $(-1, 0)$ and $(6, -8)$, determine the slope.

$$m = \frac{-8 - 0}{6 - (-1)} = \frac{-8}{7}$$

Using the point $(-1, 0)$, $m = \frac{-8}{7}$, and the point-slope form for the equation of the line, we have

$$y - y_1 = m(x - x_1)$$

$$y - 0 = \frac{-8}{7}[x - (-1)]$$

$$7y = -8(x + 1)$$

$$7y = -8x - 8$$

$$8x + 7y + 8 = 0$$

Hence, a simplified form for the equation of the line is $8x + 7y + 8 = 0$. **(Equations of lines)**

57. $2x + y < 5$

$$y < 5 - 2x$$

Hence, the required solution is $y < 5 - 2x$. **(Linear inequalities in two variables)**

58. $x - 3y > 2$

$$-3y > 2 - x$$

$$y < \frac{x - 2}{3}$$

Hence, the required solution is $y < \frac{x - 2}{3}$. **(Linear inequalities in two variables)**

59. $3x - 5y \le -2$

$\qquad -5y \le -2 - 3x$

$\qquad y \ge \dfrac{3x + 2}{5}$

Hence, the required solution is $y \ge \dfrac{3x + 2}{5}$. **(Linear inequalities in two variables)**

60. $\qquad 4x \ge 5 - 3y$

$\quad 4x - 5 \ge -3y$

$\dfrac{5 - 4x}{3} \le y$

Hence, the required solution is $y \ge \dfrac{5 - 4x}{3}$. **(Linear inequalities in two variables)**

61. $2x - 3(y - 2) < 7$

$\quad 2x - 3y + 6 < 7$

$\qquad -3y < -2x + 1$

$\qquad\quad y > \dfrac{2x - 1}{3}$

Hence, the required solution is $y > \dfrac{2x - 1}{3}$. **(Linear inequalities in two variables)**

62. $-3(x + 2) - 4(y - 5) \ge y - 3$

$\quad -3x - 6 - 4y + 20 \ge y - 3$

$\qquad -3x - 4y + 14 \ge y - 3$

$\qquad\quad -3x - 5y \ge -17$

$\qquad\qquad -5y \ge 3x - 17$

$\qquad\qquad\quad y \le \dfrac{17 - 3x}{5}$

Hence, the required solution is $y \le \dfrac{17 - 3x}{5}$. **(Linear inequalities in two variables)**

63. If $x = -3$ and $y = 5$, is $x + y > 1$?

$\quad x + y > 1$

$-3 + 5 \; ? \; 1$

$\qquad 2 > 1$ which is true.

Therefore, the ordered pair $(-3, 5)$ is a solution for the inequality $x + y > 1$. **(Linear inequalities in two variables)**

64. If x = 4 and y = −6, is 2x − 3y ≤ 5?

$$2x - 3y \le 5$$

$$2(4) - 3(-6) \ ? \ 5$$

$$8 + 18 \ ? \ 5$$

$$26 \le 5 \text{ which is false.}$$

Therefore, the ordered pair (4, −6) is *not* a solution for the inequality 2x − 3y ≤ 5. **(Linear inequalities in two variables)**

65. $3x + 2y < -2$

$$2y < -2 - 3x$$

$$y < \frac{-2 - 3x}{2}$$

If x = −1, then $y < \dfrac{-2 - 3(-1)}{2}$

$$y < \frac{1}{2}$$

Hence, if x = −1, then $y < \dfrac{1}{2}$. Therefore, y can take the values 0, −5, −23.4, and −109.5, among others.

(Linear inequalities in two variables)

66. $y > 2x - 4$

The line that separates the plane has equation y = 2x − 4 and passes through the points (0, −4) and (2, 0). This line is the boundary of two half-planes but is not included as part of the graph. Hence, the line is graphed in *dashed* form. (See Fig. 7.14.) To determine the correct half-plane, we will test the given inequality with the point (0, 0):

$y > 2x - 4$

$0 \ ? \ 2(0) - 4$

$0 > -4$ which is true.

Since (0, 0) is a solution for the inequality y > 2x − 4, the half-plane will be the one that contains the point (0, 0). The required half-plane is shaded in Fig. 7.15. **(Graphs of linear inequalities in two variables)**

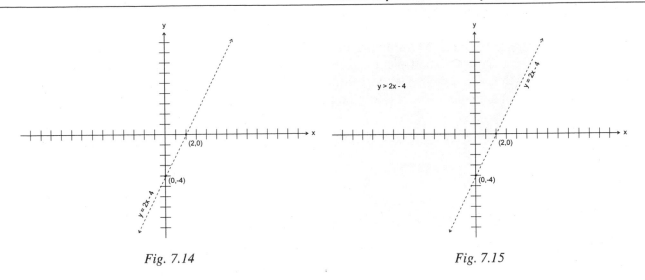

Fig. 7.14   Fig. 7.15

67. $2x - 3y < 6$

The line that separates the plane has equation $2x - 3y = 6$ and passes through the points $(0, -2)$ and $(3, 0)$. This line is the boundary of two half-planes, but is not included as part of the graph. Hence, the line is graphed in *dashed* form. (See Fig. 7.16.) To determine the correct half-plane, we will test the given inequality with the point $(0, 0)$:

$2x - 3y < 6$

$2(0) - 3(0) \ ? \ 6$

   $0 < 6$ which is true.

Since $(0, 0)$ is a solution for the inequality $2x - 3y < 6$, the half-plane will be the one that contains the point $(0, 0)$. The required half-plane is shaded in Fig. 7.17. **(Graphs of linear inequalities in two variables)**

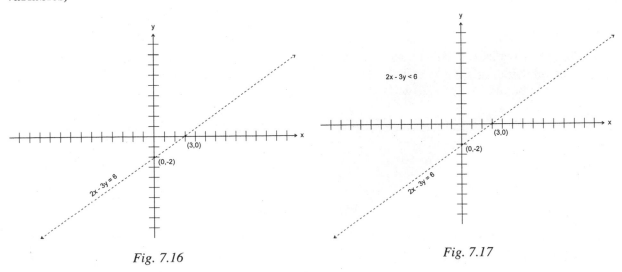

Fig. 7.16   Fig. 7.17

68. $4x - 4y \geq 8$

The line that separates the plane has equation $4x - 4y = 8$ and passes through the points $(0, -2)$ and $(2, 0)$. This line is the boundary of two half-planes and *is* included as part of the graph since $4x - 4y \geq 8$ means that $4x - 4y > 8$ or that $4x - 4y = 8$. Hence, the line is graphed in *solid* form. (See Fig. 7.18.) To determine the correct half-plane, we will test the given inequality with the point $(0, 0)$:

$4x - 4y \geq 8$

$4(0) - 4(0)$? 8

$0 \geq 8$ which is false.

Since $(0, 0)$ is *not* a solution for the inequality $4x - 4y \geq 8$, the half-plane will be the one that does *not* contain the point $(0, 0)$. The required half-plane is shaded in Fig. 7.19. **(Graphs of linear inequalities in two variables)**

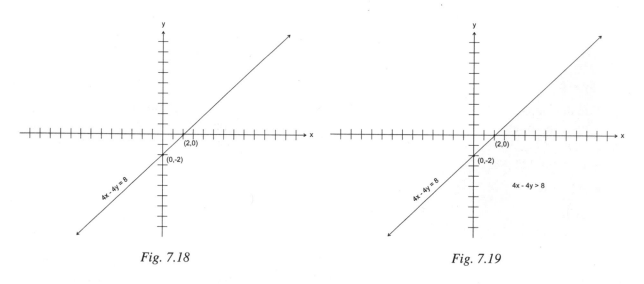

Fig. 7.18   Fig. 7.19

69. $y \leq 4x$

The line that separates the plane has equation $y = 4x$ and passes through the points $(0, 0)$ and $(1, 4)$. This line is the boundary of two half-planes and *is* included as part of the graph. Hence, the line is graphed in *solid* form. (See Fig. 7.20.) To determine the correct half-plane, we cannot use the point $(0, 0)$ since $(0, 0)$ is on the boundary line. We will test the given inequality with the point $(1, 1)$:

$y \leq 4x$

1 ? $4(1)$

$1 \leq 4$ which is true.

Since $(1, 1)$ is a solution for the inequality $y \leq 4x$, the half-plane will be the one that contains the point $(1, 1)$. The required half-plane is shaded in Fig. 7.21. **(Graphs of linear inequalities in two variables)**

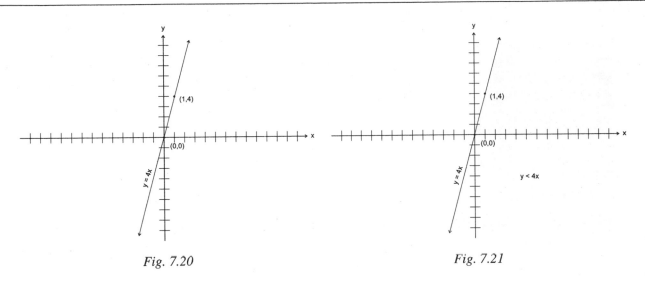

Fig. 7.20   Fig. 7.21

70. $1.2x - 2.4y > 4.8$

The line that separates the plane has equation $1.2x - 2.4y = 4.8$ (or, $x - 2y = 4$) and passes through the points $(0, -2)$ and $(4, 0)$. This line is the boundary of two half-planes, but is not included as part of the graph. Hence, the line is graphed in *dashed* form. (See Fig. 7.22.) To determine the correct half-plane, we will test the given inequality with the point $(0, 0)$:

$1.2x - 2.4y > 4.8$

$1.2(0) - 2.4(0) ? 4.8$

$0 > 4.8$ which is false.

Since $(0, 0)$ is not a solution for the inequality $1.2x - 2.4y > 4.8$, the half-plane will be the one that does *not* contain the point $(0, 0)$. The required half-plane is shaded in Fig. 7.23. **(Graphs of linear inequalities in two variables)**

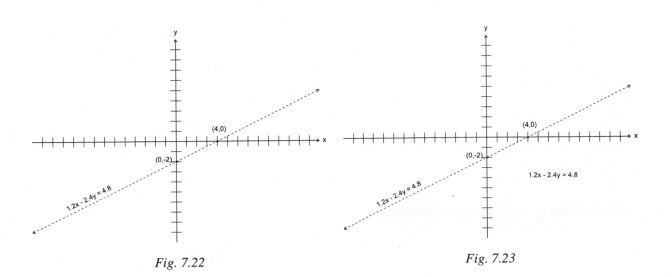

Fig. 7.22   Fig. 7.23

71. $2(x - 3) < -3(y + 1)$

The line that separates the plane has equation $2(x - 3) = -3(y + 1)$ (or, $2x + 3y = 3$) and passes through the points $(0, 1)$ and $(1.5, 0)$. This line is the boundary of two half-planes, but is not included as part of the graph. Hence, the line is graphed in *dashed* form. (See Fig. 7.24.) To determine the correct half-plane, we will test the given inequality with the point $(0, 0)$:

$2(x - 3) < -3(y + 1)$

$2(0 - 3)$? $-3(0 + 1)$

$2(-3)$? $-3(1)$

$-6 < -3$ which is true.

Since $(0, 0)$ is a solution for the inequality $2(x - 3) < -3(y + 1)$, the half-plane will be the one that contains the point $(0, 0)$. The required half-plane is shaded in Fig. 7.25. **(Graphs of linear inequalities in two variables)**

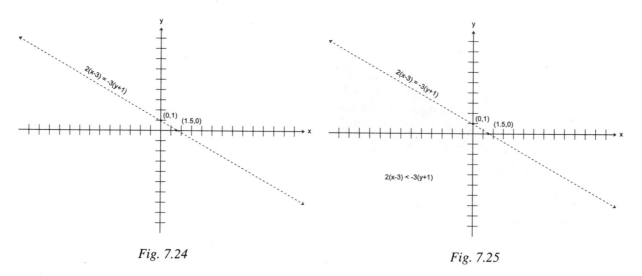

Fig. 7.24   Fig. 7.25

Grade Yourself

Circle the numbers of the questions you missed, then fill in the total incorrect for each topic. If you answered more than three questions incorrectly, you need to focus on that topic. (If a topic has less than three questions and you had at least one wrong, we suggest you study that topic also. Read your textbook, a review book, or ask your teacher for help.)

Subject: Linear Equations and Inequalities in Two Variables

Topic	Question Numbers	Number Incorrect
Rectangular coordinate system	1, 2, 3, 4, 5, 6, 7, 8	
Linear equations in two variables	9, 10, 11, 12, 13, 14, 15, 16	
Graphs of linear equations in two variables	17, 18, 19, 20, 21, 22, 23, 24, 25, 26	
Slope of a line	27, 28, 29, 30, 31, 32, 33, 34, 35, 36, 37, 38, 39, 40	
Equations of lines	41, 42, 43, 44, 45, 46, 47, 48, 49, 50, 51, 52, 53, 54, 55, 56	
Linear inequalities in two variables	57, 58, 59, 60, 61, 62, 63, 64, 65	
Graphs of linear inequalities in two variables	66, 67, 68, 69, 70, 71	

Systems of Linear Equations and Inequalities

8

8.1 Solving Systems of Linear Equations by Graphing

Two or more linear equations in two variables, when taken together, are called a **system of two linear equations in two variables**.

To solve such a system, we must determine all of the ordered pairs of real numbers that satisfy *all* of the equations in the system. In this section, we examine the graphical method for solving a system of two linear equations in two variables.

The graphical method sometimes gives only an approximate solution, depending upon how accurately the graphs of each equation are drawn and how accurately you read the coordinates of the point of intersection.

The graph of a system of two linear equations in two variables will be two lines. The following solutions are possible:

1. If the graphs are two *intersecting* lines, then there will be *exactly one* solution. (The solution will be the ordered pair representing the point of intersection of the two lines.)

2. If the graphs are two *parallel* lines, then there will be *no* solution. (That is, there are no points common to the two lines.)

3. If the graphs are *coinciding* lines (that is, the same line), then there will be *infinitely many* solutions. (All of the points on one line will also lie on the other line.)

The procedure for using the graphical method to solve a system of two linear equations in two variables is illustrated below in Fig. 8.1.

Solve the following system of equations graphically:

$$\begin{cases} x + y = 1 \\ x - y = 1 \end{cases}$$

The graph of the equation $x + y = 1$ is a line that passes through the points $(0, 1)$ and $(1, 0)$.

The graph of the equation $x - y = 1$ is a line that passes through the points $(0, -1)$ and $(1, 0)$.

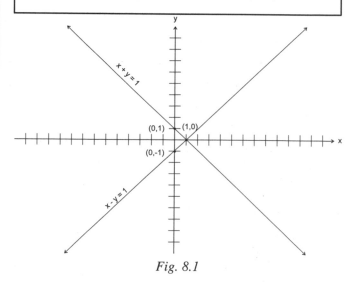

Fig. 8.1

Graph the preceding lines and determine that the *only* point that lies on *both* lines is (1, 0). (See Fig. 8.1.)

Therefore, the only solution for the given system is (1, 0).

Checking this solution in *each* of the given equations, we have

$x + y = 1$ and $x - y = 1$

$1 + 0 ? 1 \qquad 1 - 0 ? 1$

$1 = 1\sqrt{} \qquad 1 = 1\sqrt{}$

In Exercises 1-5, solve each of the given systems of equations graphically.

1. $\begin{cases} x - 2y = 1 \\ x + 2y = 1 \end{cases}$

2. $\begin{cases} x = 3 \\ y = 3x \end{cases}$

3. $\begin{cases} x + y = 0 \\ 2x - 3y = 6 \end{cases}$

4. $\begin{cases} x - y = 3 \\ 2x = 4 + 2y \end{cases}$

5. $\begin{cases} 2y - 8 - 0 \\ y = 3x - 6 \end{cases}$

Slopes of lines can be used to determine whether the lines are intersecting, parallel, or coinciding.

If two lines have *different* slopes, then the lines are *intersecting* lines.

If two lines have the same slopes but *different* y-intercepts, then the lines are *parallel* lines.

If two lines have the *same* slopes and the same y-intercepts, then the lines are *coinciding* lines.

In Exercises 6-9, use slopes to determine whether the graph of the given system consists of intersecting, parallel, or coinciding lines.

6. $\begin{cases} x + y = 3 \\ 3x - 4y = 0 \end{cases}$

7. $\begin{cases} 3x - 2y = 1 \\ 4y = 1 + 6x \end{cases}$

8. $\begin{cases} y - 2x = 7 \\ 4x = 2y - 14 \end{cases}$

9. $\begin{cases} x - 5y = 4 \\ 2x + 5y = 6 \end{cases}$

8.2 Solving Systems of Linear Equations by Elimination

There are two algebraic methods for solving a system of two linear equations in two variables. One of these, known as the **elimination method**, is illustrated in this section.

Solve the following system of equations:
$$\begin{cases} x + y = 7 \\ x - y = 1 \end{cases}$$

We can add these equations together by adding the left-hand sides, adding the right-hand sides, and setting these sums equal to each other. Observe that when we do this, the y variable is *eliminated*, and we can thus solve for x.

$$x + y = 7$$

Add: $\qquad x - y = 1$

____

$$2x + 0 = 8$$

$$2x = 8$$

$$x = 4$$

Substituting 4 for x in either of the two *original* equations (the first, for this example), we have

$$x + y = 7$$

$$4 + y = 7$$

$$y = 3$$

It now appears that the ordered pair (4, 3) is the required solution. Checking in *both* of the *original* equations, we have

$x + y = 7$ and $x - y = 1$

$4 + 3 ? 7 \qquad 4 - 3 ? 1$

$7 = 7\sqrt{} \qquad 1 = 1\sqrt{}$

Therefore, (4, 3) is the required solution.

Solve the following system of equations:

$$\begin{cases} 2x - 3y = 4 \\ 3x + 4y = 0 \end{cases}$$

If we add the two equations, a variable is not eliminated. Further, if we subtract one equation from the other, a variable is not eliminated. What can we do, then, to solve the system?

Suppose that we decide to eliminate the variable x. This can be done by multiplying the first equation by 3, multiplying the second equation by 2, and subtracting the second equation from the first equation.

$$6x - 9y = 12$$

Subtract: $6x + 8y = 0$

$$-17y = 12$$

$$y = \frac{-12}{17}$$

Substituting $\frac{-12}{17}$ for y in either of the original equations (the second, in this example), we have

$$3x + 4y = 0$$

$$3x + 4\left(\frac{-12}{17}\right) = 0$$

$$3x - \frac{48}{17} = 0$$

$$3x = \frac{48}{17}$$

$$x = \frac{16}{17}.$$

It now appears that the ordered pair $\left(\frac{16}{17}, \frac{-12}{17}\right)$ is the required solution. Checking in *both* of the *original* equations, we have

$$2x - 3y = 4 \quad \text{and} \quad 3x + 4y = 0$$

$$2\left(\frac{16}{17}\right) - 3\left(\frac{-12}{17}\right) ? 4 \qquad 3\left(\frac{16}{17}\right) + 4\left(\frac{-12}{17}\right) ? 0$$

$$\frac{32}{17} + \frac{36}{17} ? 4 \qquad \frac{48}{17} - \frac{48}{17} ? 0$$

$$\frac{68}{17} ? 4 \qquad\qquad 0 = 0 \checkmark$$

$$4 = 4. \checkmark$$

Therefore, $\left(\frac{16}{17}, \frac{-12}{17}\right)$ is the required solution.

In Exercises 10-13, solve the following systems of equations by the elimination method.

10. $\begin{cases} x - y = 4 \\ 2x + y = 2 \end{cases}$

11. $\begin{cases} 2x - 4y = 1 \\ 3x + 2y = 2 \end{cases}$

12. $\begin{cases} 5x - y = 10 \\ 2x + 2y = 4 \end{cases}$

13. $\begin{cases} 3x + 4y = 5 \\ 5x - 3y = 2 \end{cases}$

8.3 Solving Systems of Linear Equations by Substitution

A second algebraic method for solving a system of two linear equations in two variables is the method of substitution. This method is illustrated in the following example.

Consider the system of equations

$$\begin{cases} 3x + 2y = 4 \\ y = x - 3 \end{cases}$$

The second equation is already solved for y in terms of x. If we substitute x − 3 for y in the *first* equation, we have

$$3x + 2y = 4$$

$$3x + 2(x - 3) = 4$$

$$3x + 2x - 6 = 4$$

$$5x - 6 = 4$$

$$5x = 10$$

$$x = 2.$$

Now, substituting 2 for x in the *second* equation, we have

$$y = x - 3$$

$$y = 2 - 3$$

$$y = -1.$$

It now appears that the ordered pair (2, −1) is the required solution. Checking in *both* of the *original* equations, we have

$$3x + 2y = 4 \qquad \text{and} \qquad y = x - 3$$

$$3(2) + 2(-1) \;?\; 4 \qquad\qquad -1 \;?\; 2 - 3$$

$$6 - 2 \;?\; 4 \qquad\qquad -1 = -1$$

$$4 = 4\,\sqrt{}$$

Therefore, $(2, -1)$ is the required solution.

In some systems of equations, neither equation is written in the form of one variable solved for in terms of the other. In such cases, pick one of the equations and solve for a variable in terms of the other. Then, proceed as in the above example.

In Exercises 14-17, solve each of the given systems of equations by using the method of substitution.

14. $\begin{cases} y = 3x - 1 \\ x - 2y = 4 \end{cases}$

15. $\begin{cases} 4x + 3y = 5 \\ x = 5y - 2 \end{cases}$

16. $\begin{cases} 2x - y = 6 \\ 3x + 2y = 5 \end{cases}$

17. $\begin{cases} 4x - 5y = 7 \\ 3x + 4y = -2 \end{cases}$

8.4 Solving Systems of Linear Inequalities

Linear inequalities in two variables, and their graphs, were discussed in Section 7.7. To graph such inequalities, we considered the graph of the associated equations. To graph the solutions for a system of two linear inequalities in two variables, we use the same procedure.

The solution for a **system of two linear inequalities in two variables** is the totality of all of the solutions common to both of the inequalities.

Graph the solution for the following system of inequalities.

$$\begin{cases} 2x + 3y \le 6 \\ 3x - 4y > 12 \end{cases}$$

Determine the graph for $2x + 3y \le 6$. Consider the equation $2x + 3y = 6$, which is a straight line passing through the points $(0, 2)$ and $(3, 0)$. This line is the boundary of two half-planes and is graphed as a *solid* line since it *is* part of the solution. Then, using

the test point $(0, 0)$, determine that the solution for this inequality is the half-plane that does contain the point $(0, 0)$. (See Fig. 8.2.)

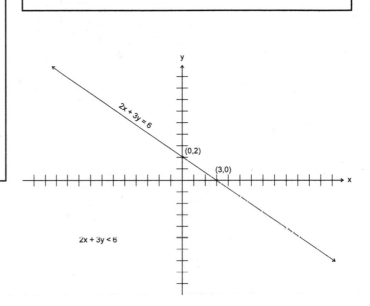

Fig. 8.2

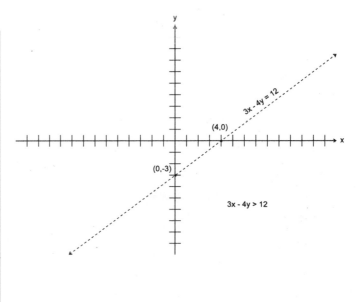

Fig. 8.3

Determine the graph for $3x - 4y > 12$. Consider the equation $3x - 4y = 12$, which is a straight line passing through the points $(0, -3)$ and $(4, 0)$. This line is the boundary of two half-planes and is graphed as a *dashed* line since it is *not* part of the solution. Then, using the test point $(0, 0)$, determine that the solution for this inequality is the half-plane that does *not* contain the point $(0, 0)$. (See Fig. 8.3.)

Determine the part of the xy–plane that is common to both of the above solutions in Figs. 8.2 and 8.3. This is the solution for the given system of inequalities. (See Fig. 8.4.)

In Exercises 18-21, solve each of the following systems of linear inequalities graphically.

18. $\begin{cases} y > 3x \\ x - y < 3 \end{cases}$

19. $\begin{cases} 2x - y < 4 \\ x - 3y < 6 \end{cases}$

20. $\begin{cases} 3x - 2y \le 6 \\ x + y > 5 \end{cases}$

21. $\begin{cases} 2x < y - 4 \\ x - 3y \ge 9 \end{cases}$

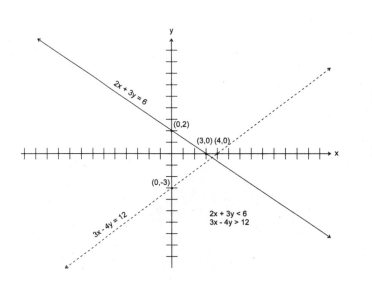

Fig. 8.4

✔ Check Yourself

1. $\begin{cases} x - 2y = 1 \\ x + 2y = 1 \end{cases}$

The graph of the equation $x - 2y = 1$ is a line that passes through the points $(0, -0.5)$ and $(3, 1)$. The graph of the equation $x + 2y = 1$ is a line that passes through the points $(0, 0.5)$ and $(3, -1)$. Graphing the two lines, in the xy-plane, determine that the *only* point that lies on *both* lines is $(1, 0)$. (See Fig. 8.5.) Therefore, the only solution for the given system is $(1, 0)$. Checking this solution in *each* of the *two* given equations, we have

$$x - 2y = 1 \quad \text{and} \quad x + 2y = 1$$
$$1 - 2(0) \ ? \ 1 \qquad \qquad 1 + 2(0) \ ? \ 1$$
$$1 = 1\sqrt{} \qquad \qquad 1 = 1\sqrt{} \quad \textbf{(Solving systems of linear equations by graphing)}$$

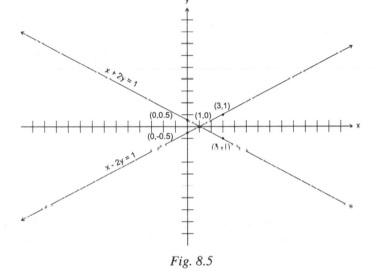

Fig. 8.5

2. $\begin{cases} x = 3 \\ y = 3x \end{cases}$

The graph of the equation $x = 3$ is a line that passes through the points $(3, 0)$ and $(3, 3)$. The graph of the equation $y = 3x$ is a line that passes through the points $(0, 0)$ and $(1, 3)$. Graphing the two lines, in the xy-plane, determine that the *only* point that lies on *both* lines is $(3, 9)$. (See Fig. 8.6.) Therefore, the only solution for the given system is $(3, 9)$. In this, and subsequent exercises, the check is left to you. **(Solving systems of linear equations by graphing)**

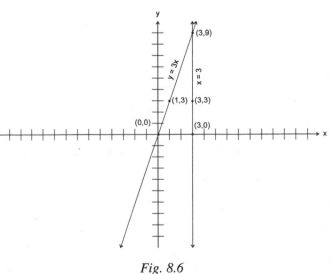

Fig. 8.6

3. $\begin{cases} x + y = 0 \\ 2x - 3y = 6 \end{cases}$

The graph of the equation $x + y = 0$ is a line that passes through the points $(0, 0)$ and $(-3, 3)$. The graph of the equation $2x - 3y = 6$ is a line that passes through the points $(0, -2)$ and $(3, 0)$. Graphing the two lines, in the xy-plane, it appears that the *only* point that lies on *both* lines is $(1, -1)$. (See Fig. 8.7.) However, this ordered pair does not check in the original equations. The actual solution is $\left(\dfrac{6}{5}, \dfrac{-6}{5} \right)$. (**Solving systems of linear equations by graphing**)

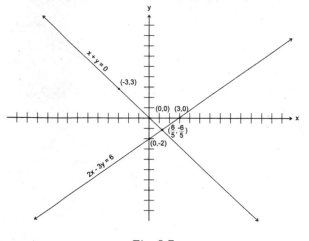

Fig. 8.7

4. $\begin{cases} x - y = 3 \\ 2x = 4 + 2y \end{cases}$

The graph of the equation $x - y = 3$ is a line that passes through the points $(0, -3)$ and $(3, 0)$. The graph of the equation $2x = 4 + 2y$ is a line that passes through the points $(0, -2)$ and $(2, 0)$. Graphing the two lines, in the xy-plane, determine that there are *no* points that lies on *both* lines. (See Fig. 8.8.) Also, note that the slope of each line is 1, but the y-intercepts are different. Hence, the two lines are parallel. Therefore, there are no solutions for the given system. (**Solving systems of linear equations by graphing**)

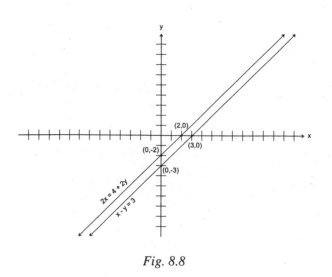

Fig. 8.8

5. $\begin{cases} 2y - 8 = 0 \\ y = 3x - 6 \end{cases}$

The graph of the equation $2y - 8 = 0$ is a line that passes through the points $(0, 4)$ and $(4, 4)$. The graph of the equation $y = 3x - 6$ is a line that passes through the points $(0, -6)$ and $(2, 0)$. Graphing the two lines, in the xy-plane, it appears that the solution is $(3, 4)$. However, this ordered pair does not check in the original equations. The actual solution is $\left(\dfrac{10}{3}, 4 \right)$. (See Fig. 8.9.) **(Solving systems of linear equations by graphing)**

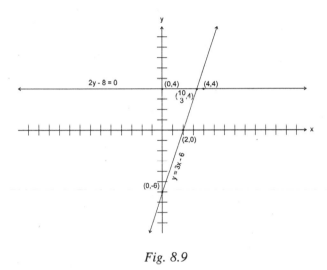

Fig. 8.9

6. $\begin{cases} x + y = 3 \\ 3x - 4y \quad 0 \end{cases}$

Rewriting both equations in slope-intercept form, we have $y = -x + 3$ and $y = \dfrac{3}{4}x$. The slopes of the respective lines are -1 and $\dfrac{3}{4}$. Since the slopes are different, the lines are intersecting. **(Solving systems of linear equations by graphing)**

7. $\begin{cases} 3x - 2y = 1 \\ 4y = 1 + 6x \end{cases}$

Rewriting both equations in slope-intercept form, we have $y = \dfrac{3}{2}x - \dfrac{1}{2}$ and $y = \dfrac{3}{2}x + \dfrac{1}{4}$. The slopes of the respective lines are $\dfrac{3}{2}$ and $\dfrac{3}{2}$. Since the slopes are the same but the y-intercepts are different, the lines are parallel. **(Solving systems of linear equations by graphing)**

8. $\begin{cases} y - 2x = 7 \\ 4x = 2y - 14 \end{cases}$

Rewriting both equations in slope-intercept form, we have $y = 2x + 7$ and $y = 2x + 7$. We can see that the two equations are the same. Their graphs have the same slopes and y-intercepts. Hence, the lines are coinciding lines. **(Solving systems of linear equations by graphing)**

9. $\begin{cases} x - 5y = 4 \\ 2x + 5y = 6 \end{cases}$

Rewriting both equations in slope-intercept form, we have $y = \frac{1}{5}x - \frac{4}{5}$ and $y = \frac{-2}{5}x + \frac{6}{5}$. The slopes of the respective lines are $\frac{1}{5}$ and $\frac{-2}{5}$. Since the slopes are different, the lines are intersecting. (**Solving systems of linear equations by graphing**)

10. $\begin{cases} x - y = 4 \\ 2x + y = 2 \end{cases}$

If we add the two equations, the y variable is eliminated. Hence,

$$x - y = 4$$
$$\text{Add : } 2x + y = 2$$
$$\overline{3x + 0 = 6}$$
$$3x = 6$$
$$x = 2$$

Substituting 2 for x in, say, the first equation, we have

$$x - y = 4$$
$$2 - y = 4$$
$$-y = 2$$
$$y = -2$$

Checking the ordered pair (2, –2) in *both* of the *original* equations, we determine that (2, –2) is the required solution. (**Solving systems of linear equations by elimination**)

11. $\begin{cases} 2x - 4y = 1 \\ 3x + 2y = 2 \end{cases}$

If we add the two equations, no variable is eliminated. Further, if we subtract one equation from the other, no variable is eliminated. However, if we multiply the second equation by 2 and add the resulting equation to the first equation, the y variable will be eliminated. Hence,

$$2x - 4y = 1$$
$$\text{Add: } \quad 6x + 4y = 4$$
$$\overline{8x + 0 = 5}$$
$$8x = 5$$
$$x = \frac{5}{8}$$

Substituting $\frac{5}{8}$ for x in, say, the second equation, we have

$$3x + 2y = 2$$
$$3\left(\frac{5}{8}\right) + 2y = 2$$
$$\frac{15}{8} + 2y = 2$$

$$2y = \frac{1}{8}$$

$$y = \frac{1}{16}$$

Checking the ordered pair $\left(\frac{5}{8}, \frac{1}{16}\right)$ in *both* of the *original* equations, we determine that $\left(\frac{5}{8}, \frac{1}{16}\right)$ is the required solution. (**Solving systems of linear equations by elimination**)

12. $\begin{cases} 5x - y = 10 \\ 2x + 2y = 4 \end{cases}$

If we add the two equations, no variable is eliminated. Further, if we subtract one equation from the other, no variable is eliminated. However, if we divide the second equation by 2 and add the resulting equation to the first equation, the y variable will be eliminated. Hence,

$$5x - y = 10$$
Add: $\quad x + y = 2$
_____

$$6x + 0 = 12$$

$$6x = 12$$

$$x = 2$$

Substituting 2 for x in, say, the first equation, we have

$$5x - y = 10$$

$$5(2) - y = 10$$

$$10 - y = 10$$

$$-y = 0$$

$$y = 0$$

Checking the ordered pair (2, 0) in *both* of the *original* equations, we determine that (2, 0) is the required solution. (**Solving systems of linear equations by elimination**)

13. $\begin{cases} 3x + 4y = 5 \\ 5x - 3y = 2 \end{cases}$

If we add the two equations, no variable is eliminated. Further, if we subtract one equation from the other, no variable is eliminated. However, if we multiply the first equation by 5, multiply the second equation by 3, and subtract the new second equation from the new first equation, the x variable will be eliminated. Hence,

$$15x + 20y = 25$$
Subtract: $\quad 15x - 9y = 6$
_____

$$0 + 29y = 19$$

$$29y = 19$$

$$y = \frac{19}{29}$$

Substituting $\dfrac{19}{29}$ for y in, say, the first equation, we have

$$3x + 4y = 5$$

$$3x + 4\left(\frac{19}{29}\right) = 5$$

$$3x + \frac{76}{29} = 5$$

$$3x = \frac{69}{29}$$

$$x = \frac{23}{29}$$

Checking the ordered pair $\left(\dfrac{23}{29}, \dfrac{19}{29}\right)$ in *both* of the *original* equations, we determine that $\left(\dfrac{23}{29}, \dfrac{19}{29}\right)$ is the required solution. (**Solving systems of linear equations by elimination**)

14. $\begin{cases} y = 3x - 1 \\ x - 2y = 4 \end{cases}$

In the first equation, y is already solved for in terms of x. If we substitute $3x - 1$ for y in the *second* equation, we have

$$x - 2y = 4$$

$$x - 2(3x - 1) = 4$$

$$x - 6x + 2 = 4$$

$$-5x + 2 = 4$$

$$-5x = 2$$

$$x = \frac{-2}{5}$$

Now, substituting $\dfrac{-2}{5}$ for x in the *first* equation, we have

$$y = 3x - 1$$

$$y = 3\left(\frac{-2}{5}\right) - 1$$

$$y = \frac{-6}{5} - 1$$

$$y = \frac{-11}{5}$$

Checking the ordered pair $\left(\dfrac{-2}{5}, \dfrac{-11}{5}\right)$ in *both* of the *original* equations, we determine that the ordered pair $\left(\dfrac{-2}{5}, \dfrac{-11}{5}\right)$ is the required solution. (**Solving systems of linear equations by substitution**)

15. $\begin{cases} 4x + 3y = 5 \\ x = 5y - 2 \end{cases}$

In the second equation, x is already solved for in terms of y. If we substitute $5y - 2$ for x in the *first* equation, we have

$$4x + 3y = 5$$

$$4(5y - 2) + 3y = 5$$

$$20y - 8 + 3y = 5$$

$$23y - 8 = 5$$

$$23y = 13$$

$$y = \frac{13}{23}$$

Now, substituting $\frac{13}{23}$ for y in the *second* equation, we have

$$x = 5y - 2$$

$$x = 5\left(\frac{13}{23}\right) - 2$$

$$x = \frac{65}{23} - 2$$

$$x = \frac{19}{23}$$

Checking the ordered pair $\left(\frac{19}{23}, \frac{13}{23}\right)$ in *both* of the *original* equations, we determine that the ordered pair $\left(\frac{19}{23}, \frac{13}{23}\right)$ is the required solution. (**Solving systems of linear equations by substitution**)

16. $\begin{cases} 2x - y = 6 \\ 3x + 2y = 5 \end{cases}$

In the first equation, solve for y in terms of x. We have

$$2x - y = 6$$

$$-y = 6 - 2x$$

$$y = 2x - 6$$

If we substitute $2x - 6$ for y in the *second* equation, we have

$$3x + 2y = 5$$

$$3x + 2(2x - 6) = 5$$

$$3x + 4x - 12 = 5$$

$$7x - 12 = 5$$

$$7x = 17$$

$$x = \frac{17}{7}$$

Now, substituting $\frac{17}{7}$ for x in the equation $y = 2x - 6$, we have

$$y = 2x - 6$$

$$y = 2\left(\frac{17}{7}\right) - 6$$

$$y = \frac{34}{7} - 6$$

$$y = \frac{-8}{7}$$

Checking the ordered pair $\left(\frac{17}{7}, \frac{-8}{7}\right)$ in *both* of the *original* equations, we determine that the ordered pair $\left(\frac{17}{7}, \frac{-8}{7}\right)$ is the required solution. **(Solving systems of linear equations by substitution)**

17. $\begin{cases} 4x - 5y = 7 \\ 3x + 4y = -2 \end{cases}$

In the first equation, solve for y in terms of x. We have

$$4x - 5y = 7$$

$$-5y = 7 - 4x$$

$$y = \frac{4x - 7}{5}$$

If we substitute $\frac{4x - 7}{5}$ for y in the *second* equation, we have

$$3x + 4y = -2$$

$$3x + 4\left(\frac{4x - 7}{5}\right) = -2$$

$$15x + 4(4x - 7) = -10$$

$$15x + 16x - 28 = -10$$

$$31x - 28 = -10$$

$$31x = 18$$

$$x = \frac{18}{31}$$

Now, substituting $\frac{18}{31}$ for x in the equation $y = \frac{4x - 7}{5}$, we have

$$y = \frac{4x - 7}{5}$$

$$y = \frac{4\left(\frac{18}{31}\right) - 7}{5}$$

$$y = \frac{\frac{72}{31} - 7}{5}$$

$$y = \frac{\frac{-145}{31}}{5}$$

$$y = \frac{-145}{155}$$

$$y = \frac{-29}{31}$$

Checking the ordered pair $\left(\frac{18}{31}, \frac{-29}{31}\right)$ in *both* of the *original* equations, we determine that the ordered pair $\left(\frac{18}{31}, \frac{-29}{31}\right)$ is the required solution. (**Solving systems of linear equations by substitution**)

18. $\begin{cases} y > 3x \\ x - y < 3 \end{cases}$

a. Graph y > 3x. Consider the equation y = 3x, which is a straight line passing through the points (0, 0) and (1, 3). This line is the boundary of two half-planes, and is graphed as a *dashed* line since it is not part of the solution. Using the test point, (2, 2), determine that the solution for this inequality is the half-plane that does *not* contain the point (2, 2). (See Fig. 8.10.)

b. Graph x − y < 3. Consider the equation x − y = 3, which is a straight line passing through the points (0, −3) and (3, 0). This line is the boundary of two half-planes, and is graphed as a *dashed* line since it is not part of the solution. Using the test point (0, 0), determine that the solution for this inequality is the half-plane that *does* contain the point (0, 0). (See Fig. 8.11.)

c. Determine the part of the xy-plane that is common to both of the above solutions in Figs. 8.10 and 8.11. This is the solution for the given system of inequalities. (See Fig. 8.12.) (**Solving systems of linear inequalities**)

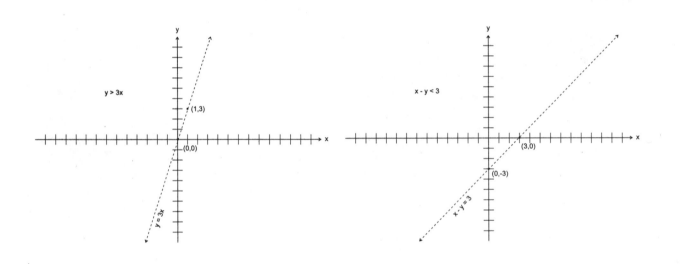

Fig. 8.10   Fig. 8.11

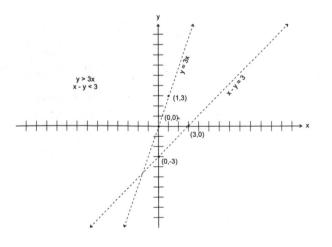

Fig. 8.12

19. $\begin{cases} 2x - y < 4 \\ x - 3y < 6 \end{cases}$

a. Graph $2x - y < 4$. Consider the equation $2x - y = 4$, which is a straight line passing through the points $(0, -4)$ and $(2, 0)$. This line is the boundary of two half-planes, and is graphed as a *dashed* line since it is not part of the solution. Using the test point, $(0, 0)$, determine that the solution for this inequality is the half-plane that *does* contain the point $(0, 0)$. (See Fig. 8.13.)

b. Graph $x - 3y < 6$. Consider the equation $x - 3y = 6$, which is a straight line passing through the points $(0, -2)$ and $(6, 0)$. This line is the boundary of two half-planes, and is graphed as a *dashed* line since it is not part of the solution. Using the test point $(0, 0)$, determine that the solution for this inequality is the half-plane that *does* contain the point $(0, 0)$. (See Fig. 8.14.)

c. Determine the part of the xy-plane that is common to both of the above solutions in Figs. 8.13 and 8.14. This is the solution for the given system of inequalities. (See Fig. 8.15.) (**Solving systems of linear inequalities**)

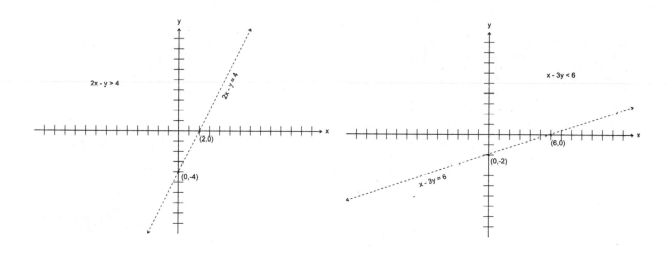

Fig. 8.13

Fig. 8.14

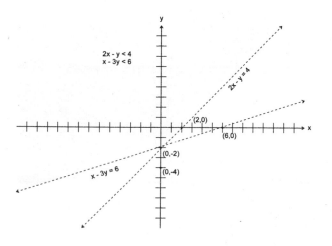

Fig. 8.15

20. $\begin{cases} 3x - 2y \leq 6 \\ x + y > 5 \end{cases}$

a. Graph $3x - 2y \leq 6$. Consider the equation $3x - 2y = 6$, which is a straight line passing through the points $(0, -3)$ and $(2, 0)$. This line is the boundary of two half-planes, and is graphed as a *solid* line since it is part of the solution. Using the test point, $(0, 0)$, determine that the solution for this inequality is the half-plane that *does* contain the point $(0, 0)$. (See Fig. 8.16.)

b. Graph $x + y > 5$. Consider the equation $x + y = 5$, which is a straight line passing through the points $(0, 5)$ and $(5, 0)$. This line is the boundary of two half-planes, and is graphed as a *dashed* line since it is not part of the solution. Using the test point $(0, 0)$, determine that the solution for this inequality is the half-plane that does *not* contain the point $(0, 0)$. (See Fig. 8.17.)

c. Determine the part of the xy-plane that is common to both of the above solutions in Figs. 8.16 and 8.17. This is the solution for the given system of inequalities. (See Fig. 8.18.) **(Solving systems of linear inequalities)**

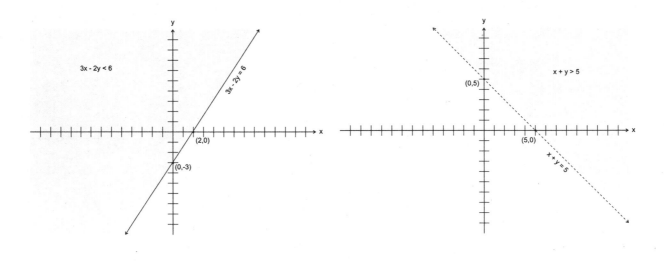

Fig. 8.16   Fig. 8.17

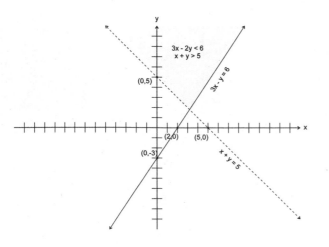

Fig. 8.18

21. $\begin{cases} 2x < y - 4 \\ x - 3y \geq 9 \end{cases}$

a. Graph 2x < y − 4. Consider the equation 2x = y − 4, which is a straight line passing through the points (0, 4) and (−2, 0). This line is the boundary of two half-planes, and is graphed as a *dashed* line since it is not part of the solution. Using the test point, (0, 0), determine that the solution for this inequality is the half-plane that does *not* contain the point (0, 0). (See Fig. 8.19.)

b. Graph x − 3y ≥ 9. Consider the equation x − 3y = 9, which is a straight line passing through the points (0, −3) and (9, 0). This line is the boundary of two half-planes, and is graphed as a *solid* line since it is part of the solution. Using the test point (0, 0), determine that the solution for this inequality is the half-plane that does *not* contain the point (0, 0). (See Fig. 8.20.)

c. Determine the part of the xy-plane that is common to both of the above solutions in Figs. 8.19 and 8.20. This is the solution for the given system of inequalities. (See Fig. 8.21.) **(Solving systems of linear inequalities)**

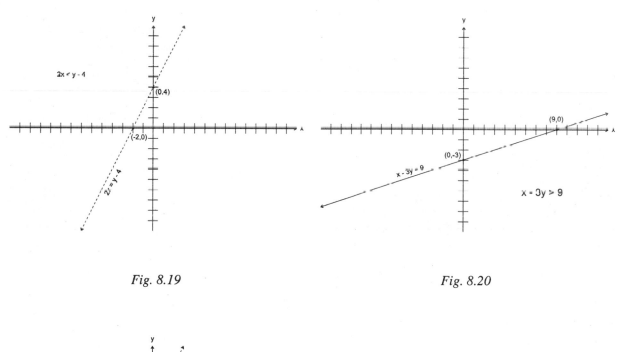

<table>
<tr><td>Fig. 8.19</td><td>Fig. 8.20</td></tr>
</table>

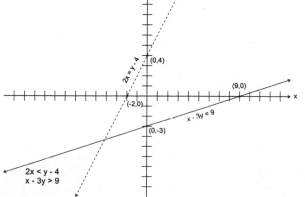

Fig. 8.21

Grade Yourself

Circle the numbers of the questions you missed, then fill in the total incorrect for each topic. If you answered more than three questions incorrectly, you need to focus on that topic. (If a topic has less than three questions and you had at least one wrong, we suggest you study that topic also. Read your textbook, a review book, or ask your teacher for help.)

Subject: Systems of Linear Equations and Inequalities

Topic	Question Numbers	Number Incorrect
Solving systems of linear equations by graphing	1, 2, 3, 4, 5, 6, 7, 8, 9	
Solving systems of linear equations by elimination	10, 11, 12, 13	
Solving systems of linear equations by substitution	14, 15, 16, 17	
Solving systems of linear inequalities	18, 19, 20, 21	

Square Roots and Radicals

9

 Test Yourself

9.1 Square Roots

To "square a number" means to multiply the number by itself. For instance, the square of 3, written as 3^2, is $(3)(3)$, or 9. The square of -5, written as $(-5)^2$, is $(-5)(-5)$, or 25.

In this section, we consider "taking the square root" of a number. We use the symbol $\sqrt{\ }$, called a **radical sign**, to represent the square root of a number. The expression under the radical sign is called the **radicand**. Only *nonnegative* real numbers have square roots that are real numbers.

Definition: If $a \geq 0$, then the **square root** of a, denoted by $\sqrt{a}$, is one of two *equal* factors of a.

The square root of 25, denoted by $\sqrt{25}$, is 5 since $5^2 = 25$. [Also, note that $(-5)^2 = 25$.]

The square root of 121, denoted by $\sqrt{121}$, is 11 since $11^2 = 121$. [Also, note that $(-11)^2 = 121$.]

From the above definition, observe that every *positive* real number has two square roots—one positive and one negative.

Definition: If $a > 0$, then the **principal square root** of a is the positive square root of a.

The principal square root of 36 is 6.

The principal square root of b^2 is b, if $b \geq 0$.

If $y < 0$, then the principal square root of y^2 is $-y$ (since $-y > 0$). For instance, $(\sqrt{(-3)^2} = 3)$

$\sqrt{-49}$ is *not* a real number since -49 is negative.

For the remainder of this text, the square root of a nonnegative number will be the principal square root, unless otherwise indicated.

In Exercises 1-8, determine the value of each of the following expressions, if it exists. If the value of the expression is not a real number, so indicate that. All variables represent positive numbers.

1. $\sqrt{81}$

2. $\sqrt{625}$

3. $\sqrt{1024}$

4. $\sqrt{4x^2}$

5. $-\sqrt{-(2-11)}$

6. $-\sqrt{3-7}$

7. $\sqrt{144x^4y^2}$

8. $-\sqrt{x^2} - \sqrt{y^6}$

9.2 Simplifying Square Root Expressions

Rule for Finding the Square Root of a Product
  If $x \geq 0$ and $y \geq 0$, then $\sqrt{xy} = \sqrt{x}\,\sqrt{y}$.

When using this rule, factor the radicand, if possible, so that one factor is the square of another expression. For instance:

$\sqrt{72} = \sqrt{(36)(2)} = \sqrt{36}\,\sqrt{2} = 6\sqrt{2}$

$$\sqrt{75} = \sqrt{(25)(3)} = \sqrt{25}\,\sqrt{3} = 5\sqrt{3}$$

$$\sqrt{a^3b^4} = \sqrt{(a)^2a(b^2)^2} = \sqrt{(a)^2}\,\sqrt{a}\,\sqrt{(b^2)^2} = ab^2\sqrt{a}$$

$$\sqrt{x^{13}y^5} = \sqrt{(x^{12})(x)(y^4)(y)} = \sqrt{(x^6)^2(x)(y^2)^2(y)}$$

$$= x^6y^2\sqrt{xy}$$

In Exercises 9-16, simplify each of the given expressions. All variables represent nonnegative numbers.

9. $\sqrt{44}$

10. $\sqrt{90}$

11. $\sqrt{108}$

12. $\sqrt{1100}$

13. $\sqrt{9a^3b^4}$

14. $\sqrt{8x^7y^9}$

15. $\sqrt{50r^2s^5t^8}$

16. $\sqrt{32x^7y^9z^{11}}$

Rule for Finding the Square Root of a Quotient

If $x \geq 0$ and $y > 0$, then $\sqrt{\dfrac{x}{y}} = \dfrac{\sqrt{x}}{\sqrt{y}}$.

$$\sqrt{\frac{16}{49}} = \frac{\sqrt{16}}{\sqrt{49}} = \frac{4}{7}$$

$$\sqrt{\frac{32}{81}} = \frac{4\sqrt{2}}{\sqrt{81}} = \frac{4\sqrt{2}}{9}$$

In Exercises 17-24, simplify each of the given expressions. All variables represent positive numbers.

17. $\sqrt{\dfrac{1}{16}}$

18. $\sqrt{\dfrac{25}{81}}$

19. $\sqrt{\dfrac{121}{64}}$

20. $\sqrt{\dfrac{50}{49}}$

21. $\sqrt{\dfrac{9x^4}{4y^2}}$

22. $\sqrt{\dfrac{8x^3y^6}{25z^6}}$

23. $\sqrt{\dfrac{162a^7b}{a^4}}$

24. $\sqrt{\dfrac{98p^5q^9r^{13}}{p^2q^4r^6}}$

Now, consider the following:

$$\frac{1}{\sqrt{2}} = \frac{1}{\sqrt{2}} \times 1$$

$$= \frac{1}{\sqrt{2}} \times \frac{\sqrt{2}}{\sqrt{2}} \qquad \text{(Writing } 1 = \frac{\sqrt{2}}{\sqrt{2}}.)$$

$$= \frac{\sqrt{2}}{\sqrt{2}\,\sqrt{2}}$$

$$= \frac{\sqrt{2}}{2}$$

The procedure illustrated above is known as **rationalizing the denominator** of a fraction. To rationalize the denominator of a fraction, multiply the given fraction by another fraction, with the same numerator and denominator, so that the denominator of the product of the two fractions will be a perfect square.

To rationalize the denominator of the fraction $\dfrac{4}{\sqrt{7}}$, proceed as follows:

$$\frac{4}{\sqrt{7}} = \frac{4}{\sqrt{7}} \times \frac{\sqrt{7}}{\sqrt{7}} = \frac{4\sqrt{7}}{\sqrt{7}\,\sqrt{7}} = \frac{4\sqrt{7}}{7}$$

In Exercises 25-30, rationalize the denominator in each of the given expressions and simplify the results. All variables represent positive numbers.

25. $\dfrac{9}{\sqrt{5}}$

26. $\dfrac{16}{\sqrt{2}}$

27. $\dfrac{2x}{\sqrt{2x}}$

28. $\dfrac{4x}{\sqrt{x^3}}$

29. $\dfrac{\sqrt{7u^3v^5}}{3\sqrt{uv^2}}$

30. $\dfrac{3\sqrt{s^4t^7}}{\sqrt{8s^3t}}$

9.3 Addition and Subtraction of Square Roots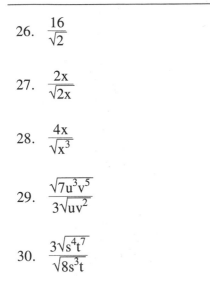

Definition: **Like square roots** are square roots that have the same radicands, after the square roots have been simplified.

Rule for Adding or Subtracting Like Square Roots

To add (or subtract) like square roots:

1. Add (or subtract) their coefficients, and

2. Multiply the sum (or difference) by the common square root.

Note: Only *like* radicals can be added or subtracted.

$3\sqrt{7} + 8\sqrt{7} = (3+8)\sqrt{7} = 11\sqrt{7}$

$x\sqrt{13} + y\sqrt{13} - z\sqrt{13} = (x + y - z)\sqrt{13}$

$\sqrt{2} - \sqrt{18} + \sqrt{32} = \sqrt{2} - \sqrt{(9)(2)} + \sqrt{(16)(2)}$

$$= \sqrt{2} - 3\sqrt{2} + 4\sqrt{2}$$

$$= (1 - 3 + 4)\sqrt{2}$$

$$= 2\sqrt{2}$$

$2\sqrt{6} - \dfrac{3\sqrt{3}}{\sqrt{2}} - \dfrac{4\sqrt{2}}{\sqrt{3}} = 2\sqrt{6} - \dfrac{3\sqrt{3}\sqrt{2}}{\sqrt{2}\sqrt{2}} - \dfrac{4\sqrt{2}\sqrt{3}}{\sqrt{3}\sqrt{3}}$

$$= 2\sqrt{6} - \dfrac{3\sqrt{6}}{2} - \dfrac{4\sqrt{6}}{3}$$

$$= \left(2 - \dfrac{3}{2} - \dfrac{4}{3}\right)\sqrt{6}$$

$$= \dfrac{-5}{6}\sqrt{6}$$

In Exercises 31-36, simplify each of the given expressions by combining like terms. All variables represent positive numbers.

31. $8\sqrt{5} - 2\sqrt{5} - 11\sqrt{5}$

32. $3\sqrt{7} - a\sqrt{7} - b\sqrt{7}$

33. $4\sqrt{12} + 5\sqrt{27}$

34. $11\sqrt{5} - 2\sqrt{20} + 4\sqrt{45}$

35. $-2\sqrt{p^3qr} + 3\sqrt{pq^5r} - 8\sqrt{p^5q^3r^7}$

36. $\dfrac{\sqrt{x}}{\sqrt{y}} + \dfrac{\sqrt{y}}{\sqrt{x}} - 3\sqrt{xy}$

9.4 Multiplication and Division of Square Roots

To multiply square roots, we use the product rule for square roots and simplify the result.

$\sqrt{3}\,\sqrt{5} = \sqrt{(3)(5)} = \sqrt{15}$

$\sqrt{8}\,\sqrt{14} = \sqrt{(8)(14)} = \sqrt{112} = \sqrt{(16)(7)} = 4\sqrt{7}$

$\sqrt{mn^2p^3}\,\sqrt{m^4np}\,\sqrt{m^3n^4p^5} = \sqrt{(mn^2p^3)(m^4np)(m^3n^4p^5)}$

$$= \sqrt{m^8n^7p^9}$$

$$= \sqrt{(m^4)^2(n^3)^2n(p^4)^2(p)}$$

$$= m^4n^3p^4\sqrt{np},$$

if $m \geq 0$, $n \geq 0$, and $p \geq 0$.

In Exercises 37-42, multiply and simplify the results. All variables represent positive numbers.

37. $\sqrt{5}\,\sqrt{10}$

38. $(2\sqrt{3})(-3\sqrt{2})$

39. $(\sqrt{3} - \sqrt{5})(\sqrt{3} + \sqrt{5})$

40. $(3\sqrt{8})(-2\sqrt{18})(-\sqrt{2})$

41. $\sqrt{a^3b}\ \sqrt{ab^5}\ \sqrt{a^3b^3}$

42. $(2a\sqrt{12})(-3\sqrt{27})(-\sqrt{45})$

To divide square roots, we use the quotient rule for square roots and the procedure for rationalizing denominators. Then, we simplify the results.

$$\frac{\sqrt{12}}{\sqrt{3}} = \sqrt{\frac{12}{3}} = \sqrt{4} = 2$$

$$\frac{p\sqrt{pq}}{q\sqrt{pq^3}} = \frac{p}{q}\sqrt{\frac{pq}{pq^3}} = \frac{p}{q}\sqrt{\frac{1}{q^2}} = \frac{p}{q} \cdot \frac{1}{q} = \frac{p}{q^2},$$
if $p > 0$ and $q > 0$.

In Exercises 43-48, divide and simplify your results. Rationalize all denominators. All variables represent positive numbers.

43. $\dfrac{4\sqrt{45}}{6\sqrt{5}}$

44. $\dfrac{3\sqrt{15}}{4\sqrt{30}}$

45. $\dfrac{5\sqrt{36} - 4\sqrt{32}}{\sqrt{2}}$

46. $\dfrac{x\sqrt{2} - y\sqrt{3}}{\sqrt{5}}$

47. $(-7\sqrt{a^3b^2c}) \div (14\sqrt{a^5bc^4})$

48. $(2\sqrt{xy^3z^2} - 4\sqrt{x^2y^5z}) \div (3\sqrt{x^2y^4z})$

9.5 Equations Involving Square Roots

If two real numbers are equal, then their squares are also equal. That is, if $a = b$, then $a^2 = b^2$. (A)

However, if the squares of two real numbers are equal, then the numbers themselves are not necessarily equal. We have: if $a^2 = b^2$, then $a = b$ or $a = -b$. (B)

For instance, $(-4)^2 = (4)^2$, but $-4 \neq 4$.

The procedure for solving equations involving square roots depends upon both (A) and (B) above.

The procedure is illustrated in the following example:

Solve the equation $8 - \sqrt{2x - 3} = 1$ for x.

First, isolate the square root term. That is, we get it all by itself on one side of the equation:

$$8 - \sqrt{2x - 3} = 1$$
$$-\sqrt{2x - 3} = -7$$
$$\sqrt{2x - 3} = 7$$

Next, square *both* sides of the equation:

$$(\sqrt{2x - 3})^2 = (7)^2$$
$$2x - 3 = 49$$

Now, solve for x:

$$2x - 3 = 49$$
$$2x = 52$$
$$x = 26$$

To determine if 26 is the correct solution, we **must** check in the *original* equation:

$$8 - \sqrt{2x - 3} = 1$$
$$8 - \sqrt{2(26) - 3} \ ? \ 1$$
$$8 - \sqrt{52 - 3} \ ? \ 1$$
$$8 - \sqrt{49} \ ? \ 1$$
$$8 - 7 \ ? \ 1$$
$$1 = 1 \ \checkmark$$

Therefore, 26 is the required solution.

Sometimes, two or more square roots are involved in an equation. Consider the following example:

Solve the equation $\sqrt{x + 1} - \sqrt{x - 2} = 4$ for x.

First, observe that there are two square roots involved. Separate them so that one is on one side of the equation and one is on the other side of the equation:

$$\sqrt{x+1} = 4 + \sqrt{x-2}$$

Next, square *both* sides of the equation.

$$(\sqrt{x+1})^2 = (4 + \sqrt{x-2})^2$$

$$x + 1 = 16 + 8\sqrt{x-2} + x - 2$$

$$-13 = 8\sqrt{x-2}$$

Square *both* sides of the resulting equation and solve for x.

$$(-13)^2 = (8\sqrt{x-2})^2$$

$$169 = 64(x-2)$$

$$169 = 64x - 128$$

$$297 = 64x$$

$$\frac{297}{64} = x$$

Is $\frac{297}{64}$ the correct solution? Check in the *original* equation.

$$\sqrt{x+1} - \sqrt{x-2} = 4$$

$$\sqrt{\frac{297}{64} + 1} - \sqrt{\frac{297}{64} - 2} \ ? \ 4$$

$$\sqrt{\frac{361}{64}} - \sqrt{\frac{169}{64}} \ ? \ 4$$

$$\frac{19}{8} - \frac{13}{8} \ ? \ 4$$

$$\frac{6}{8} \neq 4$$

Hence, $\frac{297}{64}$ is *not* the required solution. There is no solution for the original equation. Did you notice that, after squaring both sides of the original equation, we obtained the equation $-13 = 8\sqrt{x-2}$, or $\sqrt{x-2} = \frac{-13}{8}$, which states that $\sqrt{x-2}$ is equal to a negative number? The square root of a real number is never negative. Hence, we could have stopped at that point in the process.

Reminder: Always check your results in the original equation.

In Exercises 49-54, solve each of the given equations for the indicated variable. Check your results in the original equation.

49. $\sqrt{y+4} = 3$

50. $\sqrt{3u-1} - 5 = 0$

51 $9 - 2\sqrt{t+5} = 3$

52. $\sqrt{p-3} = \sqrt{2p-1}$

53. $\sqrt{x+6} - \sqrt{x-2} = 1$

54. $\sqrt{2s-3} - \sqrt{2s+1} = 2$

✓ Check Yourself

1. $\sqrt{81} = \sqrt{(9)^2} = 9$ (**Square roots**)

2. $\sqrt{625} = \sqrt{(25)^2} = 25$ (**Square roots**)

3. $\sqrt{1024} = \sqrt{(32)^2} = 32$ (**Square roots**)

4. $\sqrt{4x^2} = \sqrt{(2x)^2} = 2\,|\,x\,|$ (**Square roots**)

5. $-\sqrt{-(2-11)} = -\sqrt{-(-9)} = -\sqrt{9} = -\sqrt{(3)^2} = -3$ (**Square roots**)

6. $-\sqrt{3-7} = -\sqrt{-4}$, which is *not* a real number (since -4 is negative). (**Square roots**)

7. $\sqrt{144x^4y^2} = \sqrt{(12x^2y)^2} = 12x^2\,|\,y\,|$ (**Square roots**)

8. $-\sqrt{x^2} - \sqrt{y^6} = -\sqrt{(x)^2} - \sqrt{(y^3)^2} = -\,|\,x\,| - |\,y^3\,|$ (**Square roots**)

9. $\sqrt{44} = \sqrt{(4)(11)} = \sqrt{4}\sqrt{11} = 2\sqrt{11}$ (**Simplifying square root expressions**)

10. $\sqrt{90} = \sqrt{(9)(10)} = \sqrt{9}\sqrt{10} = 3\sqrt{10}$ (**Simplifying square root expressions**)

11. $\sqrt{108} = \sqrt{(36)(3)} = \sqrt{36}\sqrt{3} = 6\sqrt{3}$ (**Simplifying square root expressions**)

12. $\sqrt{1100} = \sqrt{(100)(11)} = \sqrt{100}\sqrt{11} = 10\sqrt{11}$ (**Simplifying square root expressions**)

13. $\sqrt{9a^3b^4} = \sqrt{(9)(a^2)a(b^2)^2} = \sqrt{9}\sqrt{a^2}\sqrt{a}\sqrt{(b^2)^2} = 3ab^2\sqrt{a}$ (**Simplifying square root expressions**)

14. $\sqrt{8x^7y^9} = \sqrt{(4)(2)(x^3)^2x(y^4)^2y} = \sqrt{4}\sqrt{2}\sqrt{(x^3)^2}\sqrt{x}\sqrt{(y^4)^2}\sqrt{y}$

    $= 2x^3y^4\sqrt{2}\sqrt{x}\sqrt{y} = 2x^3y^4\sqrt{2xy}$ (**Simplifying square root expressions**)

15. $\sqrt{50r^2s^5t^8} = \sqrt{(25)(2)(r^2)(s^2)^2s(t^4)^2}$

    $= \sqrt{25}\sqrt{2}\sqrt{r^2}\sqrt{(s^2)^2}\sqrt{s}\sqrt{(t^4)^2}$

    $= 5rs^2t^4\sqrt{2}\sqrt{s} = 5rs^2t^4\sqrt{2s}$ (**Simplifying square root expressions**)

16. $\sqrt{32x^7y^9z^{11}} = \sqrt{(16)(2)(x^3)^2x(y^4)^2y(z^5)^2z}$

    $= \sqrt{16}\sqrt{2}\sqrt{(x^3)^2}\sqrt{x}\sqrt{(y^4)^2}\sqrt{y}\sqrt{(z^5)^2}\sqrt{z}$

    $= 4x^3y^4z^5\sqrt{2}\sqrt{x}\sqrt{y}\sqrt{z} = 4x^3y^4z^5\sqrt{2xyz}$ (**Simplifying square root expressions**)

17. $\sqrt{\dfrac{1}{16}} = \dfrac{\sqrt{1}}{\sqrt{16}} = \dfrac{1}{4}$ (**Simplifying square root expressions**)

18. $\sqrt{\dfrac{25}{81}} = \dfrac{\sqrt{25}}{\sqrt{81}} = \dfrac{5}{9}$ (**Simplifying square root expressions**)

19. $\sqrt{\dfrac{121}{64}} = \dfrac{\sqrt{121}}{\sqrt{64}} = \dfrac{11}{8}$ (**Simplifying square root expressions**)

20. $\sqrt{\dfrac{50}{49}} = \dfrac{\sqrt{50}}{\sqrt{49}} = \dfrac{\sqrt{(25)(2)}}{7} = \dfrac{\sqrt{25}\sqrt{2}}{7} = \dfrac{5\sqrt{2}}{7}$ (**Simplifying square root expressions**)

21. $\sqrt{\dfrac{9x^4}{4y^2}} = \dfrac{\sqrt{9x^4}}{\sqrt{4y^2}} = \dfrac{\sqrt{(3x^2)^2}}{\sqrt{(2y)^2}} = \dfrac{3x^2}{2y}$ (**Simplifying square root expressions**)

22. $\sqrt{\dfrac{8x^3y^6}{25z^6}} = \dfrac{\sqrt{8x^3y^6}}{\sqrt{25z^6}} = \dfrac{\sqrt{(4)(2)(x^2)x(y^3)^2}}{\sqrt{(5z^3)^2}} = \dfrac{2xy^3\sqrt{2}\sqrt{x}}{5z^3}$

$= \dfrac{2xy^3\sqrt{2x}}{5z^3}$ (**Simplifying square root expressions**)

23. $\sqrt{\dfrac{162a^7b}{a^4}} = \dfrac{\sqrt{162(a^3)^2ab}}{\sqrt{a^4}} = \dfrac{\sqrt{(81)(2)(a^3)^2ab}}{\sqrt{(a^2)^2}} = \dfrac{9a^3\sqrt{2}\sqrt{a}\sqrt{b}}{a^2}$

$= 9a\sqrt{2ab}$ (**Simplifying square root expressions**)

24. $\sqrt{\dfrac{98p^5q^9r^{13}}{p^2q^4r^6}} = \dfrac{\sqrt{98p^5q^9r^{13}}}{\sqrt{p^2q^4r^6}} = \dfrac{\sqrt{(49)(2)(p^2)^2p(q^4)^2q(r^6)^2r}}{\sqrt{(pq^2r^3)^2}}$

$= \dfrac{7p^2q^4r^6\sqrt{2pqr}}{pq^2r^3} = 7pq^2r^3\sqrt{2pqr}$ (**Simplifying square root expressions**)

25. $\dfrac{9}{\sqrt{5}} = \dfrac{9}{\sqrt{5}} \times \dfrac{\sqrt{5}}{\sqrt{5}} = \dfrac{9\sqrt{5}}{\sqrt{5}\sqrt{5}} = \dfrac{9\sqrt{5}}{5}$ (**Simplifying square root expressions**)

26. $\dfrac{16}{\sqrt{2}} = \dfrac{16}{\sqrt{2}} \times \dfrac{\sqrt{2}}{\sqrt{2}} = \dfrac{16\sqrt{2}}{\sqrt{2}\sqrt{2}} = \dfrac{16\sqrt{2}}{2} = 8\sqrt{2}$ (**Simplifying square root expressions**)

27. $\dfrac{2x}{\sqrt{2x}} = \dfrac{2x}{\sqrt{2x}} \times \dfrac{\sqrt{2x}}{\sqrt{2x}} = \dfrac{2x\sqrt{2x}}{\sqrt{2x}\sqrt{2x}} = \dfrac{2x\sqrt{2x}}{2x} = \sqrt{2x}$ (**Simplifying square root expressions**)

28. $\dfrac{4x}{\sqrt{x^3}} = \dfrac{4x}{\sqrt{x^3}} \times \dfrac{\sqrt{x}}{\sqrt{x}} = \dfrac{4x\sqrt{x}}{\sqrt{x^3}\sqrt{x}} = \dfrac{4x\sqrt{x}}{\sqrt{x^4}} = \dfrac{4x\sqrt{x}}{x^2} = \dfrac{4\sqrt{x}}{x}$ (**Simplifying square root expressions**)

29. $\dfrac{\sqrt{7u^3v^5}}{3\sqrt{uv^2}} = \dfrac{\sqrt{7u^3v^5}}{3\sqrt{uv^2}} \times \dfrac{\sqrt{u}}{\sqrt{u}} = \dfrac{\sqrt{7u^3v^5}\sqrt{u}}{3\sqrt{uv^2}\sqrt{u}} = \dfrac{\sqrt{7u^4v^5}}{3\sqrt{u^2v^2}} = \dfrac{u^2v^2\sqrt{7v}}{3uv}$

$= \dfrac{1}{3}uv\sqrt{7v}$ (**Simplifying square root expressions**)

30. $\dfrac{3\sqrt{s^4t^7}}{\sqrt{8s^3t}} = \dfrac{3\sqrt{s^4t^7}}{\sqrt{8s^3t}} \times \dfrac{\sqrt{2st}}{\sqrt{2st}} = \dfrac{3\sqrt{s^4t^7}\sqrt{2st}}{\sqrt{8s^3t}\sqrt{2st}} = \dfrac{3\sqrt{2s^5t^8}}{\sqrt{16s^4t^2}}$

$= \dfrac{3s^2t^4\sqrt{2s}}{4s^2t} = \dfrac{3}{4}t^3\sqrt{2s}$ (**Simplifying square root expressions**)

31. $8\sqrt{5} - 2\sqrt{5} - 11\sqrt{5} = (8 - 2 - 11)\sqrt{5} = -5\sqrt{5}$ (**Addition and subtraction of square roots**)

32. $3\sqrt{7} - a\sqrt{7} - b\sqrt{7} = (3 - a - b)\sqrt{7}$ (**Addition and subtraction of square roots**)

33. $4\sqrt{12} + 5\sqrt{27} = 4\sqrt{(4)(3)} + 5\sqrt{(9)(3)}$

$$= (4)(2)\sqrt{3} + (5)(3)\sqrt{3}$$

$$= 8\sqrt{3} + 15\sqrt{3}$$

$$= (8 + 15)\sqrt{3}$$

$$= 23\sqrt{3} \quad \textbf{(Addition and subtraction of square roots)}$$

34. $11\sqrt{5} - 2\sqrt{20} + 4\sqrt{45} = 11\sqrt{5} - 2\sqrt{(4)(5)} + 4\sqrt{(9)(5)}$

$$= 11\sqrt{5} - (2)(2)\sqrt{5} + (4)(3)\sqrt{5}$$

$$= 11\sqrt{5} - 4\sqrt{5} + 12\sqrt{5}$$

$$= (11 - 4 + 12)\sqrt{5}$$

$$= 19\sqrt{5} \quad \textbf{(Addition and subtraction of square roots)}$$

35. $-2\sqrt{p^3qr} + 3\sqrt{pq^5r} - 8\sqrt{p^5q^3r^7}$

$$= -2\sqrt{(p^2)pqr} + 3\sqrt{p(q^4)qr} - 8\sqrt{(p^4)p(q^2)q(r^6)r}$$

$$= -2p\sqrt{pqr} + 3q^2\sqrt{pqr} - 8p^2qr^3\sqrt{pqr}$$

$$= (-2p + 3q^2 - 8p^2qr^3)\sqrt{pqr} \quad \textbf{(Addition and subtraction of square roots)}$$

36. $\dfrac{\sqrt{x}}{\sqrt{y}} + \dfrac{\sqrt{y}}{\sqrt{x}} - 3\sqrt{xy} = \dfrac{\sqrt{x}}{\sqrt{y}} \cdot \dfrac{\sqrt{y}}{\sqrt{y}} + \dfrac{\sqrt{y}}{\sqrt{x}} \cdot \dfrac{\sqrt{x}}{\sqrt{x}} - 3\sqrt{xy}$

$$= \dfrac{\sqrt{x}\sqrt{y}}{\sqrt{y}\sqrt{y}} + \dfrac{\sqrt{y}\sqrt{x}}{\sqrt{x}\sqrt{x}} - 3\sqrt{xy}$$

$$= \dfrac{\sqrt{xy}}{y} + \dfrac{\sqrt{xy}}{x} - 3\sqrt{xy}$$

$$= \left(\dfrac{1}{y} + \dfrac{1}{x} - 3\right)\sqrt{xy}$$

$$= \dfrac{x + y - 3xy}{xy}\sqrt{xy} \quad \textbf{(Addition and subtraction of square roots)}$$

37. $\sqrt{5}\sqrt{10} = \sqrt{(5)(10)} = \sqrt{50} = \sqrt{(25)(2)} = 5\sqrt{2} \quad \textbf{(Multiplication of square roots)}$

38. $(2\sqrt{3})(-3\sqrt{2}) = (2)(-3)\sqrt{(3)(2)} = -6\sqrt{6} \quad \textbf{(Multiplication of square roots)}$

39. $(\sqrt{3} - \sqrt{5})(\sqrt{3} + \sqrt{5}) = \sqrt{3}(\sqrt{3} + \sqrt{5}) - \sqrt{5}(\sqrt{3} + \sqrt{5})$

$$= \sqrt{3}\sqrt{3} + \sqrt{3}\sqrt{5} - \sqrt{5}\sqrt{3} - \sqrt{5}\sqrt{5}$$

$$= 3 + \sqrt{15} - \sqrt{15} - 5$$

$$= -2 \quad \textbf{(Multiplication of square roots)}$$

40. $(3\sqrt{8})(-2\sqrt{18})(-\sqrt{2}) = (3)(-2)(-1)\sqrt{(8)(18)(2)}$

$$= 6\sqrt{(4)(2)(9)(2)(2)}$$

$$= (6)(2)(3)(2)\sqrt{2}$$

$$= 72\sqrt{2} \quad \textbf{(Multiplication of square roots)}$$

41. $\sqrt{a^3b}\,\sqrt{ab^5}\,\sqrt{a^3b^3} = \sqrt{(a^3b)(ab^5)(a^3b^3)} = \sqrt{a^7b^9}$

$$= \sqrt{a^6ab^8b} = \sqrt{(a^3)^2a(b^4)^2b} = a^3b^4\sqrt{ab} \quad \textbf{(Multiplication of square roots)}$$

42. $(2a\sqrt{12})(-3\sqrt{27})(-\sqrt{45}) = (2a)(-3)(-1)\sqrt{(12)(27)(45)}$

$$= 6a\sqrt{(4)(3)(9)(3)(9)(5)}$$

$$= (6a)(2)(3)(3)(3)\sqrt{5}$$

$$= 324a\sqrt{5} \quad \textbf{(Multiplication of square roots)}$$

43. $\dfrac{4\sqrt{45}}{6\sqrt{5}} = \left(\dfrac{4}{6}\right)\sqrt{\dfrac{45}{5}} = \dfrac{2}{3}\sqrt{9} = \left(\dfrac{2}{3}\right)(3) = 2 \quad \textbf{(Division of square roots)}$

44. $\dfrac{3\sqrt{15}}{4\sqrt{30}} = \left(\dfrac{3}{4}\right)\sqrt{\dfrac{15}{30}} = \left(\dfrac{3}{4}\right)\left(\sqrt{\dfrac{1}{2}}\right) = \left(\dfrac{3}{4}\right)\left(\dfrac{1}{\sqrt{2}}\right) = \dfrac{3}{4\sqrt{2}}$

$$= \dfrac{3}{4\sqrt{2}} \times \dfrac{\sqrt{2}}{\sqrt{2}} = \dfrac{3\sqrt{2}}{4\sqrt{2}\sqrt{2}} = \dfrac{3\sqrt{2}}{(4)(2)} = \dfrac{3\sqrt{2}}{8} \quad \textbf{(Division of square roots)}$$

45. $\dfrac{5\sqrt{36}-4\sqrt{32}}{\sqrt{2}} = \dfrac{5\sqrt{36}}{\sqrt{2}} - \dfrac{4\sqrt{32}}{\sqrt{2}} = 5\sqrt{\dfrac{36}{2}} - 4\sqrt{\dfrac{32}{2}}$

$$= 5\sqrt{18} - 4\sqrt{16} = 5\sqrt{(9)(2)} - 4(4) = (5)(3)\sqrt{2} - 16$$

$$= 15\sqrt{2} - 16 \quad \textbf{(Division of square roots)}$$

46. $\dfrac{x\sqrt{2}-y\sqrt{3}}{\sqrt{5}} = \dfrac{x\sqrt{2}}{\sqrt{5}} - \dfrac{y\sqrt{3}}{\sqrt{5}} = \dfrac{x\sqrt{2}}{\sqrt{5}} \cdot \dfrac{\sqrt{5}}{\sqrt{5}} - \dfrac{y\sqrt{3}}{\sqrt{5}} \cdot \dfrac{\sqrt{5}}{\sqrt{5}}$

$$= \dfrac{x\sqrt{10}}{5} - \dfrac{y\sqrt{15}}{5} = \dfrac{x\sqrt{10} - y\sqrt{15}}{5} \quad \textbf{(Division of square roots)}$$

47. $\dfrac{-7\sqrt{a^3b^2c}}{14\sqrt{a^5bc^4}} = \left(\dfrac{-7}{14}\right)\sqrt{\dfrac{a^3b^2c}{a^5bc^4}} = \dfrac{-1}{2}\sqrt{\dfrac{b}{a^2c^3}} = \dfrac{-\sqrt{b}}{2ac\sqrt{c}}$

$$= \dfrac{-\sqrt{b}}{2ac\sqrt{c}} \cdot \dfrac{\sqrt{c}}{\sqrt{c}} = \dfrac{-\sqrt{bc}}{2ac^2} \quad \textbf{(Division of square roots)}$$

48. $\dfrac{2\sqrt{xy^3z^2}-4\sqrt{x^2y^5z}}{3\sqrt{x^2y^4z}} = \dfrac{2\sqrt{xy^3z^2}}{3\sqrt{x^2y^4z}} - \dfrac{4\sqrt{x^2y^5z}}{3\sqrt{x^2y^4z}}$

$$= \left(\dfrac{2}{3}\right)\sqrt{\dfrac{xy^3z^2}{x^2y^4z}} - \left(\dfrac{4}{3}\right)\sqrt{\dfrac{x^2y^5z}{x^2y^4z}}$$

$$= \dfrac{2}{3}\sqrt{\dfrac{z}{xy}} - \dfrac{4}{3}\sqrt{y} = \dfrac{2}{3}\sqrt{\dfrac{z}{xy}} \cdot \sqrt{\dfrac{xy}{xy}} - \dfrac{4}{3}\sqrt{y}$$

$$= \dfrac{2}{3}\sqrt{\dfrac{z}{xy} \cdot \dfrac{xy}{xy}} - \dfrac{4}{3}\sqrt{y}$$

$$= \dfrac{2\sqrt{xyz}}{3xy} - \dfrac{4}{3}\sqrt{y} \quad \textbf{(Division of square roots)}$$

49. $\sqrt{y+4}=3$

   $(\sqrt{y+4})^2=(3)^2$ (Square *both* sides of equation.)

   $y+4=9$

   $y=5$ (Solution ?)

Check: $\sqrt{y+4}=3$

   $\sqrt{5+4}\ ?\ 3$

   $\sqrt{9}\ ?\ 3$

   $3=3$ ✓

Therefore, 5 is the required solution.   **(Equations involving square roots)**

50. $\sqrt{3u-1}-5=0$

   $\sqrt{3u-1}=5$ (Isolating the radical)

   $(\sqrt{3u-1})^2=(5)^2$ (Squaring both sides of equation)

   $3u-1=25$

   $3u=26$

   $u=\dfrac{26}{3}$ (Solution ?)

Check: $\sqrt{3u-1}-5=0$

   $\sqrt{3\left(\dfrac{26}{3}\right)-1}-5\ ?\ 0$

   $\sqrt{26-1}-5\ ?\ 0$

   $\sqrt{25}-5\ ?\ 0$

   $5-5\ ?\ 0$

   $0=0$ ✓

Therefore, $\dfrac{26}{3}$ is the required solution.   **(Equations involving square roots)**

51. $9-2\sqrt{t+5}=3$

   $6=2\sqrt{t+5}$

   $(6)^2=(2\sqrt{t+5})^2$

   $36=4(t+5)$

   $36=4t+20$

   $16=4t$

   $4=t$ (Solution ?)

Check in the *original* equation and determine that 4 *is* the required solution. **(Equations involving square roots)**

52. $\sqrt{p-3} = \sqrt{2p-1}$

$(\sqrt{p-3})^2 = (\sqrt{2p-1})^2$

$p - 3 = 2p - 1$

$-2 = p$　　　　　　　(Solution ?)

Check: $\sqrt{p-3} = \sqrt{2p-1}$

$\sqrt{-2-3} \ ? \ \sqrt{2(-2)-1}$

$\sqrt{-5} \ ? \ \sqrt{-5}$

Observe that substituting -2 for p makes each radicand negative. Hence, there is *no* real number solution for the given equation. (**Equations involving square roots**)

53. $\sqrt{x+6} - \sqrt{x-2} = 1$

$\sqrt{x+6} = 1 + \sqrt{x-2}$　　　　　　(Separating the radicals)

$(\sqrt{x+6})^2 = (1+\sqrt{x-2})^2$

$x + 6 = 1 + 2\sqrt{x-2} + x - 2$

$7 = 2\sqrt{x-2}$

$(7)^2 = (2\sqrt{x-2})^2$　　　　　　(Squaring *both* sides again)

$49 = 4(x-2)$

$49 = 4x - 8$

$57 = 4x$

$\dfrac{57}{4} = x$　　　　　　　(Solution ?)

Check in the *original* equation and determine that $\dfrac{57}{4}$ is the required solution. (**Equations involving square roots**)

54. $\sqrt{2s-3} - \sqrt{2s+1} = 2$

$\sqrt{2s-3} = 2 + \sqrt{2s+1}$

$(\sqrt{2s-3})^2 = (2+\sqrt{2s+1})^2$

$2s - 3 = 4 + 4\sqrt{2s+1} + 2s + 1$

$-8 = 4\sqrt{2s+1}$

$-2 = \sqrt{2s+1}$

We now have $\sqrt{2s+1} = -2$, which is negative. The principal square root of a real number is never negative. Hence, there are *no* real number solutions for the given equation. (**Equations involving square roots**)

Grade Yourself

Circle the numbers of the questions you missed, then fill in the total incorrect for each topic. If you answered more than three questions incorrectly, you need to focus on that topic. (If a topic has less than three questions and you had at least one wrong, we suggest you study that topic also. Read your textbook, a review book, or ask your teacher for help.)

Subject: Square Roots and Radicals

Topic	Question Numbers	Number Incorrect
Square roots	1, 2, 3, 4, 5, 6, 7, 8	
Simplifying square root expressions	9, 10, 11, 12, 13, 14, 15, 16, 17, 18, 19, 20, 21, 22, 23, 24, 25, 26, 27, 28, 29, 30	
Addition and subtraction of square roots	31, 32, 33, 34, 35, 36	
Multiplication of square roots	37, 38, 39, 40, 41, 42	
Division of square roots	43, 44, 45, 46, 47, 48	
Equations involving square roots	49, 50, 51, 52, 53, 54	

Quadratic Equations

Test Yourself

10.1 Solving Quadratic Equations by Factoring

Definition: The **general form** for a quadratic equation in the variable x is

$$ax^2 + bx + c = 0$$

where a, b, and c are real numbers and $a \neq 0$. In the equation, a is called the **leading coefficient**.

Solving Quadratic Equations by Factoring

To solve a quadratic equation by the method of factoring:

1. Write the equation in its general form.

2. Factor the polynomial part, if possible.

3. Set each factor equal to 0 and solve the resulting equations.

Solve the equation $2u^2 = 3 - u$ for u.

1. Write the equation in its general form:
    $$2u^2 + u - 3 = 0$$

2. Factor the lefthand side:
    $$(2u + 3)(u - 1) = 0$$

3. Set each factor equal to 0 and solve the resulting equations:
    $$(2u + 3)(u - 1) = 0$$

    $$2u + 3 = 0 \quad \text{or} \quad u - 1 = 0$$

    $$2u = -3 \qquad\qquad u = 1$$

$$u = \frac{-3}{2}$$

4. Checking the results in the *original* equation, determine that $\frac{-3}{2}$ and 1 are the required solutions.

A linear equation in a single variable has one solution. A quadratic equation in a single variable has two solutions.

A special case of the quadratic equation occurs when the constant term, c, is equal to 0; that is, when we have the equation
$$ax^2 + bx = 0.$$
Solve the equation $2x^2 - 3x = 0$.

1. Since the equation is already in its general form, factor the lefthand side:
    $$2x^2 - 3x = 0$$

    $$x(2x - 3) = 0$$

2. Set each factor equal to 0 and solve the resulting equations:

    $$x(2x - 3) = 0$$

    $$x = 0 \quad \text{or} \quad 2x - 3 = 0$$

    $$2x = 3$$

    $$x = \frac{3}{2}$$

3. Checking in the *original* equation, determine that 0 and $\frac{3}{2}$ are the required solutions.

Note: Whenever c = 0, 0 will be one of the two solutions for the equation.

In Exercises 1-6, solve each of the given equations by the method of factoring.

1. $t^2 - t - 12 = 0$

2. $3p^2 - 10 = 13p$

3. $7r^2 - 12r = 0$

4. $6x^2 = 17x - 12$

5. $5y^2 + 13y = 6$

6. $4q^2 - 9q = 0$

10.2 Solving Quadratic Equations by the Square Root Method

Consider the equation $x^2 = 9$. Rewriting it as $x^2 - 9 = 0$ and using the method of factoring, we have

$$x^2 - 9 = 0$$
$$(x + 3)(x - 3) = 0$$
$$x + 3 = 0 \quad \text{or} \quad x - 3 = 0$$
$$x = -3 \qquad\qquad x = 3$$

Hence, the solutions are −3 and 3. Observe that both −3 and 3 are square roots of 9, with 3 being the principal square root of 9.

Note: The method used above works only when $b = 0$.

Using Square Roots as a Method of Solving Quadratic Equations

If $c > 0$, then the solutions for the equation $x^2 = c$ are $x = -\sqrt{c}$ and $x = \sqrt{c}$, or simply, $x = \pm\sqrt{c}$.

The above technique can be extended as illustrated in the following example:

Solve the equation $(x - 4)^2 = 9$.

$$(x - 4)^2 = 9$$
$$x - 4 = \pm\sqrt{9}$$
$$x - 4 = \pm 3$$
$$x = 4 \pm 3$$

Hence, $x = 4 + 3 = 7$, or $x = 4 - 3 = 1$. Checking

both of these values in the *original* equation, determine that 1 and 7 are the required solutions.

Now, consider solving the equation $x^2 - 4x + 4 = 1$. Before attempting to rewrite this equation in its general form, observe that the lefthand side of the equation is factorable and that the two factors are equal. Hence, we have

$$x^2 - 4x + 4 = 1$$
$$(x - 2)(x - 2) = 1$$
$$(x - 2)^2 = 1$$
$$x - 2 = \pm\sqrt{1}$$
$$x - 2 = \pm 1$$

Therefore, the required solutions are $x = 2 + 1 = 3$, and $x = 2 - 1 = 1$.

In Exercises 7-12, solve the given equations by the square root method.

7. $x^2 - 64 = 0$

8. $y^2 - 225 = 0$

9. $9u^2 - 25 = 0$

10. $(2t - 1)^2 = 16$

11. $p^2 - 6p + 9 = 3$

12. $r^2 - 14r + 49 = -5$

10.3 Solving Quadratic Equations by Completing the Square

The methods of Section 10.1 and Section 10.2 cannot always be used to solve quadratic equations. However, the method of **completing the square** can always be used.

Completing the Square for the Expression $x^2 + px$:

To complete the square for the expression $x^2 + px$:

1. Take one-half of the coefficient of x, obtaining $\frac{1}{2}p$.

2. Square $\frac{1}{2}p$, obtaining $\frac{1}{4}p^2$.

3. Add $\frac{1}{4}p^2$ to the given expression, obtaining

$x^2 + px + \frac{1}{4}p^2.$

4. The resulting quadratic trinomial can be factored with two equal linear binomial factors as

$$x^2 + px + \frac{1}{4}p^2 = \left(x + \frac{p}{2}\right)\left(x + \frac{p}{2}\right) = \left(x + \frac{p}{2}\right)^2$$

Solve the equation $x^2 + 6x - 1 = 0$ by the method of completing the square.

Since $x^2 + 6x - 1$ is *not* a perfect square, rewrite the given equation as

$x^2 + 6x = 1.$

Next, complete the square on the lefthand side of the equation.

$$x^2 + 6x + \left(\frac{6}{2}\right)^2 = x^2 + 6x + 9$$

Adding 9 to both sides of the given equation, we have

$x^2 + 6x + 9 = 1 + 9$

Solving the resulting equation, we have

$x^2 + 6x + 9 = 1 + 9$

$x^2 + 6x + 9 = 10$

$(x + 3)^2 = 10$

$x + 3 = \pm\sqrt{10}$

$x = -3 \pm \sqrt{10}$

Hence, the required solutions are $-3 \pm \sqrt{10}$.

In the next example, we consider what happens when the leading coefficient is not 1.

Solve the equation $2y^2 - 8y + 5 = 9$

Proceed as follows:

$2y^2 - 8y + 5 = 9$

$2y^2 - 8y = 4$

$y^2 - 4y = 2$ (Divide both sides of the equation by 2, to obtain a leading coefficient of 1.)

$$y^2 - 4y + \left(\frac{-4}{2}\right)^2 = 2 + \left(\frac{-4}{2}\right)^2$$

$y^2 - 4y + 4 = 2 + 4$

$(y - 2)^2 = 6$

$y - 2 = \pm\sqrt{6}$

$y = 2 \pm \sqrt{6}$

Therefore, the required solutions are $2 \pm \sqrt{6}$.

In Exercises 13-18, solve the given equations by the method of completing the square.

13. $x^2 - 2x - 8 = 0$

14. $y^2 + 10y + 3 = 0$

15. $u^2 - 12 = 5u$

16. $15t = 2 - 8t^2$

17. $4p^2 - 12p = -9$

18. $9q^2 - 6q + 1 = 13$

10.4 Solving Quadratic Equations by the Quadratic Formula

Another method than can always be used to solve a quadratic equation is known as the *quadratic formula*. It is based upon the method of completing the square and involves only the coefficients of the quadratic equation.

The Quadratic Formula

Consider the equation $ax^2 + bx + c = 0$, which is the general form of the quadratic equation in the variable x, where a, b, and c are real numbers and $a \neq 0$. Then, the solutions for the equation are given by the formula

$$x = \frac{-b \pm \sqrt{b^2 - 4ac}}{2a}$$

This formula is called the **quadratic formula**.

In the equation $2x^2 - 4x + 5 = 0$, a = 2, b = -4, and c = 5. In the equation $3 - 7x - 3x^2$, a = -3, b = -7, and c = 3. In the equation $4x^2 - 5 = 0$, a = 4, b = 0, and c = -5. The equation $3 - 5x^2 = 9x$ can be rewritten as $5x^2 + 9x - 3 = 0$, with $a = 5$, $b = 9$, and $c = -3$.

Using the quadratic formula, solve the following equation:

$$2x^2 - 3x - 5 = 0$$

For this equation, $a = 2$, $b = -3$, and $c = -5$. We have

$$x = \frac{-b \pm \sqrt{b^2 - 4ac}}{2a}$$

$$x = \frac{-(-3) \pm \sqrt{(-3)^2 - 4(2)(-5)}}{(2)(2)}$$

$$x = \frac{3 \pm \sqrt{9 + 40}}{4}$$

$$x = \frac{3 \pm \sqrt{49}}{4}$$

$$x = \frac{3 \pm 7}{4}$$

$$x = \frac{3 + 7}{4} \quad \text{or} \quad x = \frac{3 - 7}{4}$$

$$x = \frac{5}{2} \qquad\qquad x = -1$$

Checking in the *original* equation, determine that -1 and $\frac{5}{2}$ are the required solutions.

If the expression $b^2 - 4ac$, called the **discriminant**, is negative, then there are no real number solutions for the equation.

In Exercises 19-26, use the quadratic formula to solve each of the given equations. If there are no real number solutions, indicate that fact.

19. $3x^2 - 4x - 1 = 0$

20. $4y^2 + y = 8$

21. $u^2 + 6 = 2u$

22. $5t^2 + 2t = 3$

23. $3s = 6s^2 - 9$

24. $7z^2 = 5 - 4z$

25. $8r - 7 = 2r^2$

26. $11 + 3q + 2q^2 = 0$

✓ Check Yourself

1. $\quad t^2 - t - 12 = 0$

$\quad (t - 4)(t + 3) = 0$

$\quad t - 4 = 0 \quad$ or $\quad t + 3 = 0$

$\qquad t = 4 \qquad\qquad t = -3$

Checking in the *original* equation, determine that -3 and 4 are the required solutions. **(Solving quadratic equations by factoring)**

2. $\qquad 3p^2 - 10 = 13p$

$\quad 3p^2 - 13p - 10 = 0$

$\quad (3p + 2)(p - 5) = 0$

$\quad 3p + 2 = 0 \quad$ or $\quad p - 5 = 0$

$\qquad 3p = -2 \qquad\qquad p = 5$

$\qquad p = \frac{-2}{3}$

Checking in the *original* equation, determine that $\frac{-2}{3}$ and 5 are the required solutions. **(Solving quadratic equations by factoring)**

3. $7r^2 - 12r = 0$

$r(7r - 12) = 0$

$r = 0 \quad$ or $\quad 7r - 12 = 0$

$\qquad\qquad\qquad 7r = 12$

$\qquad\qquad\qquad r = \dfrac{12}{7}$

Checking in the *original* equation, determine that 0 and $\dfrac{12}{7}$ are the required solutions. (**Solving quadratic equations by factoring**)

4. $\qquad\qquad 6x^2 = 17x - 12$

$6x^2 - 17x + 12 = 0$

$(2x - 3)(3x - 4) = 0$

$2x - 3 = 0 \quad$ or $\quad 3x - 4 = 0$

$\quad 2x = 3 \qquad\qquad\quad 3x = 4$

$\quad x = \dfrac{3}{2} \qquad\qquad\quad x = \dfrac{4}{3}$

Checking in the *original* equation, determine that $\dfrac{4}{3}$ and $\dfrac{3}{2}$ are the required solutions. (**Solving quadratic equations by factoring**)

5. $\qquad 5y^2 + 13y = 6$

$5y^2 + 13y - 6 = 0$

$(5y - 2)(y + 3) = 0$

$5y - 2 = 0 \quad$ or $\quad y + 3 = 0$

$\quad 5y = 2 \qquad\qquad\quad y = -3$

$\quad y = \dfrac{2}{5}$

Checking in the *original* equation, determine that -3 and $\dfrac{2}{5}$ are the required solutions. (**Solving quadratic equations by factoring**)

6 $\quad 4q^2 - 9q = 0$

$q(4q - 9) = 0$

$q = 0 \quad$ or $\quad 4q - 9 = 0$

$\qquad\qquad\qquad 4q = 9$

$\qquad\qquad\qquad q = \dfrac{9}{4}$

Checking in the *original* equation, determine that 0 and $\dfrac{9}{4}$ are the required solutions. (**Solving quadratic equations by factoring**)

7. $x^2 - 64 = 0$

$$x^2 = 64$$

$$x = \pm\sqrt{64}$$

$$x = \pm 8$$

Checking in the *original* equation, determine that -8 and 8 are the required solutions. **(Solving quadratic equations by the square root method)**

8. $y^2 - 225 = 0$

$$y^2 = 225$$

$$y = \pm\sqrt{225}$$

$$y = \pm 15$$

Checking in the *original* equation, determine that -15 and 15 are the required solutions. **(Solving quadratic equations by the square root method)**

9. $9u^2 - 25 = 0$

$$9u^2 = 25$$

$$u^2 = \frac{25}{9}$$

$$u = \pm\sqrt{\frac{25}{9}}$$

$$u = \pm\frac{5}{3}$$

Checking in the *original* equation, determine that $\frac{-5}{3}$ and $\frac{5}{3}$ are the required solutions. **(Solving quadratic equations by the square root method)**

10. $(2t - 1)^2 = 16$

$$2t - 1 = \pm\sqrt{16}$$

$$2t - 1 = \pm 4$$

$$2t = 1 \pm 4$$

$$t = \frac{1 \pm 4}{2}$$

$$t = \frac{1 + 4}{2} \quad \text{or} \quad t = \frac{1 - 4}{2}$$

$$t = \frac{5}{2} \qquad\qquad t = \frac{-3}{2}$$

Checking in the *original* equation, determine that $\frac{-3}{2}$ and $\frac{5}{2}$ are the required solutions. **(Solving quadratic equations by the square root method)**

11. $p^2 - 6p + 9 = 3$

$(p - 3)^2 = 3$

$p - 3 = \pm \sqrt{3}$

$p = 3 \pm \sqrt{3}$

Checking in the *original* equation, determine that $3 \pm \sqrt{3}$ are the required solutions. (**Solving quadratic equations by the square root method**)

12. $r^2 - 14r + 49 = -5$

$(r - 7)^2 = -5$

$r - 7 = \pm \sqrt{-5}$

Since $\sqrt{-5}$ is not a real number, there are *no* real number solutions for the given equation. (**Solving quadratic equations by the square root method**)

13. $x^2 - 2x - 8 = 0$

$x^2 - 2x = 8$

$x^2 - 2x + \left(\dfrac{-2}{2}\right)^2 = 8 + \left(\dfrac{-2}{2}\right)^2$

$x^2 - 2x + 1 = 8 + 1$

$(x - 1)^2 = 9$

$x - 1 = \pm \sqrt{9}$

$x - 1 = \pm 3$

$x = 1 \pm 3$

$x = 1 + 3 \qquad \text{or} \qquad x = 1 - 3$

$x = 4 \qquad\qquad\qquad x = -2$

Checking in the *original* equation, determine that -2 and 4 are the required solutions. (**Solving quadratic equations by completing the square**)

14. $y^2 + 10y + 3 = 0$

$y^2 + 10y = -3$

$y^2 + 10y + \left(\dfrac{10}{2}\right)^2 = -3 + \left(\dfrac{10}{2}\right)^2$

$y^2 + 10y + 25 = -3 + 25$

$(y + 5)^2 = 22$

$y + 5 = \pm \sqrt{22}$

$y = -5 \pm \sqrt{22}$

Checking in the *original* equation, determine that $-5 \pm \sqrt{22}$ are the required solutions. (**Solving quadratic equations by completing the square**)

15. $$u^2 - 12 = 5u$$

$$u^2 - 5u = 12$$

$$u^2 - 5u + \left(\frac{-5}{2}\right)^2 = 12 + \left(\frac{-5}{2}\right)^2$$

$$\left(u - \frac{5}{2}\right)^2 = 12 + \frac{25}{4}$$

$$\left(u - \frac{5}{2}\right)^2 = \frac{73}{4}$$

$$u - \frac{5}{2} = \pm\sqrt{\frac{73}{4}}$$

$$u - \frac{5}{2} = \frac{\pm\sqrt{73}}{2}$$

$$u = \frac{5}{2} \pm \frac{\sqrt{73}}{2}$$

$$u = \frac{5 \pm \sqrt{73}}{2}$$

Checking in the *original* equation, determine that $\dfrac{5 \pm \sqrt{73}}{2}$ are the required solutions.   **(Solving quadratic equations by completing the square)**

16. $$15t = 2 - 8t^2$$

$$8t^2 + 15t = 2$$

$$t^2 + \frac{15}{8}t = \frac{1}{4} \qquad \text{(Divide \emph{both} sides by 8 to get leading coefficient of 1.)}$$

$$t^2 + \frac{15}{8}t + \left(\frac{15}{16}\right)^2 = \frac{1}{4} + \left(\frac{15}{16}\right)^2$$

$$\left(t + \frac{15}{16}\right)^2 = \frac{1}{4} + \frac{225}{256}$$

$$\left(t + \frac{15}{16}\right)^2 = \frac{289}{256}$$

$$t + \frac{15}{16} = \pm\sqrt{\frac{289}{256}}$$

$$t + \frac{15}{16} = \pm\frac{17}{16}$$

$$t = \frac{-15}{16} \pm \frac{17}{16}$$

$$t = \frac{-15 \pm 17}{16}$$

$$t = \frac{-15 + 17}{16} \quad \text{or} \quad t = \frac{-15 - 17}{16}$$

$$t = \frac{2}{16} \qquad\qquad t = \frac{-32}{16}$$

$$t + \frac{1}{8} \qquad\qquad t = -2$$

Checking in the *original* equation, determine that -2 and $\frac{1}{8}$ are the required solutions. (**Solving quadratic equations by completing the square**)

17. $\quad 4p^2 - 12p = -9$

$$p^2 - 3p = \frac{-9}{4}$$

$$p^2 - 3p + \left(\frac{-3}{2}\right)^2 = \frac{-9}{4} + \left(\frac{-3}{2}\right)^2$$

$$\left(p - \frac{3}{2}\right)^2 = \frac{-9}{4} + \frac{9}{4}$$

$$\left(p - \frac{3}{2}\right)^2 = 0$$

$$p - \frac{3}{2} = 0$$

$$p = \frac{3}{2}$$

Checking in the *original* equation, determine that $\frac{3}{2}$ is the required solution. (**Solving quadratic equations by completing the square**)

18. $\quad 9q^2 - 6q + 1 = 13$

$$9q^2 - 6q = 12$$

$$q^2 - \frac{2}{3}q = \frac{4}{3}$$

$$q^2 - \frac{2}{3}q + \left(\frac{-1}{3}\right)^2 = \frac{4}{3} + \left(\frac{-1}{3}\right)^2$$

$$\left(q - \frac{1}{3}\right)^2 = \frac{4}{3} + \frac{1}{9}$$

$$\left(q - \frac{1}{3}\right)^2 = \frac{13}{9}$$

$$q - \frac{1}{3} = \pm\sqrt{\frac{13}{9}}$$

$$q - \frac{1}{3} = \frac{\pm\sqrt{13}}{3}$$

$$q = \frac{1}{3} \pm \frac{\sqrt{13}}{3}$$

$$q = \frac{1 \pm \sqrt{13}}{3}$$

Checking in the *original* equation, determine that $\frac{1 \pm \sqrt{13}}{3}$ are the required solutions. **(Solving quadratic equations by completing the square)**

19. The equation $3x^2 - 4x - 1 = 0$ is quadratic in the variable x, with a = 3, b = −4, and c = −1. Hence,

$$x = \frac{-b \pm \sqrt{b^2 - 4ac}}{2a}$$

$$x = \frac{-(-4) \pm \sqrt{(-4)^2 - 4(3)(-1)}}{2(3)}$$

$$x = \frac{4 \pm \sqrt{16 + 12}}{6}$$

$$x = \frac{4 \pm \sqrt{28}}{6}$$

$$x = \frac{4 \pm 2\sqrt{7}}{6}$$

$$x = \frac{2 \pm \sqrt{7}}{3}$$

Checking in the *original* equation, determine that $\frac{2 \pm \sqrt{7}}{3}$ are the required solutions. **(Solving quadratic equations by the quadratic formula)**

20. The equation $4y^2 + y = 8$ is quadratic in the variable y, with a = 4, b = 1, and c = −8. Hence,

$$y = \frac{-b \pm \sqrt{b^2 - 4ac}}{2a}$$

$$y = \frac{-1 \pm \sqrt{(1)^2 - 4(4)(-8)}}{2(4)}$$

$$y = \frac{-1 \pm \sqrt{1 + 128}}{8}$$

$$y = \frac{-1 \pm \sqrt{129}}{8}$$

Checking in the *original* equation, determine that $\frac{-1 \pm \sqrt{129}}{8}$ are the required solutions. **(Solving quadratic equations by the quadratic formula)**

21. The equation $u^2 + 6 = 2u$ is quadratic in the variable u, with a = 1, b = −2, and c = 6. Hence,

$$u = \frac{-b \pm \sqrt{b^2 - 4ac}}{2a}$$

$$u = \frac{-(-2) \pm \sqrt{(-2)^2 - 4(1)(6)}}{2(1)}$$

$$u \ \frac{2 \pm \sqrt{4 - 24}}{2}$$

$$u = \frac{2 \pm \sqrt{-20}}{2}$$

Since −20 is negative, $\sqrt{-20}$ is not a real number. Hence, there are *no* real number solutions for the given equation.   **(Solving quadratic equations by the quadratic formula)**

22. The equation $5t^2 + 2t = 3$ is quadratic in the variable t, with a = 5, b = 2, and c = −3. Hence,

$$t = \frac{-b \pm \sqrt{b^2 - 4ac}}{2a}$$

$$t = \frac{-2 \pm \sqrt{(2)^2 - 4(5)(-3)}}{2(5)}$$

$$t = \frac{-2 \pm \sqrt{4 + 60}}{10}$$

$$t = \frac{-2 \pm \sqrt{64}}{10}$$

$$t = \frac{-2 \pm 8}{10}$$

$$t = \frac{-2 + 8}{10} \quad \text{or} \quad t = \frac{-2 - 8}{10}$$

$$t = \frac{3}{5} \qquad\qquad t = -1$$

Checking in the *original* equation, determine that −1 and $\frac{3}{5}$ are the required solutions.   **(Solving quadratic equations by the quadratic formula)**

23. The equation $3s = 6s^2 - 9$ is quadratic in the variable s, with a = 6, b = −3, and c = −9. Hence,

$$s = \frac{-b \pm \sqrt{b^2 - 4ac}}{2a}$$

$$s = \frac{-(-3) \pm \sqrt{(-3)^2 - 4(6)(-9)}}{2(6)}$$

$$s = \frac{3 \pm \sqrt{9 + 216}}{12}$$

$$s = \frac{3 \pm \sqrt{225}}{12}$$

$$s = \frac{3 \pm 15}{12}$$

$$s = \frac{3 + 15}{12} \quad \text{or} \quad s = \frac{3 - 15}{12}$$

$$s = \frac{3}{2} \qquad\qquad s = -1$$

Checking in the *original* equation, determine that -1 and $\frac{3}{2}$ are the required solutions.   (**Solving quadratic equations by the quadratic formula**)

24. The equation $7z^2 = 5 - 4z$ is quadratic in the variable z, with a = 7, b = 4, and c = −5. Hence,

$$z = \frac{-b \pm \sqrt{b^2 - 4ac}}{2a}$$

$$z = \frac{-4 \pm \sqrt{(4)^2 - 4(7)(-5)}}{2(7)}$$

$$z = \frac{-4 \pm \sqrt{16 + 140}}{14}$$

$$z = \frac{-4 \pm \sqrt{156}}{14}$$

$$z = \frac{-4 \pm 2\sqrt{39}}{14}$$

$$z = \frac{-2 \pm \sqrt{39}}{7}$$

Checking in the *original* equation, determine that $\frac{-2 \pm \sqrt{39}}{7}$ are the required solutions.   (**Solving quadratic equations by the quadratic formula**)

25. The equation $8r - 7 = 2r^2$ is quadratic in the variable r, with a = 2, b = −8, and c = 7. Hence,

$$r = \frac{-b \pm \sqrt{b^2 - 4ac}}{2a}$$

$$r = \frac{-(-8) \pm \sqrt{(-8)^2 - 4(2)(7)}}{2(2)}$$

$$r = \frac{8 \pm \sqrt{64 - 56}}{4}$$

$$r = \frac{8 \pm \sqrt{8}}{4}$$

$$r = \frac{8 \pm 2\sqrt{2}}{4}$$

$$r = \frac{4 \pm \sqrt{2}}{2}$$

Checking in the *original* equation, determine that $\frac{4 \pm \sqrt{2}}{2}$ are the required solutions.   (**Solving quadratic equations by the quadratic formula**)

26. The equation $11 + 3q + 2q^2 = 0$ is quadratic in the variable q, with a = 2, b = 3, and c = 11. Hence,

$$q = \frac{-b \pm \sqrt{b^2 - 4ac}}{2a}$$

$$q = \frac{-3 \pm \sqrt{(3)^2 - 4(2)(11)}}{2(2)}$$

$$q = \frac{-3 \pm \sqrt{9 - 88}}{4}$$

$$q = \frac{-3 \pm \sqrt{-79}}{4}$$

Since -79 is negative, $\sqrt{-79}$ is not a real number. Hence, there are *no* real number solutions for the given equation. **(Solving quadratic equations by the quadratic formula)**

Grade Yourself

Circle the numbers of the questions you missed, then fill in the total incorrect for each topic. If you answered more than three questions incorrectly, you need to focus on that topic. (If a topic has less than three questions and you had at least one wrong, we suggest you study that topic also. Read your textbook, a review book, or ask your teacher for help.)

Subject: Quadratic Equations

Topic	Question Numbers	Number Incorrect
Solving quadratic equations by factoring	1, 2, 3, 4, 5, 6	
Solving quadratic equations by the square root method	7, 8, 9, 10, 11, 12	
Solving quadratic equations by completing the square	13, 14, 15, 16, 17, 18	
Solving quadratic equations by the quadratic formula	19, 20, 21, 22, 23, 24, 25, 26	